CAMERON BROWN

The Warrior Teacher

Shaping the Well of Being

First published by Cameron Brown 2026

First edition

ISBN (print): 978-1-7646406-1-9
ISBN (digital): 978-1-7646406-3-3

This book was professionally typeset on Reedsy.
Find out more at reedsy.com

This is a message of thanks and appreciation to all
Teachers, Coaches, Instructors, Lecturers, Leaders, and Parents.
The work you do to create individual change is amazing.
Whether it is teaching in a classroom, boardroom, pool, lab,
sports field, or dining table.
Whether you are explaining Mathematics, Leadership, First Aid, Dancing,
Running, or Spelling.
I am in awe of the work you are doing.
Big change happens when individuals such as yourself put in the work.
This book is for you.

Contents

VIII How Does It End?

IX Final Considerations

I

The world opens

"The basic difference between
a warrior and an ordinary person
is that a warrior takes everything as a challenge,
while an ordinary person takes everything
as a blessing or a curse."
—Carlos Castaneda

"We are warriors. We take the road untraveled.
Not because it is easy, but because someone must."
—Marvel, What If ...?

The Classroom: The Day Begins

Wednesday Morning

8:30 a.m.

I sit at my desk and survey the room and my planning, and I consider my day. The timetable is on the board, so the students know what to expect. The work is laid out neatly, and I begin to visualize what will happen. But then, my thoughts turn to what happened the day before. The defiance and the disrespect that I received. I was up last night going through what was said on both sides. How did it get to this? What could have been done differently? But I must remove those thoughts, as I lost too much sleep last night.

It is a new day today.

There are students in the class who are great and inspiring and deserve the best teaching and learning that they can get. They really make teaching worth it with their ideas, humor, and dedication to improving. This moment of joy is punctured by the realization that they are not getting the best learning because of ...

Stop. Don't think about the past.

Today is a new day.

A glance at the clock.

8:45 a.m.

Time to get the class.

I arrive at the front of the line. The students are mostly all there. They are eager to see me. Smiles and comments are made back and forth between the students and me. A quick scan of the line. Yes, those students are here today. They are always here. They never miss a day.

"No matter," I remind myself.

Today is a new day.

The class filters into the classroom. Bags are unpacked; equipment is either stored in cupboards or on desks. Water bottles go under desks, and once I am satisfied that all students are in attendance, I check the clock again.

9:00 a.m.

The roll is marked, and the students are ready to begin the day. I go through the day's timetable and give another reminder about class expectations. I do not mention what happened yesterday. Some students will remember; most will not. Some may have experienced far worse at home last night.

But today is a new day.

I invite the students to take out their books for work. Again, 93% of students comply and are eager to learn. But then, I observe the two students from yesterday. One has their iPad out and is playing games. The other is drawing pictures. Both are ignoring me.

9:01 a.m.

Surely not again.

Today is a new day.

My heart begins to race a bit faster. I do not want a repeat of the events from yesterday. I again remind the two students to get their work out, and again, they ignore me. The rest of the class is now settled with their work. Some have begun looking at the interaction between the two students and me. I recognize that this defiance is now being watched. My heart rate has risen again.

I also recognize that there are three other students in the class who are watching and learning. They are interested in how far the two students can go, what the response will be, and when they may be able to try something themselves.

This thought begins to raise increasing concern for me. I have to make a decision: do I insist on compliance to the detriment of the lesson and the classroom environment, or do I ignore it and continue the lesson while teaching the rest of the class that defiance works and students don't have to work if they don't want to? My heart rate rises again, as does my anger, and the sweat begins to accumulate.

9:03 a.m.

Today is a new day.

I raise my voice, and the environment changes. If this is how the day starts, then I begin to recognize that it will be a long day. The battle between teaching and learning, between students and teachers, between protecting and challenging student's is just beginning.

But the battle is not with pedagogy or curriculum. It is not with the student and the system. The real battle that is taking place is between me and my thinking, me and my well-being, and me and my mental health, which at this stage is not positive, not future-focused. The battle is to regain control of the first environment: my thoughts. I will need to do this to continue to teach.

Who is going to win this battle? Will there be a winner? Should there be a winner?

This can be reflected in hindsight, but at this moment, 9:04 a.m., I feel like I am losing, and the stress, sleepless nights, and trauma caused yesterday are growing exponentially and spiraling around me. I question my career, my ability to communicate, to teach, to lead. But that is a 3:00 p.m. question.

9:05 a.m.

How hard is it to get your book out?

Today is not a new day.

Introduction

I am a teacher.

I need to be a warrior.

A teacher steps into this classroom to teach.

A warrior steps into this classroom prepared to engage in the many elements that will impact learning.

I step into the world of teaching knowing that I have to change mindsets, thinking, beliefs, and the opinions of students, parents, and the community.

I need to be a warrior teacher, but this can mean many things to many people. I can be supportive and strong. I can be caring and courageous. I can be relational and reserved. I can be pedagogically sound and practically ambitious.

The warrior teacher also recognizes the key elements of mental health and well-being, as the greatest battles can take place in fields and arenas far from the observing eye: the mind of the teacher. We are not immune to the dangers, turmoil, and hidden mental traps that can hold us in their sway. It is the role of the warrior teacher to be environmentally aware and mentally agile, to have a clear strategy in any teaching situation. It is important that we have plans and processes in place before we teach so we can react positively to the challenges we may come across. Negative well-being will impact my teaching if I am not in control. Positive well-being will impact my teaching if I am.

The Warrior Teacher seeks to reveal, respond, and reassert the importance of teaching. Through these considerations, I hope you may find a chapter, a consideration, or an idea that may be helpful or make you rethink your processes.

The first chapter is Who Are You? You are being asked who you are as a person. What kind of person steps into the classroom? The person, the thinking, and the beliefs that you are outside the classroom will emerge inside the classroom. It is important that before a teacher takes the first step, they are clear about their motivation and belief system. They need to understand their own triggers and history. This area needs to be thought over and defined before they engage with the students whose academic growth they are challenged to improve.

The next chapter is to consider the well-being of teaching. Once you know who you think you are, you will be challenged in the classroom with your mental health. Teaching is a relational sport. You will engage with students and form relationships. But this is a two-way process, and that may cause a relationship imbalance that can impact the very nature of who you are and how you see yourself. This chapter encourages all teachers to strategize and be tactical in their well-being and mental health. It is your energy and drive that will enable great teaching, but that energy must come from somewhere.

The next chapter is focused on the war of teaching. This is where the tactical, purposeful, and strategic elements of teaching are found. Using the familiar theme of battles, teachers are encouraged to link teaching with flags, war cries, armory, uniforms, and maps as it relates to creating better learning. This chapter delves into the enemies that teachers may face, the allies they can make, and how the challenge of teaching is serious and impactful. While the concept of war may sound unsettling or even outright inappropriate, it is important to consider that a professional soldier, teacher, or someone in any other profession is planned, prepared, and ready to use whatever is at their disposal to ensure success.

The chapter that follows is the battle of learning. There are many elements in the day that can impact a teacher's role, lesson, or influence in the classroom. Maybe it is the importance of time or safety. Interesting concepts like magic and domestication make their entrance in this chapter as we explore ways in which teaching and learning can fall away under the pull of various gravitational forces. As teachers, we explore ways to consider, counteract, and even exploit these points of difference for our educational gain.

In navigating the defenses, it is important to note again that there are forces at work outside the classroom that affect our students and us as teachers. The defenses formed against learning can be expressed in the motivation to learn. We explore the importance of resistance that can enable teachers and students to not be able to demonstrate their full capacity, and all teachers are encouraged to both recognize and plan accordingly.

It is vital to recognize in the next chapter what can be achieved through planning. Teachers can create an impregnable fortress of learning if we evaluate the language we use, the questions we ask, and the little changes that we can make if we play the long game. If we have our sights fixed on what we can achieve, we lift our vision of the lesson and ourselves. Teachers need to be encouraged that differences can be made.

Then, we consider the end. What does death look like for teachers? What does peace look like? How can we plan for both? Do we know what failure looks like, and can/should we avoid it? Can we identify what victory looks like and how to plan for it?

We conclude by considering the importance of wisdom, the impact of gardening, and beginning our first step towards being the great teacher we can be, and we all need. It is important to respect the professionalism and opportunities of being a teacher.

And finally, sometimes I write 'I', and sometimes I write 'you', or 'we' in an inconsistent way. This is to indicate that I am also on this journey, making mistakes and learning. I wrote this book for me as much as anyone!

- A teacher should be a warrior as they are focused, driven, and goal-orientated.
- A teacher should be a fighter, as they are brave despite the hits and trials they face.
- A teacher should be a samurai as they are disciplined, deliberate, and calm.
- A teacher should be revolutionary, as they are challenging the status quo of old ideas.
- A teacher should be a martial artist as they are mentally balanced, flexible, and adaptable.
- A teacher should be a chess grandmaster as they are strategic, can "see the board", and have a plan.
-

"Thus, it is that in war the victorious strategist only seeks battle after the victory has been won, whereas he who is destined to defeat first fights and afterwards looks for victory."
—Sun Tzu, The Art of War

Consider the Warrior Teacher

(Recommended Reading:
Be Water, My Friend:
The True Teachings of Bruce Lee
by Shannon Lee)

"If you have the mental image of a warrior as someone who runs bravely and determinedly into battle, translate that image instead into the image of someone who takes on whatever life throws at them with grace, determination, someone who does not turn away from a challenge or from acknowledging their own shortcomings, someone who does not seek an ideal image but an ideal soul. That's a modern-day warrior and hero."
—Shannon Lee

It is important to begin by exploring the concept of the warrior teacher. Shannon Lee has written a book about the teachings, philosophy, and commitment of her father, Bruce Lee. Bruce Lee is known the world over for his approach to martial arts. He displayed discipline and quality in how he demonstrated his expertise in martial arts. Shannon explains that her father was not a naturally gifted individual. He did not have the height or eyesight that one might expect of such a famous fighter. Rather, it was his dedication, commitment, and fanatical approach to his unique fighting style that took him on a journey all the way to Hollywood movies. Bruce

Lee could be considered a warrior. But his journey was not through talent, luck, or natural ability. His journey was through hard work, focus, and repetition. It was no accident that he became great; he simply adopted a warrior mindset.

But what does a warrior mindset need? This is where the real adventure begins. Bruce Lee was committed to learning. He wanted to learn and improve. He wanted to know what his body could do and how to do it better. He wanted to learn from others and employ their techniques, equipment, and thinking in his own style. Bruce Lee was the ultimate teacher, and the person he was teaching was himself. Every kick, every punch, every time he demonstrated his speed and skill, he was also demonstrating his ability to be a learner.

Bruce Lee was a warrior teacher who undertook training to improve and become a learner not only of martial arts but also of himself. Shannon demonstrated that underlying his physical movements and actions, there was philosophy and deep thought attached to it. Bruce studied philosophy as a way to learn how to think and how to respond. The topic of the book, and the thinking that permeated his life, was to "be water". It was important for Bruce that every engagement, conversation, or fight became open in his mind. He did not waste time applying his own thinking, opinions, and perceptions to what he was facing. Rather, he became like water and moved with, around, and even through it. When one approaches life from a philosophical perspective, one is challenged to reveal how one thinks.

It was also identified that Bruce Lee had opponents or adversaries. In this book, we will also investigate and identify enemies. Shannon explored the idea of opponents and adversaries as opportunities. An opponent will come at you with a different opinion and perspective, and an adversary will challenge how you think and react. These are not to be avoided. In fact, it is recognised—and hopefully demonstrated throughout this book—that it is through our opponents, adversaries, and enemies that we learn. If we go through life with no challenges and never change our approaches, life could become stagnant. Worse still, when life throws an event at you, it may undermine your confidence in yourself and your abilities. When Bruce faced many opponents and obstacles, either in fighting conditions or in other environments, his open-minded, "be water", learner-focused mentality allowed him to learn about his opponent, but ultimately to learn about himself.

Bruce Lee was a warrior teacher. He was a fighter philosopher. He was physically committed and mentally aware. Bruce Lee learned to control the only environments he could: his body and then his mind. He then proceeded to learn as much as he could about everything else, and applied what he could to his thinking, his routines, his art, and his life.

Bruce Lee could be just one example as we move through the book.

"Adapt what is useful, reject what is useless,
and add what is specifically your own."
—Bruce Lee

Consider the Well of Being

(Recommended Reading: ***Wisdom Takes Work*** by Ryan Holiday)

"Learning is discovery,
the discovery of the cause of our ignorance...
It is discovering what is there in us.
When we discover we are uncovering our own abilities,
our own eyes ... to see what is going on,
to discover how to enlarge our lives."
—Bruce Lee

Water is a macroscopically formless, microscopically structured inorganic compound that can effortlessly shape itself into the container that it has been poured into. If gravity continues to be the force interacting with everything, water will continue to find every part inside that shape. Bruce Lee demonstrated the importance of being like water in his fighting and thinking strategies. He recognized the elements of water and its remarkable capacity, and how we should also be formless like water, so we can adjust and adapt ourselves to situations. But water needs to be poured into a shape, that shape will have boundaries, and there needs to be consideration regarding what the shape will look like. As a thought exercise, let's consider the shape that the water is being poured into. Let's see if we can use both it and "water" to develop ourselves.

We need to form and create a shape that can hold water. As the creator of the shape, we need to be less focused on the water and focus more on the depth and design of the shape that can hold water. We need to create a vessel for ourselves. If the shape is small and shallow, then not much water will gather, and the little water we have will be unable to fill or nourish ourselves. But if the shape is deep and round, then more water will be able to fill such a generous space. If we continue to be deep and create many levels, then the water will take great joy in exploring and enveloping us. It is not the job of water to create the shape. It is the creator who makes the shape. The creator's goal should not be to become full and stop any more growth, but to have the capacity to take in and hold as much as possible. We need to be less focused on what hold, and more focused on how much we can potentially hold.

We are beings that need to be filled emotionally, intellectually, spiritually, and relationally, but we can only be filled as much as we allow in. Our focus should be on our being, and our being should be like a well. We need to dig deeper and extend our ideas, imaginations, relationships, philosophies, and understanding of ourselves. The deeper we dig within ourselves and explore the passages and locked doors of our history, identity, loves and dislikes, passions and cravings, and trauma and mistakes, the more we understand our role in the world and the more we will be filled.

Digging deep also creates foundations for us to build upon. The higher the building, the deeper the foundations. With ourselves, the higher we explore and grow, the deeper the foundations we need to create in our thinking, philosophies, and understanding of ourselves. The more we extend ourselves upwards, the more it needs to be supported by a strong understanding of who we are. The foundations of learning, reading, discussing, and exploring our responses, reactions, and emotions are what allow those foundations to be dug. Embracing the uncomfortable conversation, person, or idea and digging into it more deeply is how extended foundations are created.

"It is a thorny undertaking, and more so than it seems,
to follow a movement so wandering as that of our mind,
to penetrate the opaque depths of its innermost folds,
to pick out and immobilise the innumerable flutterings that agitate it."
—Michel de Montaigne

But when you dig down, there is dirt and mud, the taint of our history that may be hard to physically and mentally work through. It is important that we dig, remove, and deal with the dirt because that is the only way to find the precious resources that may be buried there. As you dig, you might find the resource of resilience or strength, or a new skill, or imagination, or an idea, or even a passion that you buried years ago. The real "you" may be buried under the history and compaction of dirt, expectation, and "should haves" from your life. It is through digging down, reflecting, reading, and dealing with who you are, or who you were, that these precious resources can be found.

The deeper you dig, the harder it becomes, so you need tools to help you uncover and deal with the dirt and history of your life. This is where you may need to employ the help of a professional "miner": a counsellor, chaplain, psychiatrist, or psychologist who can enable you to dig safely. They provide support to ensure you are not buried by your feelings and emotions, helping to light the way and strengthen the walls of your well—your being.

But what is the purpose of a well? It is to find water. Developing who you are and creating a safe, deep place that you have shaped yourself will allow you to strike water. You then become nourished and supported by the water and the resources that you have. You do not need water to be poured externally because you have found the comfort, satisfaction, and resources within you. The deeper it goes, and the greater its capacity to grow, the more water—opportunities, relationships, growth, and even ideas — will take hold.

We create a well of our beliefs, thinking, and being, and this can *become* our well-being. The water that flows from life that is found in relationships, adversaries, and experiences will mix with the personal water of your soul, your beliefs, and strengths. The mixing of the water creates a stronger person, a confident human, and a better teacher.

As a teacher, my well of being also extends to pedagogy, behavior management, curriculum, relationships, planning, and feedback. The deeper my well is dug to include these elements of my profession, the more I can hold, work, and grow within my profession. This knowledge base and confidence will extend my well of being as a teacher, improve my well of being as a leader, increase my well of being as a learner, and maximize my well of being as a human being.

"Self-leadership is about digging out your hidden endowment and making them known and useful to those who need it most."
—Israelmore Ayivor

II

Who Am I?

"In preparing for battle, I have always found the plans are useless, but planning is indispensable."
—Dwight Eisenhower

"Everyone has a plan, until they are punched in the face."
—Mike Tyson

The Classroom: Questions are asked

I wonder why I became upset today in the classroom. This person, who became emotional and slightly unhinged in the class, is not who I am. Who was this person who was feeling, responding, and reacting that way? Or is this the way I am? I want to be a responsible teacher, a relational teacher, and a curious teacher, but all that went out the window today, and over what?

That kid's comments were annoying, so is that all it takes? I was up late last night trying to finish a show I have been watching. Is that the reason? My lessons are falling behind the rest of the cohort. Is that the explanation?

I try to see my life as a representation of the television screen. An American police officer on the TV shows that I watch wants to "protect and serve." I see myself as a member of Star Trek as I "seek out new life and new civilizations." But instead, I am really like the theme of Mission: Impossible, "Your mission, should you choose to accept it ..." And then, just like that, I dissolve in a waft of smoke when the mission becomes real.

It is easy to blame the student, the attractiveness of the television show, or the lesson planning, but I need to be curious about myself. It is easy for me to look elsewhere, but somewhere inside me, there is a person who reacted in a way that was inconsistent with the ideal person that I try to manifest in my dreams.

It is time to wake up.

Luckily, no one in the class knew what I felt or said to myself. I kept that inside this time. But for me to keep teaching, I will need to unpack the person inside the body, rummage through the feelings and history, and explore who I am.

I do know that the way I felt scared me a bit. And my thoughts inside me were a brief, uncalculated, lack-of-self-control microsecond away from becoming real.

And then the whole class would see a very different version of me.

I had better reveal who I am to myself before I reveal who I could be to the class.

Consider the Education of Me

(Recommended Reading: ***The Fourth Pillar*** by Martin Moffitt)

I am a teacher. I am a warrior.
I can be an educator, but I need to educate myself.
I can be a teacher, but first I need to teach myself.
I can be a trainer, but I need to train myself first.

But before I can go out and be something, I must first look in
and think about it.
I can be a leader in the classroom, but I need to lead myself first.
I can only talk about discipline, perseverance, and learning
if I demonstrate them.
I can talk about well-being, mental health, and overcoming challenges
after I have quietly taught myself how.

To believe in others, I need to believe in myself first.
If I am going to listen to others, I need to listen to myself first.
If I am going to question others, I need to ask myself first.
If I am going to challenge others, I need to challenge myself first.

A teacher should not sit on the sidelines and passively participate.
A warrior teacher actively involves themselves in the game.
I use the philosophy I teach during tough times and good times.

As a warrior teacher, I position myself as a revolving door.
Constantly moving.
Information coming in and coming out.
Welcoming and accepting ideas and thoughts.
Removing and ejecting aspects that do not allow me to develop.
Always revolving around a single thought, philosophy, or belief
that keeps me centered when traffic is flowing.
Challenges are coming and going.
It allows me to move and be in control.

I am a teacher.
I am a warrior.
I have not become great.
I train myself every day to be great.
I move, I think, I challenge, I reflect, I learn.
Then I engage, I teach, I educate.
I am a teacher. I am a warrior.

Consider Why

(Recommended Reading: ***Start with Why*** by Simon Sinek)

"Regardless of WHAT we do in our lives,
our WHY—our driving purpose, cause or belief—never changes."
—Simon Sinek

Some fundamental questions must be asked and answered before a soldier enters a battlefield, a player steps onto the field, or a lawyer steps into a courtroom.

Why am I here?

Why am I a teacher? Why am I willing to engage in this profession? Why do I want to engage in the battle of learning with students?

Explain why:

-

There will be a lot of what, when, how, and where explained in this book, but if I am unable to adequately outline the why, then a teacher, even a great teacher, will battle within themselves to solve all the other questions that will be asked of them.

There is no correct answer; there is only my answer. But I must first recognize if my answer is about me, or if it is about the students? Is my answer "Because I am an amazing teacher?" Or is it because I want to learn?

The answer to why I want to be a teacher could be the reason that I am going to be successful, but it could also be the first step to failing. As the challenges mount and the expectations grow, I will need to fall back on why I am a teacher.

I need to spend time reflecting on the question and my answer. Share my answer with others. Continue to meditate on the why, and as I teach, investigate whether it can withstand the challenges, complexities, and setbacks found in teaching.

- Is my why giving me the adrenaline push to overcome and grow as a teacher?
- Is my why creating an anchor for my growth, and needs to be re-evaluated?
- Remember that as a teacher, I will change, and my whys can change as well.
- In fact, they must for me to remain relevant.
- If I can fall back on the why, I will be able to create the momentum to move my teaching forward despite the setbacks.

A strong and confident 'why' will overcome any 'how'.

I may need to go back to my 'why' from time to time. I may need to change it or adapt to it. And if I have to, it will enable me to continue to develop as I embark on my professional journey.

"Working hard for something we do not care about is called stress, working hard for something we love is called passion."
—Simon Sinek

Consider My Story: Part One

"Stories have power.
They delight, enchant, touch, teach, recall, inspire, motivate, and challenge.
They help us understand."
—Janet Litherland

Every movie, book, and play has a story embedded in it. If it didn't, it would be boring. Someone walking down the street is not interesting unless there is a reason they are doing it: something or someone to get, something or someone to avoid. The story is interesting because of the journey the main character goes on. Do they learn something? Is there tension in their life that they must overcome? Who they meet along the way creates challenges or problems and provides weapons or removes opportunities. Are they part of a team, and is there an enemy they will have to face? The tension in the story makes the character, makes people watch or read, and makes the story.

I am the main character of my life, and I am a teacher. This means that I have a story to tell, a journey to go on. I have tension that I will create, and there is tension in my life that I will walk into. I will create situations that I will have to navigate. I will also need to avoid, learn from, or embrace events independent of me.

Who I am now should not be who I am in ten years' time: as a person, a teacher, a family member, and a member of the human race. I need to be on a journey and embrace the challenges. I also need to recognize that, as a teacher, I will be shaping, molding, and supporting the stories of many children who sit in front of me every day.

Life is amazing and traumatic; it is exhilarating and depressing. It is a journey of mountains, rivers, plains, deserts, peasants, and monsters.

Your well-being can be like a story, full of ups and downs. But you are the author and the creator. You have the capacity to fulfill your dreams or create your nightmares.

How you see the world that you create is up to you. Don't blame the curriculum, department, students, or parents. They are part of your journey, and how you see them is how you see yourself.

See your teaching career as a story. See your well-being as the guiding force that enables you to overcome monsters. See your monsters as the challenges that create meaning, purpose, and direction in your story. See yourself as an adventurer or hero. I am the creator of my story. I can include characters who add value. I can include personalities who provide resources for me and my story. I can give time to characters who are essential to the timeline of my story. My story is not determined by the students. My story is not guided by students' parents. I am in control of my story.

Be a storyteller who has a story worth telling.

"Listen, and you will realize that we are made not from cells or from atoms. We are made from stories."
—Mia Couto

Consider My Story: Part Two

(Recommended Reading: ***The Soul: A History of the Human Mind*** by Paul Ham)

"If you have built castles in the air, your work need not be lost;
that is where they should be.
Now put the foundations under them."
—Henry David Thoreau

The walls of castles are thick, strong, and high. The defenses of those walls are armed and patrolled regularly. Throughout history, the places that are important are protected, up-to-date, and prepared. All attacks are seen before they arrive, and there is no way of attacking that no one has already envisaged. Those who have not prepared have fallen; those who have prepared remain strong. There is a foundation to the structure, and it is created with careful consideration of the forms of repetitive attack that must be endured. Nothing is left to chance. Everything is considered, and the formation of the defense is constantly monitored, patrolled, repaired, and never underestimated.

The castle is the story you have created about yourself. It is where you live, what you believe, and how you see the world around you. Your story of who you are allows you to make decisions, and the strength of the walls is the strength of your well-being. It creates a prism that you look through, and it can be clear and strong, tinted and flowery, or dark and depressing. It can withstand attacks against you, or it will buckle under the complications of life. The mind of a teacher needs to have a level of protection to support their mental health.

But where does this protection come from? What is the history that makes the structure? What is the narrative that creates the bricks? What is the thinking that establishes the mortar between the bricks that allows them to be strong? What are the beliefs that add depth to the castle of well-being?

Exploring this involves considerable thinking and reflection on the habits, practices, beliefs, philosophies, strengths, and weaknesses that are used to create the story of your well-being castle. How well do you know your own thinking? How much have you considered your own thoughts? Do you know where your thinking has come from, and are you exposing yourself to attacks from an enemy that can exploit your ill-considered approaches to life?

The history of humankind is a study of learning, growing, and developing ideas. It is about creating, pruning, supporting, destroying, and evolving the ideas of previous generations. The animistic beliefs and superstitions found in African, Native American, and Australian cultures. The Egyptian gods and the worship directed toward them, and the control they believed these gods had over the elements. The Hindu belief system of karma, reincarnation, and a caste system where people are born into a certain class. The Confucian philosophies which focus on understanding yourself, and introduce the yin and yang in all things. The Buddhist approach that seeks enlightenment and nirvana through cycles of suffering and renewal. The Christian and Muslim traditions, where life is controlled by an all-knowing and all-seeing God. The Socratic questioning that encourages us to "know thyself." The Stoic philosophers who challenge us to consider what we can and cannot control. Nietzsche believed that people could create their own meaning in life to avoid nihilism. And there are many others.

Whether you believe in the above or not, or whether you have considered it or not, the fact is that there are parts of your life that you may recognize in the paragraphs above. You may not have even realized that they direct you in your decision-making, in your relationships with people, with material things, with your beliefs, and with your career. A lack of understanding of your incredibly strong beliefs can create challenges for you in the classroom.

If you have a strong belief in karma, then you may expect that things will happen to you, and others, in an appropriate fashion. If you are superstitious, there may be routines that you follow to create allegedly better teaching. You may believe that the gods control the elements or that a god controls your life. None of these are problems, as they are belief systems you have developed in your life, inherited from your family, or passed down through generations. It is part of who you are, and you should not be afraid of it, but you do need to consider it as it relates to the story of your well-being.

If it is something you just think about, then it is a weak spot, and it may be exploited. You will need to strengthen your beliefs and consider how they may be challenged by students, parents, teachers, and the administration. You need to create iron-clad reasons for your thinking and be prepared to defend them. The more you think about them, the more you may begin to change and refresh your story. This is a good thing. As you change, you begin to accept that others have stories that are different from yours and that others also have a story about you.

Your well-being is directly related to your beliefs, as it is a reflection of who you are as a person. You cannot afford to allow who you are to be based on a foundation of weak thinking or a paper-thin construct of a family decision that was simply handed down to you. If you place your beliefs in a house of straw, your well-being will be blown away at the first sign of trouble.

Don't forget that others will join you in the classroom with their own sets of beliefs and philosophies. But they can be more dangerous because they often arrive with belief systems that have not been tested or explored but simply inherited. A belief system that has been inherited is one that is assumed to be correct, and without the insight of deeper thinking, it can result in a rigid confidence that may not only sink them, but you as well, if you remain too close. When combined with the other twenty-odd students in the classroom and the belief systems of their parents as well, it becomes important that you create firm foundations for what you believe. Understand the story of who you are and what you believe and accept. Be prepared to embrace the wave that may crash down onto your well-being.

Also consider that some may have the same belief system as you. So, while you use your belief system to prepare for a good day of teaching, someone else may be using that same belief system to hope that you are away sick for the day.

***"A warrior is not defined by their armor or weapons, but by their courage, resilience, and ability to protect what they believe in."* —Brené Brown**

Consider the Emotional Call to Teach

(Recommended Reading: ***The E-Myth Revisited*** by Michael Gerber)

"Picture the typical entrepreneur...
a man or woman standing alone,
windblown against the elements, bravely defying insurmountable odds,
climbing sheer faces of treacherous rocks.
My experience tells me they are rare."
—Gerber, The E-Myth Revisited

When a soldier sets out to fight in a war, they go with a heart full of patriotism, to follow the impassioned cry of a charismatic leader, or to defend their land. They step out onto the battlefield with a cause and a goal, and victory is what they seek. But in every battle, there are costs to be paid. Sometimes those costs take place in the battle, but sometimes they take place in the days, weeks, months, and years afterwards. These costs occur because a change has taken place. Soldiers fight to create change in others or defend against change themselves. Are the soldiers aware of the costs of fighting over change before they enroll?

Teachers also have emotional calls to teach. They have been inspired by someone or something. But what is it that they have seen that has created that desire to be a teacher? Most people want to be a teacher based on their idea of what a teacher is. They may base this on their own experiences of being a student or on their love of children, learning, or that age group. But what do they really know? Their understanding of the role of the teacher is limited, as there are costs that they need to identify.

In the book *The E-Myth Revisited*, the author Michael Gerber looks at how small businesses work and the disconnect between working in a business and believing you can run your own. Gerber writes about the three conceptual areas of a business: the entrepreneur, manager, and technician. It is usually the technician who is skilled at creating the product. They fall under the misconception that they can go out on their own and start their own business. The technician fails to understand how the roles of manager and entrepreneur ensure that the business is successful. This lack of understanding of the roles means that the technician becomes frustrated by the elements of the business that they either don't know or didn't think were important.

The same thought process can also be applied to education. Most people want to get involved in teaching based on their idea of what a teacher is, drawn from their own experiences. They saw a teacher and watched them in class. They believe that they have an understanding of the role. How hard could it be? "O, Captain! My Captain!" So, they go to training based on their background knowledge. Here is a list of roles that a teacher takes on. See if you can identify the ones that a new teacher understands.

- Curriculum understanding
- Behavior management strategies
- Weekends spent marking
- Recognition that the role extends further than 9:00–3:00
- Quality relationships
- Professional development activities
- Having conversations with parents regarding marks, concerns, and student behavior
- Assessment and reporting
- Pedagogical knowledge

- Applying diagnostic and summative assessments
- Differentiation (and explaining it to parents)
- Subject-specific understanding and specialization

I would suggest that most people are drawn to teaching because of the quality of the relationships they had with their teachers. The role of teaching is far more extensive and complicated than that. As the book says, the technician who goes to work and expects to be successful will fail because they don't realize the importance of the other roles.

It is important to recognize this since young men and women arrive to be trained as teachers based on an emotional call to make a difference, and this is an incomplete picture of the role. Reality hits them after they are dropped into a classroom. They leave the teaching profession as the complications and stress associated with all the other roles become clearer. Teachers need the quality relationships aspect of teaching, but they also need to understand that teaching is about change.

And just like the soldier, teaching is about creating change in others or about being willing to accept change within themselves. And change comes at a cost. We need teachers who are willing to pay the price of change, understand the different roles, and embrace the challenges of complexity, as that is when they become the great teachers they witnessed when they were a student.

***"Contrary to popular belief,
my experience has shown me that the people who are
exceptionally good in business aren't so because of what they know
but because of their insatiable need to know more."
—Michael E. Gerber, The E-Myth Revisited***

Consider Everything About Myself

"Your vision will become clear only when you can look into your own heart. Who looks outside, dreams; who looks inside, awakes."
—Carl Jung

Just as a teacher needs to know why, they will also need to go further into the depths of their personality and recognize who they are. This is important, as your personality, beliefs, and values will be entering the class with you. I cannot separate my teaching self and my home self, so it is important that I am clear as to what I value and believe. Then I can reflect on what I value and believe as it relates to teaching, learning, and students.

- What are my values?
-
- What are my beliefs?
-
- What are my values and beliefs about teaching?
-
- What are my values and beliefs about learning?
-
- What are my values and beliefs about students?
-
- How familiar am I with my mental health?
-
- What are my values and beliefs about discipline in my life, and for

students?

-
- What is my personal mission statement?
-
- Who is my inspiration as a teacher?
-
- Why?
-

Before I know the curriculum, pedagogy, behavior plans, and the students, I need to know myself first. I may have unresolved issues, thoughts, strategies, and expectations buried within layers of history, experience, family, and tradition. It is best to recognize and resolve those beliefs now before they become an unwilling influence on how I see the world. It is better to open the door and view the world than to continue judging myself and everyone else through the keyhole of my beliefs and values.

You may not be able to answer these questions confidently now, but hopefully this book will begin to unlock your questions.

"Knowing others is intelligence;
knowing yourself is true wisdom."
—Lao Tzu

Reflective Considerations

- I am a teacher, and I am a warrior.
- I can improve students when I believe in and demonstrate improvements in myself.
- I have a story to tell, but I also have a story to develop.
- My future story can be built from my past, or I can create my own understanding of who I am while I build my story, and that allows me to adjust and learn.
- I am conscious of the emotions behind teaching.
- I need to be clear about who I am before I work with other people.

III

The Well-Being of Teaching

(Recommended Reading: The Well of Being
by Jean-Pierre Weill)

You never lose your ability,
but well-being is about how you think.
So, you can lose your capacity to think appropriately.
And your thinking affects your ability.
What is it that is changing your thinking
and impacting your ability?

The Classroom: Anxiety creeps in

I sit at home and stare at the television.

The colors and sounds blur together, and I pretend to watch and listen. I am present physically, but mentally, I am back in the classroom.

Today took its toll.

The frequent comments by students. The constant disrespect from the children in the room. It did not stop, and I am worn out. I tried to turn it around by making a joke. It wasn't about Sarah...but it was. I was convinced that it would land and turn the class to my side. Show my entertaining, cool self. It was a chance to show that I can be funny and make learning alive and unpredictable.

It didn't work. I lost Sarah. I lost the class.

I lost my self-respect and my self-esteem today.

My husband walks into the room and tries to engage in conversation with me. I nod and pretend to listen while he talks about his day. I act the way I am supposed to act when the conversation and topics are not about me. But this is good, as the more he talks, the more I can hide myself, my feelings, and my emotions. I can hide behind the face of a dutiful wife while my emotions and mental health plummet as I relive my day ... and Sarah's face.

At least the face that I saw before she gave me that look of shock and dejection. Then the head dropped, and all I saw was her neat hair. Her ponytails on both sides of her head, with the part at the top of her head that could have been used as a ruler. That is all I saw from her for the rest of the day.

I think back to the lunchtime session when I saw two of my peers talking. They looked at me when I walked in, quietly spoke some more, and then they both walked out as I sat at the table. I am sure they weren't talking about me, yet maybe they were. Did they know about the class and the behavior breakdown? Did they hear about the joke I made that caused Sarah to be upset?

I think I am spiraling. I am creating monsters in my head, and my imagination is making them worse. But still, I cannot stop thinking that I lost my class and my peers in one session.

I don't know if I can go back tomorrow. I don't know if I can face the class, Sarah, or my peers.

My husband keeps talking, and the television keeps flashing, but the darkness begins to envelop me. It is dragging me further down and down as the images of the day play on repeat in my head.

Who can I talk to about this? No one. No one would understand. People who aren't teachers would not know why a comment to a little girl would affect me this way. I cannot talk to my peers as they probably know and think less of me, or they don't know, and when they do, they will think less of me. Or maybe they just wouldn't care, as they have their own class to deal with.

My husband stopped talking. He is now distracted by whatever is on television. He is happy he was able to talk about his day. I guess my facial expression showed that I was interested or concerned about it. Maybe I even laughed at the right time. I cannot remember.

I sit surrounded by color, music, and happiness while at the same time I question my teaching, commitment to learning, well-being, and purpose in life.

This is not how the day was supposed to end.

Consider the Distractions to Well-Being

(Recommended Reading:
The Myth of Normal by Dr. Gabor Maté,
Brain Rules by John Medina,
The Body Keeps the Score by Bessel van der Kolk, and
Why Zebras Don't Get Ulcers by Robert Sapolsky)

"Whether we realize it or not, it is our woundedness, or how we cope with it, that dictates much of our behavior, shapes our social habits, and informs our ways of thinking about the world."
—Gabor Maté, The Myth of Normal

I am the center of my world, and I need to be in control of my well-being and mental health. But my world is surrounded by many distractions. Who I am as a person has been shaped by my history, relationships, and my vision of who I am or want to be. To begin to understand who I am, I need to first recognize the four main factors that will impact me as a teacher and as a person.

The first step is the relationship between the mind and the body. The body contains muscles, ligaments, internal organs, and all the blood and bone that create the form that we see. The body also contains a nervous system. The nervous system, when combined with our five senses, is how we identify and respond to the world around us. The nervous system sends all messages to the brain. The brain contains the mind that interprets the five senses and allows us to make decisions.

The body, as recognized by the senses and interpreted by the brain, can be affected by pain. Maybe I dropped a rock onto my foot, walked on hot concrete, or was poked by a splinter. All these pain signals were activated, and my mind decided how the body would react. I put ice on my foot, got off the hot concrete, or removed the splinter.

But the mind has its own experiences as well. It interprets the world according to my own judgements. I dropped the rock onto my foot because I was incompetent to carry it. I walked on hot concrete because I was too stupid to wear shoes. I got a splinter because I was confident that I could move the wood without wearing gloves. Or all of that could be untrue. We know that physical actions often have physical solutions, but mental or thinking actions do not always have clear ones. Or worse, we believe that what we think about ourselves in those situations is true.

Studies have revealed that the brain does not clearly differentiate between physical and mental pain. Getting a splinter in the hand or abuse from a parent can cause pain. But for one, we remove the splinter, but for the other we...endure it?

The first part of the target is recognizing that sometimes we need to focus on the body and other times, we need to focus on the mind. We need to choose to react, respond, and recover both the body and the mind when they have been affected. This first act is crucial for our well-being.

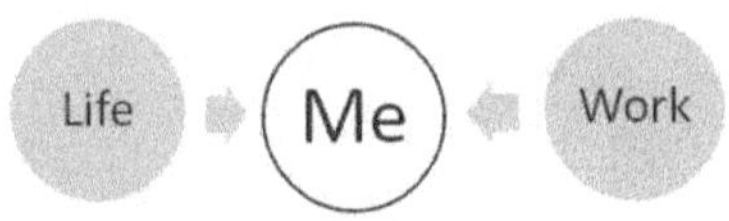

The next part of the target is work and your life. There is no such thing as work/life balance. There is only work, and then there is the rest of your life. As a teacher whose day of teaching is limited to when students are in the classroom, there is a need, or possibly a temptation, to work longer hours before school, after school, and at home. These hours of work are important for planning, marking, and providing feedback. But they can also slowly reveal themselves to be more important than they need to be.

Your other life—the life you live when you are not a teacher—is the resource that provides you with the strength, compassion, energy, humor, and sleep required to be successful as a teacher. As you consider who you are and your mental health routine, it is important to recognize that you are not targeting the work aspect of your life over life itself.

In the same way, the life aspect is fun and tempting. It is full of adventures, people, and relationships. There is too much life to enjoy. Do not worry about your work. If this becomes your focus, the time will come when planning, feedback, and student marking will suffer. You have to be conscious if you are aiming too far left or right. The well-being aim is to consider the story and either move up for the concerns of the mind, or then drop down to reveal the pain and pleasure of the body. It is also moving left to consider the work that must be done, then moving right to ensure that your family, relationships, and rest are being considered.

Mental health does not always manifest as a pure mental problem. It can become a physical problem. What happens in the mind can affect the body through stress, ulcers, panic attacks, the rising of the heart rate, or sweating profusely. These are indications that the body is under threat from the mind's recognition that something is not right.

When I am physically struck by a child or verbally abused by a parent, it can develop into a mental health problem. A mental health problem can create a physical problem. A mental health problem can become something as mild as headaches or as serious as cancer. Dr. Maté, in the book above, recommends treating the mental health concern at the same time as the physical concern, as one invades the other.

Treating the mind and body as different and unrelated elements and keeping work and life separated ensures that I do not deal with what is happening to me in a supportive way. The five senses can create a story of the world that our mind interprets as healthy or unhealthy. I can then react accordingly, and this thinking can affect relationships, emotions, and eventually teaching. Our physical reactions to stress can imprint the brain with negative or positive emotions. The link between the two is medically observed and physiologically impactful.

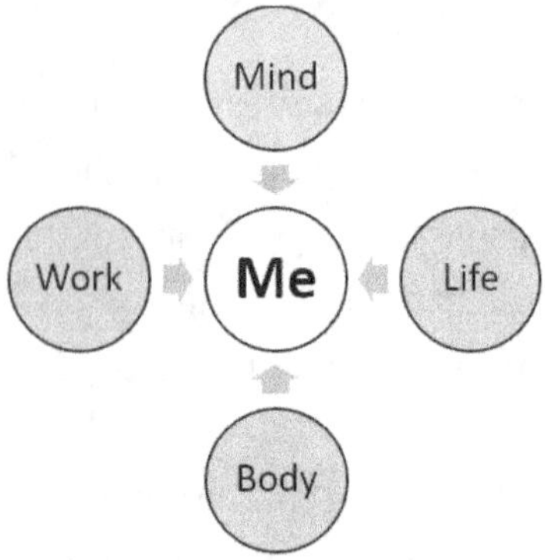

As we begin exploring the idea of myself and the various distractions that can take place in identifying who I am, I begin to realize that mind v body and work v life are not the only distractions that I can focus on. There is also the discrepancy between what I believe and what I experience. Beliefs, as we have previously described, come from history, family, and tradition. They keep you centered and focused on the task at hand. They enable you to think quickly and solve problems without having to address the various elements that may be hidden. You believe something, and that makes it true to you, so you focus your attention and decision-making on that.

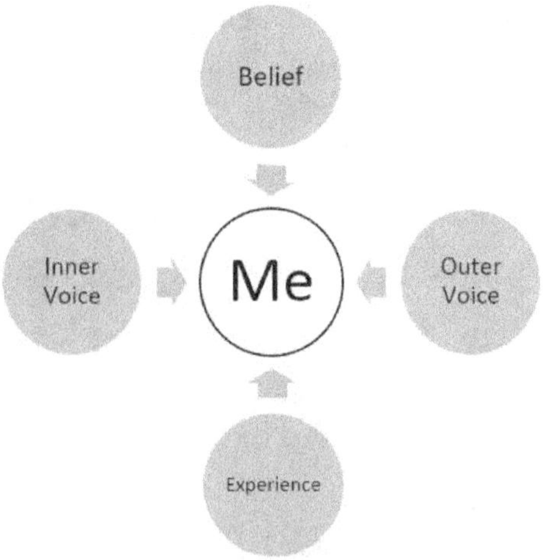

But experience can be a thorn in the side of beliefs. You may believe one thing, but then you experience something else that questions your beliefs. The experiences you face or that you have witnessed others face, the real-world events, impacts, and consequences, can have a troubling effect on your beliefs. Do you focus your attention on what you believe is true, or do you reconcile yourself to what you have seen is true? As a teacher, you are constantly fixing your attention. The system believes in one thing, but your experience has shown you something different. Mental health and well-being can be affected by the divide between belief and experience.

Another factor influencing your well-being is the difference between your inner voice and your outer voice. What does your inner voice say and think? How strong is that voice, and can it affect your decision-making and thinking? How effective is it at controlling your decisions? Does your inner voice respond to and believe in both the beliefs and experiences that you have encountered? Or do they confuse you even more, and then you argue and complain inside your head about the injustices and unfairness?

But what does the outer voice say? The one that everyone can hear is loud or quiet, but can still be heard. The one that makes jokes, talks to friends, tries to make romantic connections, supports a team, tribe, or community. Does the outer voice represent the real you, or is it the inner voice? Does the outer voice create a G-rated version of the inner voice's thoughts?

The inner voice that you have can be incredibly powerful when thinking about yourself and your students, peers, and school. What is the inner voice telling you, and what impact is it having on your mental health? So too is the outer voice. What are you expressing to others? Is it helpful and uplifting, or is it sarcastic and downgrading? Do the inner voice and outer voice match each other? Are you saying what you are thinking? Or are you revealing someone else to the outside and suppressing your true feelings? Neither of these are right nor wrong, but it is important to take ownership of these thoughts, as they will impact your well-being.

When I recognize that I am in the center of my own thinking, it allows me the chance to understand what I am thinking and why I am thinking it. I am able to realize that if my well-being is off, then my aim may be off at my target. I am spending too much time on my inner voice and beliefs. Or I am expressing my outer voice with my beliefs that don't align with my experience. I am listening to my inner voice, which is worried about issues in my mind, not realizing that it is having a physical effect on my body.

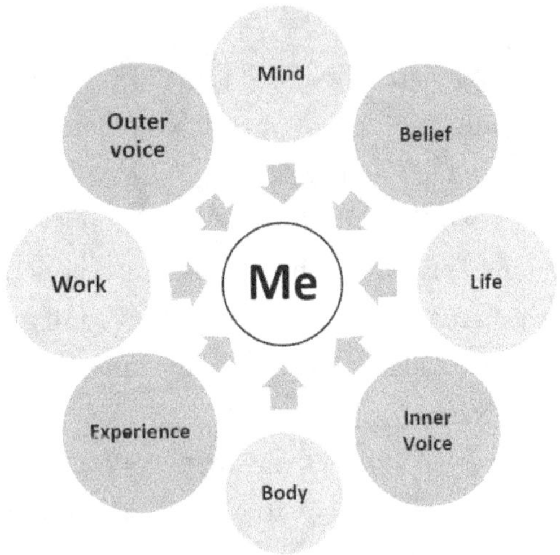

Combined, it can look like this, but this is a limited example, as there are many other factors that come together to form your perception of yourself as a person and a teacher. There are other external factors like changing curriculum, behavior management, personal circumstances, and social media. The list goes on.

I can add as many circles of "truth" as I want.
But they remain in a fixed position.
The only thing that moves is me and my aim.

The goal here is not to create an exhaustive list but to learn to be a warrior for my own mental health. To vigilantly recognise what I aim for. To strategically create an accurate perception of myself. To tactically address the problems. To control and ignore the ones I cannot use.

"And finally, this question,
the mystery of whose story it will be.
Of who draws the curtain. Who is it that chooses our steps in the dance?
Who drives us mad?
Lashes us with whips and crowns us with victory
when we survive the impossible?
Who is it that does all of these things?
Who honors those we love for the very life we live?
Who sends monsters to kill us,
and at the same time sings that we will never die?
Who teaches us what's real and how to laugh at lies?
Who decides why we live and what we'll die to defend?
Who chains us? And who holds the key that can set us free...
It is you.
You have all the weapons you need.
Now fight!"
—Sucker Punch

Consider the Safety Net

(Recommended Reading: ***The Paramedic Mindset*** by Leigh Anderson)

"Mistakes don't define you. How you respond to them does."
—Leigh Anderson

Every journey has a backup plan. Every purchase has insurance. Every Plan A has a Plan B. Steps have a handrail, electricity boards have a safety switch, and a gymnast has a mat. To get through life, it is imperative that there is something to catch us physically, financially, psychologically, or metaphorically when we fall. It is not a negative expectation that we will fail, but rather that on this journey of life, there will be moments or events that will come up fast on us that we will not expect. It is in those moments that a safety net of sorts is available for you to use.

In teaching, there should also be a net to catch you when you fall. This net in teaching needs to be a combination of your professional and mental support. The safety net to catch you should be a tapestry that is as strong as it is light, as flexible as it is durable. The interlocking, through its flexibility, will enable you to be caught and returned to a state of preparedness.

The safety net should be created from four interlocking strands.

Pedagogy for a teacher is extremely important. It is how you present information to a class that will enable them to learn. The curriculum is not important as that will change, but the pedagogy will be that which enables the curriculum, in all its different forms, to be moved forward.

A Feedback strand moves in the opposite direction of pedagogy. When pedagogy goes out, feedback comes in. It may be information from students about what is not working, or it may be your own reflections. It is the reflective direction a teacher must accept to grow professionally.

Pedagogy and feedback work together as it allows the constant reflection of what is working, what is being delivered, what is being learnt, and how all that can improve. They are the safety net for teachers.

To create the tapestry of the safety net, you need two more strands that can go either direction to create the support that you need.

Overlapping with pedagogy and feedback is the strand of personal values. Personal values, mission statements, philosophies, and beliefs create the strand that makes you who you are. You are committed to a certain vision, and you can access and interpret information from a belief system that you have developed over time. This is very important, as nothing upsets mental health more than not knowing who you are and what you believe. Without a core purpose and focus, you are going to be easily led by anyone or anything, from the latest curriculum to the newest pedagogy. Time must be spent recognizing what you believe and stand for as both a person and a teacher. The strength of your position will be the strength of your ability to rebound when life becomes challenging.

In the other direction from personal values is the importance of positive social interaction. The teacher who stands alone and spends evenings and weekends focusing on pedagogy, feedback, student improvement, and system expectations will be the teacher who falls. The strength of every teacher should be the team, relaxed moments of levity, and release from the stresses of the role. It is time spent with people who are not teachers and have no knowledge or interest in what you do that enables you to recover, restore your sanity, and build your reserves for another day.

A safety net is simply a beautiful interlocking tapestry that contains ideas and wisdom, mistakes and failures, improvements and adventure. While it may look fragile, it is the individual's experience that gives it its strength. It is the time spent creating the tapestry that gives it power. It is the time spent developing networks that provide support. It is the tapestry of beauty that creates the bounce and color in your life.

The tapestry of the safety net should be something to be proud of and should provide the different shades of who you are, but it is also the strength you need to support you when you fall. It is also flexible enough to propel you back to your optimal state after you have fallen.

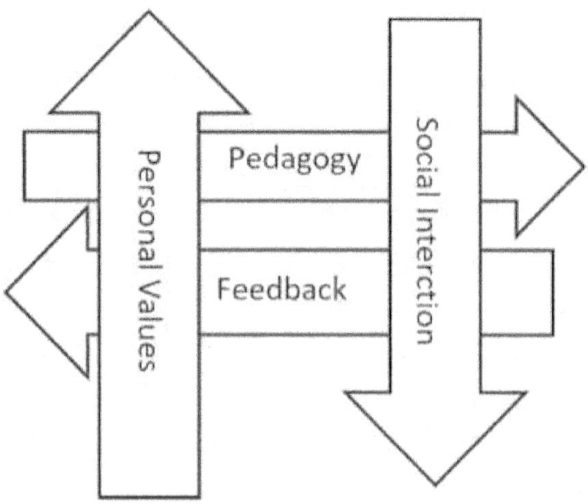

You need to create your own safety net. It does not need to contain the same strands as outlined above, as it needs to be created personally. You should create your own tapestry of identity, strength, and support, but it is important that you create this. You need to be strategic in your planning, thinking, and recovery options now. You cannot create a tapestry of a safety net while you are falling. You shouldn't wait for Plan A to fail before creating Plan B. You cannot buy insurance after the item is stolen, so neither should you hope that nothing will happen as a teacher. You are a warrior teacher, so you need to plan for this. Your well-being needs to be shaped by you now. There is no shame in falling, but spend the time creating your safety net before you start so that your educational journey does not slow down.

The tension in the net must be exact so that I can recover, but the tension of the net may not be consistent, so the recovery will be different every time. I may not recover and rebound to my original position. But that is a good thing. When I fail, make a mistake, or uncover a challenge, I will fall, but my safety net will support me, catch me, adjust to the new experience or event, and then bring me back. But I will be different. I will have changed, learnt, or adapted. I don't want to be the same person who failed, and I don't want to return to my old ways of thinking. I want to move as a teacher. My well-being, teaching, and improvement only happen when I learn. I cannot learn without failing, but in failing, I can bounce forward, improve, and absorb what I learnt to create more strings on my safety net. When I have built a safety net of support, I can move confidently into a lesson and look forward to the challenges, complexities, and failure, as it enables me to become better. I always want to bounce forward.

"For better or worse,
we did not get where we are today by bouncing back to normal."
—Harry Moffitt, The Fourth Pillar

Consider the Economics of Mental Health

"It takes a big heart to help change little minds."
"I touch the future. I teach."
"A good education can change anyone. A good teacher can change everything!"
"Children learn more from who you are than what you teach."
"You cannot stop a teacher when they want to do something. They just do it."
"Teachers are those who help find strengths, wipe away tears, overpower demons, and conquer fears."
"It is the teacher that makes the difference, not the classroom."
"Education is not the filling of a pail but the lighting of a fire."
"A good teacher is like the rising sun that comes to fill empty and dark minds with the light of education."

These are some of the quotes that can be found on web pages, in books, on classroom walls, and in teacher diaries. They all proclaim the greatness of being a teacher. They preach about your ability, inspiration, and motivation to create better learners. It is like the famous USA Army quote, "I want YOU for the US Army." This call to arms was devoted to motivating regular American men and women to leave the safety of their lives and join the war effort.

But the unspoken truth of that call was that many men and women who answered it never came back. The call to war was also a call to surrender your freedoms, family, and life. War takes a toll, and the quote to join the war effort was not so much a call for men and women to join as it was a way to replace the men and women who had already fallen. The call that they needed YOU was less about your unique skill set and more about the heartbeat that you had.

The quotes above for teaching are similarly inspiring and motivational. But the unspoken concept behind the mantra is that it is all up to me. I have to be the change. I have to be the inspiration, to have a big heart and fire. It is all on me to create this. The problem with this wishful thinking is that while those statements may inspire me to be a teacher, they can also push me out the door as my mental health strains to be what is expected from those "motivational" statements.

It is the goal of this book to recognise that mental health is an economic choice. The value I bring to the classroom is expected to come from me, but I am not a limitless source of emotion, motivation, energy, and strength. I pay an economic price for my energy, and this will run out if it is not replenished. Teams are a big focus in all areas of life. The best player in the world on a team will be celebrated for their success, but will give a shout-out to the team that allows that creative player, marketer, businessperson, or writer to perform at the highest level.

- Mantras for sports teams are about working together.
- Mantras for educators are about being on your own.

But behind the mantras and the easy-to-believe mindset ("It is just teaching children. How hard can it be?") there is a recognition. People are falling behind, struggling with the realities of the profession that look vastly different from the inspirational quotes they follow, or in some cases, simply not returning. The underlying thought behind those quotes is that you are giving something: your time, flame, effort, inspiration, ideas, and your love. But where does your time, effort, and love come from?

The economics of a teacher's mental health is that they need to inspire and create learning, but they must also replenish that energy. If I keep taking money from my bank, eventually I will run out. The same is true with teaching. Teachers need to be economical about their ability to perform. How are they going to replenish their energy and ideas? Who are they going to turn to for support in their teaching and learning? When are they going to ensure that there is a conscious effort to engage in the practice of recovery and restocking?

The rewards can be a gift: the smile of a child, the knowledge of a job well done, the improvement of students over the course of a day, term, or year. But what if that is not what you receive? I need to consider the steps I take, the people I talk to, the books I read, and the strategies I develop and use to enable me to keep moving forward. My mental health is crucial in creating great teaching. How I support myself and develop my skills is crucial in creating the mental strength needed to be a great teacher.

The mantras you don't hear are:

- You need to be selfish to ensure your mental health can cope with creating learning.
- You need to balance the negative with the positive every day.
- If you cannot listen to yourself, why do you think students will listen to you?

The teaching quote that should be considered is:

I get what I pay for. I can have great students, great lessons, and a great career, but it will come at a cost. There is a cost for everything. Sometimes that cost is worth it in the smile and improvement of students. There is value in that moment for teaching. But sometimes the cost is great, with emotional and physical hardships. There is value to be found in teaching, to be sure, but never underestimate the economics of teaching. Always consider, "How much I'm willing to pay, and who is going to pay me back?"

A mentally strong, self-aware teacher who has a range of strategies, both academically and emotionally, can create great learning in the classroom. But it does not just happen, and for the sake of my school, my students, and especially myself, I need to get a team together to work on this.

"In the economy of action, effort is a cost, and the acquisition of skill is driven by the balance of benefits and costs."
—Daniel Kahneman

Consider My Emotions

(Recommended Reading: ***The Laws of Human Nature*** by Robert Greene)

"Our ability to process information
is hamstrung by our emotional need to validate ourselves."
—Mark Manson, Everything Is F*cked

Our lives are emotional, and we make decisions based on emotion more than we think.

The strategic element of war is to distract the enemy. The best way to distract them is to use their emotions against them. Comments about them, their family, their supporters, or their country could be used to create conflict. But it is not the conflict they are looking for as much as it is the emotional state the other party falls into that will enable that party to make mistakes. Decisions made in a heightened emotional state can lead to mistakes and victory for the opposition. Martial artists work not only at developing the skills to defend themselves but also at reaching an emotional balance, so they are not pulled into small conflicts.

Mental health and well-being are important every day, but this is ineffective if it does not lead to one thing: healthy self-reflection. Teachers are people, and people have emotions. The teacher's ability to control their emotions and the self-reflective ability to consider whether those emotions are creating a barrier to learning are important.

To be effective as a teacher, it is imperative that I am emotionally stable. An emotional teacher will look inwards, and all comments, moments, and actions will be interpreted as an attack on the teacher. An emotional teacher may use students as a validation tool to bring joy and importance into the teacher's life. The perceived affection and interest students bring to the teacher becomes the emotional proof they need to get through the day. Some teachers may be so fragile in their own opinion of themselves that they are unable to process regular classroom information. Teachers who need to validate themselves, to make themselves feel important and knowledgeable, are ineffective. Teachers who need to have respect from students have already lost the conversation—and the class. If your emotional stability is going to be affected so easily by students, then that is the first step towards recognizing that you have some work to do as a teacher.

This is not healthy.

Students will find that weakness and chase after it. If you show this weakness while at the same time trying to validate yourself, then you are going to struggle. This can be changed with honest self-reflection. I need to be honest about my ability to deal with the class. I need to be honest about my capability to work on my own emotional journey. Walking into a classroom knowing I am hamstrung by my own emotional pitfalls can be avoided through self-reflection. Students need a teacher who is capable and ready to engage with the emotional turbulence of the classroom.

An emotionally stable person will look at the classroom and become a healthy observer. An emotionally stable teacher will look at the students as young people who need support.

Every person has good and bad days, and teachers are not immune to the emotional waves that can flow over us during the course of our lives. The supports are available to enable teachers to stand firm in those waves. Frameworks exist that teachers can cling to when times get tough. But the students are not the support that will enable me to get through the day. They will create joy and frustration in equal measure, but do not cling to their childlike ways as a lifeboat for your emotions, or you will get swept away.

Thinking that teaching is a beautiful profession and that it is a privilege to work with children demonstrates that you are not prepared for the battle ahead.

The teacher who wants to make a difference is driven by emotions. I want to be a teacher who is a learner who recognizes and controls emotions.

***"Expanding your body physiologically prepares you to be present;
it overrides your instinct to fight or flee,
allowing you to be grounded, open, and engaged."
—Amy Cuddy***

Consider "Fuck Parkinson's"*

Watch Apple TV show –* ***Shrinking*
(Recommended Reading:
Four Thousand Weeks: Time Management for Mortals
by Oliver Burkeman)

"Work expands so as to fill the time available for its completion."
Parkinson's Law

The Apple TV show *Shrinking* tells the story of families dealing with life in humorous, and often deeply moving ways. The focus of the stories are the therapists who manage their own trauma and joy, as well as counselling others. One of the main characters recognises he is beginning down a difficult path as he finds that he has Parkinson's disease. Parkinson's disease is a terrible affliction that affects the brain and nervous system. The patient slowly loses control of their physical condition. The character plays the role of dealing with Parkinson's disease, and on the way, he spends time with Michael J Fox, a famous actor who, in the real world, is also afflicted by Parkinson's. Their humorous way of dealing with it is to simply say "Fuck Parkinson's". This simple act of defiance is the actor's way of saying that the time taken away from them (both fictionally and actually) due to this disease does not stop them from living in the time that they have.

C. Northcote Parkinson, in 1955, wrote a satirical essay where he expressed the idea that it is time and not work that dictates our lives. This is known as Parkinson's Law. An activity that takes one hour will take two hours if two hours are allowed. It is not necessarily the activity that controls us and dictates time, but the time that we give ourselves to undertake the activity. This is a cause of concern and frustration for many people who can literally witness their work, their time, or their lives fritter away in useless or meaningless activities. The time given to other unproductive tasks seems to grow and become more important. The Parkinson law lives in the wasted time and lives of everyone.

The tragedy of life is that it is the moments when our life is at the end, or compromised, or threatened, that we suddenly become hyper-focused. The weekly assignment that is due on Monday is suddenly very clear to students on a Sunday afternoon. The marking for the report card becomes a panicked focus 48 hours before they are due, despite the weeks that lay dormant beforehand. The illness in the lives of our loved ones, or even ourselves, causes a moment to reflect on the time wasted on meaningless disputes or worthless pursuits.

In creating our well of being, it is easy to be distracted by shiny objects or moments of interest that deter us from the real purpose in our lives. We dig thinking we have all the time in the world, or even worse, we don't dig as that is something we can do after we finish school, tertiary education, get a job, get married, have a baby, become 'experienced', or retire. That is the Parkinson law affecting our thinking and our judgements. We should not allow ourselves to be slaves to the whims of the world, led by unelected ideas, or distracted by the bushfires that others have created.

Our war cry in that moment is to "Fuck Parkinson's".

"The only route to psychological freedom
is to let go of the limit-denying fantasy of getting it all done,
and instead to focus on doing a few things that count."
-Oliver Burkeman

Consider My Quadrant

(Recommended reading: ***Mastery*** by Robert Greene)

"It is what we know already that often prevents us from learning."
—Claude Bernard

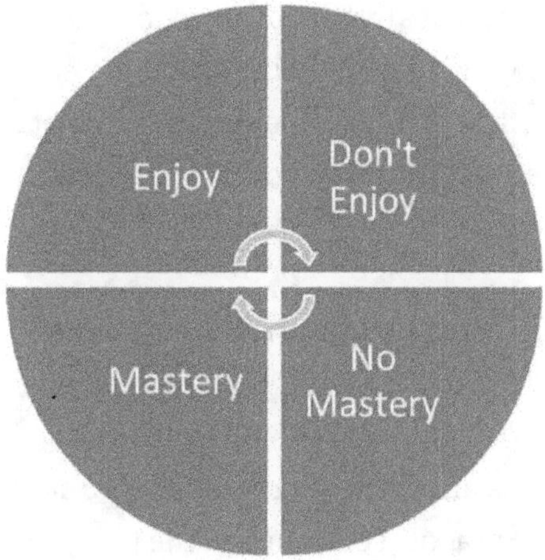

The well-being of a teacher can be affected in multiple ways. As humans travel on life's journey, they are directed to follow the trail that has been created for them. This path may offer four aspects. It may be something that you enjoy, something that you don't enjoy, something that you don't enjoy but do well, or something that you don't enjoy and don't do well. The recognition of these four quadrants will affect how you see yourself, the path you are on, and the opportunities to make different decisions. This can confuse and upset the equilibrium of a teacher, or a human being, who is geared towards finding pleasure and avoiding pain.

Before we move forward, it is important to recognise the four quadrants.

Enjoy – This is an activity that you enjoy doing and may find pleasure in. This does not mean the activity is something that you are good at, but in enjoying it, you may well improve with time. The enjoyment provides the dopamine hit that allows you to keep coming back. What do you enjoy about teaching?

Don't Enjoy – This is an activity that you do not enjoy doing, and it does not provide the psychological lift that you need to complete your day. Maybe you have been doing this for some time, and the enjoyment has passed, but the mastery is there and can support others. What is it that you do not enjoy? What is the reason, and do you have the skills to support or teach others?

Mastery – This is an activity that you excel at, have developed mastery over, and can use to lead others. What is it that you have shown mastery in?

No Mastery – This is an activity that you have no skill or understanding. The theoretical and practical elements of the task are beyond you. It will take considerable time and effort to gain even close to mastery of these skills. However, the application of these skills may provide some measure of enjoyment, whether through accepting failure, the promise of potential, or even the peer friendships that are formed by teammates with similar skill levels. What is it that you are not a master at?

It is important that, as you progress through your teaching years, you always look back at the continuum. This can support your professional development and your well-being. If you can complete activities that you are a master at and enjoy, then your work and well-being will be lifted. If you continue to do activities that you can do but with no enjoyment, your well-being will eventually be affected.

If you continue to take part in activities that you are not a master at but you enjoy, your well-being will be lifted, and you may well not only improve your own skills but also create an environment that others enjoy working in with you.

If you spend your time doing activities that you are not a master at, have no chance of being a master at, and do not enjoy, it does not take a degree to know that your perception of yourself as a person of influence will take a hit, and your well-being will fall.

If you continue to do activities that you enjoy and can do but are afraid of change and relearning, then you are affecting your professional development. By not growing, you are becoming less valuable as a teacher. So, before you embark on the journey of being a teacher, maybe it is time to reflect on what skills and enjoyment you can bring, and what you need to avoid. What do you ...?

- Enjoy and master in education
- Don't enjoy, but master, in education

Now consider this for your well-being. What is it that you can bring to the world that makes it better and improves your well-being at the same time? What is it that creates a negative emotion in you that limits your chance of growing and developing as a person?

What do you…?

Enjoy and have Mastery of for your Well-being	Don't Enjoy but have Mastery of for your Well-being
No Mastery but Enjoy for your Well-being	Don't enjoy and don't master and affects your Well-being

As a classroom teacher, you may be limited in your capacity to either enjoy and/or demonstrate mastery over a particular subject, pedagogy, or personality. This is when the warrior comes out to work. The warrior identifies the specific element that you need. Do you need to find enjoyment in something that you do, or do you need to develop mastery over something that you do in the classroom? The warrior then becomes strategic and disciplined in improving that outcome for either your professionalism or your well-being. It is the coward who says, "I hate this" or "I am not good at this," yet continues to sit in their discomfort without even trying to break free and create new boundaries.

I need to take ownership of my life, direction, professionalism, and well-being.

If I am not in control of it, then someone else will be.

"Become who you are by learning who you are."
—Robert Greene, Mastery

Consider the Daily Battle

"Discipline is often a battle against procrastination ...
It wasn't a thing you arrived at; it was a daily practice. It was a habit.
And in this daily practice, we become who we are ... or not."
—Ryan Holiday

Your teaching, well-being, pedagogy, mental health, and relationships—none of these just happen. They need to be carefully cultivated, nurtured, and developed, and habits need to be formed, practiced, and moderated. There is a constant battle every day for your attention, time, and effort. It takes considerable skill to be able to focus on what is important and ignore the rest. The idea of a battle taking place for your skills, attention, and time is hard to justify if you do not see it, but it is the business model for parents, students, the system, social media, and family. To be effective, you need to consider the impacts that are taking place in your life, and identify what is healthy and what is not, what is effective and what is not, and what creates time, space, and energy—and what removes it.

Your teaching is your profession. It is more than just a job. A job is where you are paid at an hourly rate. A profession is one where there is an expectation of higher education, and you can build a career on your experience, education, and skills. Teaching inspires and expects discipline. Teaching is a battle when the status quo of learning and student engagement is constant. The teacher must be disciplined to ensure that learning takes place every day. Teaching does not happen without battling distractions, tiredness, and the misguided belief that learning will just happen. To be a teacher is to be disciplined every day. This is not to produce quality teaching. (That should be a given.) It is to be considered professional.

Your well-being and mental health are battles that all teachers and humans need to consider. Your ability to be effective in life is determined by the discipline you place in your thinking strategies and how you deal with conflict, stress, and disappointment. The decisions you make when things go well or poorly relate to your mental health. The professional teacher also considers that they are dealing with many other personalities and challenges every day, so the need to be disciplined is even more important. A focus on ensuring the battle of thinking correctly, thinking responsibly, and thinking from the perspective of a healthy condition is very important.

"The mind never lives in the present.
In order to survive, it has to anticipate the future,
and it has to regret the past....
What the ego hates is having nothing to do.
Because then it's afraid that it no longer exists.
So it keeps itself busy dreaming up problems of the future.
And inventing regrets from the past.
Of course, neither one of them has any reality,
And therefore you stay in a state of non-reality."
—David R Hawkins

Consider the Pygmalion Effect

"Every man is his own Pygmalion and spends his life fashioning himself. And in fashioning himself, for good or ill, he fashions the human race and its future."
—I. F. Stone

There is no greater battle than the one in the teacher's heart and mind. There is a constant battle in the narrative teachers tell themselves about themselves, and the one they tell of the students in the classroom. This battle in the mind dictates the success, or otherwise, of the teacher, which in turn determines the future of the students. The battle for control of themselves will manifest itself irreconcilably in the classroom.

The story of Pygmalion is about a sculptor who created a beautiful statue. After finishing the sculpture, he stared at it and fell so deeply in love with it that the statue came to life. The story of the Pygmalion effect deeply impacts the way we think of ourselves and others. Another term for this effect is self-fulfilling prophecy.

Never underestimate the effect of expectation as it relates to the relationships and progress of students. What you think of the class will be what you find when you are in the room.

Set your mind to a high standard and consider what these students can achieve with the proper guidance. Set your mind against negativity, low expectations, and fear. These will come to life in your classroom and with the students.

- The Pygmalion effect may single-handedly destroy classrooms.
- The Pygmalion effect may single-handedly lift learning.

The Pygmalion effect is especially strong in a teacher who wants to make a difference. They will look at the class and have high expectations of what they can do to help the class achieve. When the class does not respond to their teaching, then the class may manifest as something disappointing and poor.

The Pygmalion effect for a teacher who is a learner will see a class that has potential. They will determine that everyone can succeed, but the teacher will need to learn how to make that happen. The "statue," in this case, will come to life because it learns how to "live."

If you consider a student worthy of praise and learning, and you go out of your way to deliver it, then you will reap what you sow.

Think about the students who apply the same Pygmalion effect to the teacher. They will also look to create the vision they have of the teacher. You will not only battle against the usual opposition towards learning, but you may also battle against the ideal teacher they have in their mind. The teacher who always gives free time, who lets them out to play earlier, and who always brings chocolate. If this is the teacher that they are expecting, then you may have to change their prophecy.

The strong effect of expectation on a child, by a teacher, will determine all future conversations, teachings, learning, and feedback opportunities. There is a lot of research around the impact of the spoken word. Do not underestimate the way in which you can change the life of a student or change your own life.

This effect also works with teachers as they look upon themselves. What they see and believe in themselves is the greatest predictor of their success in the classroom and in themselves. The story they tell, the philosophies they believe in, and the myths they create about themselves and their ability. The mental gymnastics they use to make themselves the hero or the villain in every story, the force or the forced, and the bystander or the upstander. These can all create the image of you in your head, and likely or not, you are going to teach, relate, behave, and act accordingly.

Your well-being is the Pygmalion you make of yourself.

Don't underestimate your impact.

***"Knowledge has many authors, knowledge has many facets,
it looks different to each person, and it changes moment to moment.
A piece of knowledge is not a description of something,
it is a way of relating to something."
—Stephen Downes***

Consider My Role

"The important thing is not to stop questioning. Curiosity has its own reason for existing."
—Albert Einstein

"How/Why/When/Where do...?"

Education begins at the end of a question. That is where education always begins. But actually, there is a lot more to it than that. Education begins with curiosity. Something has happened, and we do not know the answer, so we become curious. That curiosity moves to a why or how question. The depth of curiosity will lead to a deeper willingness to find the answer. Once the answer has been found, the person has been educated.

At no stage was anyone involved in this process, apart from the person who was curious. So, what is the role of the teacher?

Is their role to create curiosity? Is it to create the question? Is it to create the capability to find the answer? The short answer is yes. The longer question is how can we create the curiosity that begins the process?

This is the role of the teacher. Too often, the teacher enters the classroom with the curriculum goal that leads to the assessment task and begins the lesson. The teacher needs to understand that the role of the teacher starts with engaging the student's curiosity in the learning.

In sports, wars, operations, and court cases, there does not need to be a why question, as the reason that everyone is there is clear from the very beginning. The role of the operator in this instance does not need to be explained. But how often have students asked, "Why are we learning this?" This needs to be a call to action. If that statement is expressed by a student, then the teacher has not engaged the most important part of the child: their curiosity.

Once curiosity is established, the student will then ask their own questions. And when they ask that question, they are more willing to find the answer. The teacher can guide and teach the capabilities to find the answer, but the searching and the ultimate education are performed by the student.

Teachers may well argue that some things have to be learned. I then ask in return: if they must be learned, but there is no curiosity or bigger picture that they fill, then do they have to learn it? I also ask that a part of the role of a professional teacher, it is my responsibility to create that curiosity in the child. If I cannot see the reason, if the child cannot see the reason, or I cannot sell the reason for learning, then I may well ask myself if it is worth it in the long run. Students are quick to identify paint-by-numbers teaching, and my lack of enthusiasm for the content will be exposed quickly.

My role is to create curiosity. But I need to be curious to begin with.

"Why is it that when one man builds a wall,
the next man immediately needs to know what's on the other side?"
—George R.R. Martin

Consider Marcus

(Recommended Reading: ***Meditations*** by Marcus Aurelius)

"External things are not the problem.
It is your assessment of them.
Which you can erase right now."
—Marcus Aurelius

Marcus Aurelius was a leader in Rome. He was a leader of people, the military, and politics. But he did not use his power to become famous, he did not use his position to become wealthy, he did not use his military to conquer nations, and he did not use his politics to dictate the lives of others. He wished to be a leader of one thing only, and that was himself. Marcus used his knowledge of Stoicism to create a lifestyle for himself that he worked on correcting and focusing on what he could control, and looked with bemusement at the areas of his life that impacted him that he could not control.

Stoicism focuses on self-control, reason, and virtue. It seeks to establish an understanding of what you can control, and in demonstrating discipline of what you control: your thoughts, actions, environment, and decisions.

Teachers work in environments that are increasingly out of control, and this lack of control can lead to poor decision-making, poor self-esteem, and poor well-being. Yet, teachers live in a world far removed from the constant pressure of Marcus Aurelius (a Roman emperor), or Seneca (the consul of the Roman tyrant Nero), who eventually ordered him to commit suicide, or Epictetus (who was a slave), who became a philosopher under the tutelage of Stoic teaching. Yet teachers look at the classroom, the behaviors, school, and consider it difficult.

Well-being under Stoic philosophy would disagree with teachers. It is important that teachers directly understand what is in their control: their teaching, behavior management, time, pedagogy, and relationships. Focused and proactive attention on aspects of the profession that can be controlled is the first step towards positive mental health. Focused and reactive attention to aspects of the profession that teachers cannot control is the first step to negative mental health.

Teachers should be encouraged to write down the names of the students in the classroom. Name the students who provide predictable responses to lessons, and write down the students who are unpredictable in their nature. This creates a direct link to learning what control will look like in the classroom. Poor well-being in the classroom is linked to the unpredictable nature of the environment and students. If teachers begin by recognizing where the unpredictable behavior will come from, then the surprises will be minimized.

You will not be able to control the behavior, but the expectation that it is going to happen can take the power away from the student who is seeking that moment of indecision or shock from the teacher. Use this process to recognize those who will learn, and those who will not. Those who will listen and those who will not. Those who will work independently and those who will not. Those who will respond to learning and those who will not. This will create a picture of elements of the classroom that you can control and those that you cannot. This does not mean that you ignore that which does not want to work; you must continue to try to develop learning for all students. But poor well-being is placing your ability to teach at the feet of students, and those who walk over it make a direct impact on your well-being.

Continue to provide learning for all students, but do not attach your well-being to those who choose not to be involved. Instead, attach your well-being to the learning that you have created and that has been embraced. If you gain learning for those who do not wish to be involved, then this can add to your positive mental health. Create a baseline for yourself and then build it from there.

The same approach can be applied to class expectations, unit and lesson plans, policies expected, and other aspects of the profession that you can control. This will take time, but this is the profession, and this is being proactive about teaching and learning, about mental health and well-being.

Well-being is a battle that teachers will need to face. Whether they seek to engage with this enemy is up to them, but the enemy of low self-esteem will attack whether I am prepared or not, whether I believe it or not. Remember the thinking about Stoicism and learn about ways of thinking that can improve positive well-being and mental health.

- Recognize what can be controlled.
- Recognize what cannot be controlled.
- Have a tactical plan to address both.

"The chief task in life is simply this:
to identify and separate matters so that I can say clearly to myself
which are externals not under my control,
and which have to do with the choices I actually control.
Where then do I look for good and evil?
Not to uncontrollable externals,
but within myself to the choices that are my own."
—Epictetus

Consider Conversational First Aid

(Recommended Reading: ***Thick Face, Black Heart*** by Chin Ning Chu)

***"If you are not concerned about the outcome of a circumstance,
you will experience no fear.
Whatever the outcome will be, will be, whether you fear it or not."
—Chin Ning Chu, Thick Face, Black Heart***

The soldier is lying on the field of battle, and they are in pain. They are screaming in agony and saying words that are inappropriate and rude. They may even begin to swear at you and make you feel uncomfortable with their comments and abusive language. If you are so offended, you may swear back and list the reasons why what they are saying has made you feel uncomfortable. You may need to admonish them on their use of language and chastise them for the way they have made you feel. You may even report them to the higher authorities for the way they have acted around you. If they are a higher rank, you could report them for bullying; if they are a lower rank, you could report them for not respecting the chain of command. Your feelings have been hurt, and you can do all these things, or consider them, as the person is lying in front of you with their foul language, abusive comments, and deliberately hurtful rhetoric.

The problem is that they are screaming because they are injured. As a medic, first aid responder, or a friend, your role is to ignore the comments and words that are being expressed and recognize the reason for the anger. The reason for their anger is pain. It could be a splinter, a broken bone, or internal injuries. The language could be for many reasons, but it will not help to focus on what they are saying, but rather on asking questions to identify and triage the real hurt.

This scenario may sound simplistic and self-explanatory, but it is, in fact, a common occurrence in schools. Parents will come to school and be a raging fount of emotions, opinions, and beliefs. The teacher needs to conduct first aid on this "patient" by being patient and applying DR ABC. Ignore the screaming and comments and start with:

D – Danger

What is the reason for the comments? Listen to what they are saying. What can you discover without approaching? Keep your distance both physically and verbally, and use your eyes and ears to make assumptions about their state of being. Look at the clothes, skin, and footwear. Who is with them? Are they all talking and angry? Is there one who is leading the pack, and the others are following?

R – Response

Now begin to question. Introduce yourself and make them feel welcome. This will allow you to gauge how they respond to a welcome and friendly manner. Do they change the tact, or do they become angrier? Can they respond? Do they match your (hopefully) calm voice? Does your slower and considered speech pattern allow them to also regulate how they speak? Lead them to a safe place to sit and ensure the right temperature is in the room.

A – Airway

Open the airway of the conversation and ask them how you may help them. Allow them the chance to talk and open their airway. Do not constrict it with your ideas, opinions, answers, suggestions, and criticism. Allow the parents to speak and get into a flow while you take notes. Within the notes and verbal barrage, you will start to identify a theme. Maybe it is a theme that is not as drastic as they make it out to be. Maybe it is a theme that is hidden behind previous trauma or discontent, and it has emerged. Or maybe they have a genuine concern that will need to be addressed.

B – Breathing

Slowly breathe oxygen into the conversation by asking for more specific information regarding what you know about the incident. Repeat what they have said to allow them to be sure that you have heard them. Slow down the breathing and allow time to pass between an answer and the next question. Take notes to also slow down the breathing. Slowly, the person will begin to take charge of their emotions and think a bit more clearly, and you can begin to direct the conversation onto the topic that is of concern. This will allow the emotion to be removed, and first aid can begin being applied to the now-stated "injury."

C – Compression

Begin applying pressure to the reason for the pain. You have identified it, and now the compression of focused questions and focused ideas begins. It is your role to be consistent in your questioning, just like compressions. Do not go too fast, do not slow down. Do not change the topic of conversation, make a joke, or not take their concerns seriously. Continue to explore ways that they may be able to find a solution. Offer ways that the school can support. Be consistent with your understanding of the problem and your desire to help.

Remember, first aid gives you the assistance you need until a professional medical authority becomes involved. Schools should be no different. The parent may have calmed down, but that does not mean that more support should not be wrapped around them. They may need a GP or mental health specialist. Their child may need professional support both externally and internally. Negotiate this with the parent. This demonstrates that you care and also ensures that you will not have to triage this incident again, as support will be provided.

At some stages, like in first aid, the patient may start to become unsettled. And just like first aid, you may need to start again.

Danger – Did you say or do something that created this new outburst?

Response – begin the conversation again.

Airway – allow them to talk and identify if there is a new cause or if you did not appreciate the original one. You continue first aid until the patient can breathe or think on their own without emotion guiding their decisions.

Parents will always come to school in a fit of emotions as it affects their child. This should be acknowledged and accepted. The role of the teacher is to identify the reason for the emotion, the seriousness of the emotion, and the response to the cause of the emotion. Do not waste time trying to solve the emotion itself. It may be buried under years of discontent, and you do not have the time, authority, or skillset to uncover this hurt. Focus on the student, focus on the reason, and set the path towards healing, and let the parent deal with themselves.

Use DRABC on yourself during times of trauma. Identify what the danger is. Maybe it is the parent who has come to me angrily, and I need to recognize that I feel that danger. Am I able to respond, and can I respond correctly? I will need to open up my airway to breathe, as sometimes the stress of the situation can prevent me from breathing or cause me to take shallow breaths, and this is not the time to lack oxygen. Breathing slowly allows for better questions of myself. Am I in danger, or is it in my imagination? Compression means to feel the rhythm of my body, my heart, my breathing. Am I able to feel the temperature and rhythm of the room? Am I able to center myself and create a rhythm of listening, watching, speaking, listening, watching, speaking, repeat ...

"Silence, along with modesty, is a great aid to conversation."
—Michel de Montaigne

Consider Pleasure

"Many of us pursue pleasure with such breathless haste that we hurry past it."
— Søren Kierkegaard

For pleasure to be created, there needs to be tension. The tension before the event can enhance pleasure. It is the joke before the punchline, the build-up of play before they score; it is asking the question of romance before the response of the partner. The tension created can affect your nervous system as you eagerly await the response, and the response can be such a release that it can fill the nervous system with pleasure-enhancing chemicals. Pleasure is to be sought after and experienced by all.

But pleasure can only be experienced with tension. A punchline with no joke, a goal scored with no competition, a declaration of love without the pursuit seems cheap. There is no pleasure to be gained without tension and the pursuit of discomfort. The chemicals within the body will not be activated in this scenario, and the pleasure will not be accessed. Pleasure can only be released after tension has been created. It is a scientific fact that when you apply pressure to something, it creates an opportunity for release.

"We talk about tension like it is a bad thing.
But the only way to launch a rubber band across the room
is to pull it backwards, creating tension ...

And tension keeps us focused on the world around us."
—Seth Godin, This Is Strategy

This can also happen in classrooms. If my students are learning everything and getting everything correct, then that may mean that I am not challenging them. I am not creating tension in learning. This tension should be created for the students' benefit and for me. Witnessing students being placed under pressure through learning that is intentionally shaped to create tension is the goal. The release of learning and the thrill of achieving is a pleasure that the students and I will experience. The pleasure of learning then creates intrinsic motivation to delve deeper, explore further, and develop a greater understanding. The pleasure that I think students gain from stickers or sweets is dwarfed by the natural chemicals of achievement flowing through their bodies as they experience the release from the tension of not knowing to the pleasure of now understanding.

As a teacher, I will also gain that pleasure and feel the impact of chemicals sweeping through my body when I recognize that the tension I created in the room with my teaching has produced the release of learning. That look of understanding and acknowledgement from the student, who may not have realized what I created, is all the pleasure I seek.

Pleasure can also be a fine line to tread. If I seek to create pleasure by increasing tension, but the pressure becomes too much, then I will not create a release, and I can squash the learning and creativity. As a teacher, it is imperative that I monitor, with the range of students in the room, the level of tension that I am creating and ensure that the release is both academic and profitable for intrinsic motivation. Remember also that the release of pleasure is only measured in relation to the tension that created it. If the tension and pressure of the moment were greater than the small amount of release and pleasure that was created, then students will be unwilling to commit to the stress of learning in the future.

Teaching is the constant balance between learning and understanding, tension and release, or pain and pleasure.

"For without pain, there can be no pleasure.
Without sadness, there can be no happiness.
Without misery, there can be no beauty."
—Harlan Ellison

Consider Pain

(Recommended Reading: The Most Important Question of Your Life, https://markmanson.net/question, Mark Manson)

***"What pain do you want in your life?
What are you willing to struggle for?"
—Mark Manson***

You may know what you want, but what are you willing to sacrifice to get what you want? You may have a goal but consider what nightmares you are willing to endure to reach the goal. The goal is important, but the struggle is the only way to get there. The bigger and better the goal, the harder and more complicated the struggle. It is easy to walk to the shops, and it is harder to walk to Mt. Everest. Yet, the view and accomplishment of Mt. Everest dwarfs (literally) the experience of going to the shops, and it is worth the effort, pain, and exhaustion.

Warriors throughout history, both men and women—on the battlefield, the sporting field, or in the business world—only became successful by recognizing the physical, psychological, and emotional sacrifices that they would have to accept to improve. They needed to discipline their body, thinking, decisions, relationships, and weaknesses to be successful. They willingly embraced the pain and the hardship as they knew that was the only path towards success. While success is not guaranteed, the journey will always encounter diamonds along the way for those who are strong enough to embrace the pain and walk the path.

Teachers all want great students and inspiring classrooms, but what are you willing to do to create that environment? What are you willing to ignore to ensure learning happens? What are you not going to accept to create a positive learning environment? How much time will you spend after school, on weekends, and on holidays? How much are you willing to sacrifice to ensure that students learn?

What are you willing to endure? What pain are you willing to accept? What sacrifices are you willing to make to improve your teaching or your thinking? If you think teaching is a noble profession that you can walk into, then you do not appreciate the blood, sweat, and tears drawn from successful people in places away from the spotlight where real learning, strength, and endurance were created.

That student's behaviour is relentless and annoying, but is it also the pain needed to strengthen patience? The curriculum is confusing and non-linear, or is it the struggle needed to dig deeper into my planning to solve this question? Students are always noisy and disrespectful when they come to the classroom after a break, or is this the challenge of learning to engage, or to set boundaries, weeks ago? The assessment task does not make sense, and the students are guaranteed to fail, or is this the frustration needed to ensure the assessment tasks were clear when I was planning this unit to begin with? The winging of girls, or the machismo of boys, is something I do not need in my life....or maybe I do, as this is the pain that I need to strengthen my empathy, relationships, or understanding of students.

What will I need to do to experience success as a teacher? Where do I need to go, and who do I need to see to ensure my teaching practice has the strength and fortitude to hold up when the pain hits? What strategies will I have created to roll through the tough times?

- What are some things you would give up to be a great teacher?
- What sacrifices are you willing to make to improve your teaching?
- What pain and time will you accept to ensure your teaching remains relevant?

"Take chances; make mistakes. That's how you grow.
Pain nourishes your courage.
You have to fail in order to practice being brave."
—Mary Tyler Moore

Consider the Identity Anchor

(Recommended Reading: **Quit** by Annie Duke)

"When it comes to quitting,
the most painful thing to quit is who you are."
—Annie Duke

I am a teacher. I am a male. I am a female. I am funny. I am loud. I am a reader. I was almost a sportsperson. I travelled around the world. I worked in another industry. I am a parent. I have children. I am single. I am married. I am a maths teacher. I am an English teacher. I am interesting. I am shy. I have a lot to offer. I am still learning. It is just who I am.

Having an identity is important. It tells the world who you are and what you stand for. It allows you to make decisions using your anchor as a guide. The anchor of your well-being is like the anchor of a boat. It provides you with the strength and comfort to keep you in a fixed position so you can ride the waves of challenges, the currents of emotion, and the winds of unpredictability that crash against you. These elements try to push the boat off course. With a strong anchor and a solid identity, this will be a fool's errand.

But the anchor is heavy and does not allow you to move. In fact, it can stop progress, and when the environment changes, the anchor must be allowed to move. Identity can become fixed, or a fixed mindset, and the anchor could ignore the signs that you have to change. Blockbuster had an identity, and it was renting videos and DVDs. Kodak had an identity, and it was producing rolls of film for cameras. Nokia and Blackberry had an identity, and it was producing the best mobile phones. All these companies failed because their identity did not allow them to change, adapt to feedback from the market, or respond to competitors. They happily kept the anchor of their identity in place while the world moved on without them.

The well-being of a teacher should be like an anchor. It should be a comfort, but it also needs to be lifted when life changes, when the curriculum changes, when the pedagogy changes, when behavior changes, and when the complexities change. You need to move with your growth and ideas. You need to explore the edges of who you are, then drop your anchor and be that person.

Maybe you are an early-year teacher who loves Math. But you can also identify as an upper-year teacher who enjoys exploring English. You may be a loud and funny teacher who hides your identity behind your opinions. You could become a quiet, reflective teacher who listens more to others' opinions.

As an anchor, you will need to recognise the difference between the storms of change and the storms of turbulence. Storms of change may challenge you to move and think differently, and may allow you the chance to obtain a new identity. Storms of turbulence can rage around you and distract you from who you are, without wanting to improve who you are.

Do not hide behind your anchor, and do not ride the storms of change while clinging tightly to it. Find the identity that embodies you: kind, friendly, pedagogy-focused. Then feel free to use your anchor to be a teacher who is also a learner.

"When your identity is what you do,
then what you do becomes hard to abandon,
because it means quitting who you are."
—Annie Duke

Consider Game Theory

(Recommended Reading: ***The Art of Strategy*** by Dixit & Nalebuff)

"I know what you're thinking:
'Did he fire six shots or only five?'
... you've got to ask yourself one question:
'Do you feel lucky?' Well, do you, punk?"
—Dirty Harry, Clint Eastwood

The world is less about the decisions we make and more about the responses those decisions create. Dirty Harry is asking a question and playing a game. The game is whether you roll the dice and try your luck or capitulate. The game is not about the decision; it is about what happens after you make it. Often, we feel like we are playing with a one-sided dice. We believe in one outcome and act accordingly. We are then surprised when we encounter two-sided outcomes, or four, or forty different outcomes that can occur when the opposition responds to the challenges that we have laid in front of them.

"What the other player will actually do,
not what you think they will do in their shoes."
—Dixit and Nalebuff, The Art of Strategy

Game theory should be a focus for teachers in behavior management. It asks participants to consider what the options are before making a decision.

Often, we consider what we will do, but not what the other party will do. Sometimes we make our intentions clear by outlining what we will do if they act in a certain way.

Teaching, however, involves decisions for both students and teachers. Teachers decide where to teach, when to teach, how to teach, and sometimes who to teach. Students are affected by those decisions, and they react to them. Sometimes they go with the flow and follow the teaching, or at least appear to be. Others consider the choices in front of them and make different decisions. Game theory is about recognizing there are other decisions that could be made, including by the teacher. It is about recognizing what we do not know and determining what possible courses of action are available to both teachers and students.

In a game, every action has an equal and opposite reaction. Actually, that statement is true of many things, except teaching. Sometimes an action produces an unequal and wholly oppositional reaction. When teachers are working on learning and encounter hostility, it is usually in the form of verbal or physical misconduct towards the teacher or peers. This outburst is not a proportional response to learning about writing or mathematics. It is an emotional response with layers that are not known or have not been observed by the teacher.

The problem for teachers is that the response makes no sense. When asked to get their book out, the response of a child could be to get it out and throw it across the room, rip it out, or refuse to get it out altogether. This is not within the realm of events that should occur as a response to simply getting a book out. As teachers, we need to recognize that even the simplest instruction can lead to challenging responses.

Game theory is never about a single event. It recognizes that one event may have several outcomes, and it is the role of the teacher to identify and respond to the outcomes that students may produce. By knowing your students, you are in the best position to determine how they may respond when learning comes their way. When a concept is taught or a lesson is presented, your job when using game theory is not to ask what you think they will do, but what they will do if you try to walk in their shoes. Good lesson planning may have strategic steps outlined, but perhaps one of those steps was not understood. Perhaps one was not seen as relevant.

Game Example

Teacher: "If you don't write the work down, you will be kept in at lunch."

The teacher has outlined the game and provided what they think will be the consequence. Students, however, may not want to play that game and will likely create their own scenario. As teachers, we need to consider the different ways they can play and then predict the responses. We often consider what we will do, but hardly ever consider what others will do. We hope the threat of being "kept in at lunch" is enough of a strategy. But that is not always the case.

e.g. responses:

- The student writes everything down, but it cannot be read.
- The student rips the paper up.
- The student throws books across the room.
- The student immediately runs from the room.
- The student begins swearing at classmates.

None of these scenarios were in the plan stipulated by the teacher, and were not expected. While it may be hard to ask teachers on a busy day to consider all alternatives, students will be doing exactly that. They will make a move and see what you will do. Game theory is about creating a scenario to see how the opponent responds. That response then creates another reaction, and the game is afoot. Sometimes it is about seeing how far the teacher can go before the student is caught. Sometimes it is about seeing how far they can go before the teacher gives up. Sometimes it is to see if the teacher is bluffing. Students are crafty and always considering their options. Teachers need to recognize the game theory at play.

"Every battle is won before it is fought."
—Sun Tzu

One of the game strategies from Dixit and Nalebuff is called looking ahead and reasoning backward. If you ask the student to write out the lines, the teacher needs to look ahead at the options and reason backwards. Game theory teachers could put a probability number on the possible options and structure a plan in case it occurs. If you know the student, it may result in the student abusing classmates and have a probability rating of 78%, in which case you have a plan to respond.

Some simple games like rock, paper, and scissors, or choose a number between one and a hundred. These all focus on the odds that are in favour of the person setting up the scene. To do it correctly, you need to predict what strategies they are going to use and consider ways to counter them. The same applies to behaviour management in teaching. If the teacher does not set down strategies, they are allowing the student to create the game and the rules. The teacher then plays catch-up for the entire interaction, as they respond to the strategies of the student.

Game theory looks at identifying possible responses to actions. If I put an X in a tic-tac-toe square, I need to recognise that the other person is going to put an O down as well. But they will not put the O down in a haphazard way. They will either create a defensive move against the position of my X, or they will use an offensive move against me. These are the only two options.

Teachers should expect the same thing in the classroom. Students will either produce a defensive move against you and/or your teaching, or they will create an offensive move. If they move defensively, what are they protecting? If they move offensively, what weakness can they see in you?

Defensive moves:

Why are you always making us write?

Why do we have to do this?

Offensive moves:

This is rubbish, and so are you.

I am over this work, and there is nothing you can do to make me (while ripping the sheet).

Our whole life is spent attacking or defending. We are either attacking a position/person/idea that we don't like, or else we are defending our position/person/idea from others. It is a part of life that we create these boundaries, both physical and metaphorical, that are integral to who we are. It is perfectly understandable that when our perception of who we are comes under threat, we respond. In fact, it is a healthy person who will respond in such a way under such conditions. It is the unhealthy person who allows others to storm their castle of ideas without creating some defense.

Students are the same. They have been challenged in their thinking. Their position/person/idea of who they are as a learner is under attack. They need to defend their position, or they need to attack others who are seeking to storm the castle of who they think they are. This should not be taken lightly, nor should it be considered a character flaw. The only flaw in this process is that we, as teachers, did not appreciate the depth of meaning that learning something new would have for them. Game theory would look at this situation unfavorably. You walked into a room to play a new game with opponents and never told them the rules. Never gave them the tools to play, never explained what success mean and didn't explore how long the game was going to go for. The opponents in your class are going to respond. The ones who don't are either eager to play the game, have played the game before, or are too small in nature to question your motives. And if you are attempting to develop critical thinking, then their position of who they are will need to be explored.

Game theory recognizes that if you put an X on a square, pass a ball on the wing in a game of soccer, or charge into an online room fully armed in a computer game, you are trying to create a response. You either want to see what your opponent will do or you want to surprise your opponent. Students may not think at this high level of reasoning, and so the response is less thought-out and calculating and more emotional, but as a teacher, it is your role to have played this game already in your head. You need to recognise the possible responses a student will provide, and you must either have set up plans to avoid the confrontation or a response plan.

Control yourself. Be a learner. Be encouraged to learn about the students. Do not pity or excuse their behavior, but allow their behavior to teach you about themselves and their weaknesses, responses, or fears. Create learning opportunities and devise strategies that encourage growth. If the student embraces it and makes a 1° turn, then you have made a difference. As 1°, over time, can be the difference. You will not make a change by being the difference in the future; you will make a change by focusing on the present.

"Never let the future disturb you.
You will meet it, if you have to,
with the same weapons of reason
which today armed you against the present."
—Marcus Aurelius

Consider My Journey

(Recommended Reading: ***Strong Ground*** by Brené Brown)

"Our strong ground is made up of two elements:
(1) Our own footing, including our values, a clear sense of our contribution, our curiosity, and our humility.
(2) Our connection to another person or group of people who are also grounded."
-Brené Brown

"Individuals and organisations are building new muscles. Finding our strong ground, that athletic stance, is the only thing that can provide both unwavering stability in a maelstrom of uncertainty, and a platform for the fast, explosive change that the world is demanding".
-Brené Brown

As we start the journey, we all individually have to take responsibility for the certainty that we believe we stand on. Our well of being begins when our certainty is explored, and our understanding of ourselves grows. The deeper we dig, the stronger the ground and the more capacity to build our lives and teaching. The individual journey becomes easier and more exciting when others join us on the adventure. When an organization or a school joins, then the journey really begins.

My individual journey starts at the bottom of the pyramid.

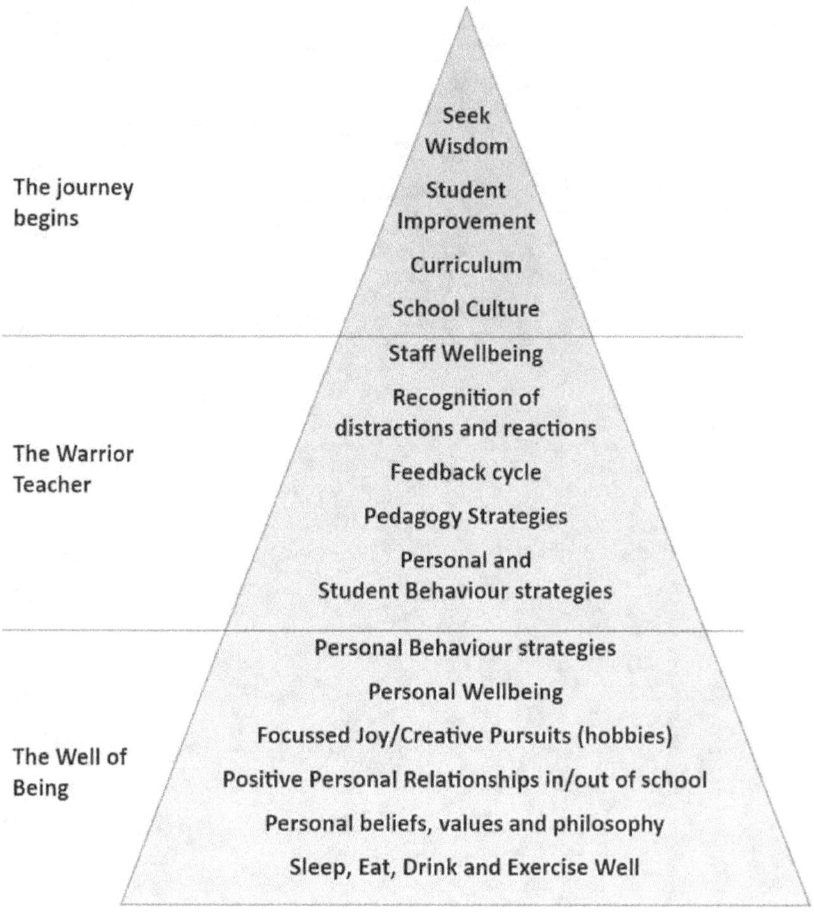

If all staff participate and create the circle, how much stronger can the school become?

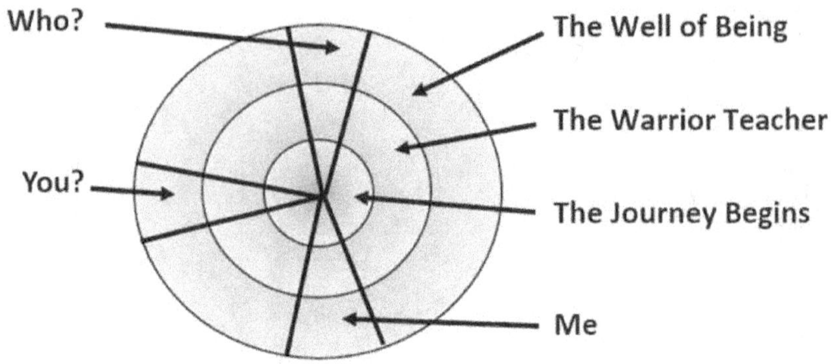

Consider...Now

Honour the moment.
Respect the moment.
Be present.
Now.

The now is fleeting and is never still.
The past comes before the now, but it cannot be changed.
The future comes after the now, but it is relatively unknowable.
There is only that fraction of a second in my life that is now.
There is a sliver of a moment that separates the past from the now.
There is a sliver of a moment that separates the now from the future.
The sliver of a moment is the key to everything.
How you perceive, and what you do with that sliver,
will impact what "now" looks like.

I consider my now as a direct reflection of my past.
It does not need to be.
I consider my future fixed from now.
It does not have to be.
That lesson, that behaviour, that comment that has happened.
It was in the past.

My well-being concerns, my planning problems,
my pedagogy inefficiencies.

They are in the past, and they are not me now.
I need to honour and respect the moment I am now in.
I don't need to allow that past to direct my now.
I need to use my now to support, prepare, plan, and organise my future.

My future will be the new now, but will it be the old teacher?
My future can be the new teacher, but will it be the old practitioner?
The past should not be the wall that holds me back ...
unless the wall holds a large mirror
Now I am present in the now.
There is power, learning, honesty, and feedback in my past ...
that can positively impact my now.

Tools, strategies, and challenges have been my past.
Ideas, opportunities, and battles will be my future.

It is only now that I can identify what is useful and what is not.
What will support me and what will not?
What will engage my teaching and move my learning forward?
The more I encounter, choose, direct, and impact in my teaching now,
the better my well-being and self-esteem will be now ... and in the future.

Since I started reading this, there are 20, 30, or 50 more.
I had many choices I could have made:
I could have stopped reading.
I could have started doomscrolling.
I could have spoken to a friend.
Watched television.
I could have observed the scenery.
I could have gone to the gym.
I could have read another book.

Don't waste any moment.
Honour the moment.
Respect the moment.
Be present.
Now.

Reflective Considerations

- It is important to be focused on what our focus is to ensure positive well-being.
- When we fall, we need to have the capacity and capability not to bounce back, but forward.
- Recognize the pleasure and appreciate the pain, as they will follow and teach you, but they should not control you. It will deepen your well of being and reaction.
- Learn about game theory; there is much to learn and apply in the classroom to extend your well of decision-making.
- Learn about the theory of economics and apply it to teaching and mental health; it will create a deeper well of being and responding.
- Marcus Aurelius is just one philosopher; there are more. Research others to create a deeper well of being.
- Reflect on the pyramid of success for you and your school.
- Know your role, check your anchor, and excavate your well of being.
- Do it now.

IV

The War of Teaching

"Almost every student you meet may be fighting a battle you know nothing about.
Stop, think, then make your response accordingly."
—Robert John Meeham

"A real soldier does not fight because he has something that he hates in front of him.
He fights because he has something that he loves behind his back."
—G.K. Chesterton

The Classroom: The improvement begins

I sit at my desk and prepare for the day.

What happened yesterday that worked, and what did not?

I look at the room. The desks are all lined up in rows, like soldiers on a field of battle. The chairs are tucked in neatly, for now. The feeling in the room is calm, with peace and quiet, and yet I am alert for the coming intrusion of the students.

What do I need to work on?

There is Sarah. I told a joke to the class that I thought would land and bring her and the class together. It did not land, and Sarah dropped her head and did not participate for the rest of the day. I tried to see her at the end of the day, but she escaped quickly and quietly. I need to see her before class starts to apologize. This is how the day should start.

I look out the window and see the class lining up. Stella is barking instructions to one of her peers. She will be in the classroom giving me looks, rolling her eyes, and expecting the world to work around her. I will need to be present to provide her with the attention that she needs, whilst purposefully avoiding the looks that will take place. She is the queen.

I need to be aware of Brian and Emily. They are bored in class and are not joining in. I recognize now that they are working at a much higher standard than what

I am teaching. I am strategically prepared for them. I have extension material that will be harder and more challenging than what I have provided previously. I cannot wait to see the looks in their eyes when I take them aside and offer them the opportunity to really stretch their knowledge, their imagination, and their intelligence. This will be a high point of my day.

There are Rob and Percy. I thought it was a good tactical move to have them sitting together to nullify the behaviour of one and provide the other with a chance to mentor. That did not work out as planned. I have had to change my tactics and separate them between Stacey. She will be a good shield for their conversations and their behavior. I will try this today and assess whether it is worth pursuing or whether I will need to move them again.

I am still unsure about Erica. She engages in some activities but not others. She has great friends one day and sits by herself on others. She refuses to participate in assessments, but in her workbook, she displays a clear voice in her writing and has a perceptive way of looking at maths problems. How do I activate her passion and her interests? I have tried relationship building and different pedagogies. I will try some more today. I will evaluate their effectiveness, and then I will possibly try something different tomorrow. Erica is an enigma yet to be solved.

I need to remember that there will be comments today from the students. I do not predict that the day will be the most exciting one. As much as I can tactically avoid this, there is no getting around the learning that will have to take place. The topics, themes, and expectations are going to be a dry, hard slog today. I will need to remove my well-being from the comments and questions; I cannot let them change me or the lesson plan.

Today begins again.

Today is a new day.

Consider the Tug of War

"Life is one big tug of war between mediocrity and trying to find your best self."
—David Goggins

In schools, camps, and social clubs around the world, there is a version of this game that follows the same rules and structure as the tug of war. Why is it called the tug of war? Because it involves tugging, pulling, and physically moving the opposition away from their side of the field and onto yours. Why is it called war? Because that is what war is. It is two sides coming together on a field of their choosing and trying to convince the other side that not only are they wrong, but that one side is the right side. They tug, pull, connive, convince, bribe, barter, bully, and bash their way to ensure the other side is pulled into their way of thinking.

It is a game that is as old as time itself, and the core concepts of that game are felt in schoolyards and camps, boardrooms and legal dramas, football fields and battlefields to this day. Education is the same battle.

Two combatants enter the classroom with the same goal: to convince the other that their way is the right way. A student may enter and grip the rope of not changing, not thinking, not wanting to reassess their belief structure. A teacher may enter the classroom with the desire to create new learning and thinking, to challenge the old way of looking at the world.

Both grip the rope at the beginning of the day, and it is where that rope is, and the position that the person finds themselves in at the end of the day, that will determine the success, or otherwise, of the day.

This is not always the case, though. Some students grasp the rope of learning and are ready to engage, only to find that the teacher is not holding the rope. So, the student stands unmoved with a limp rope in their hand. Maybe the teacher is spending all the time explaining the rules of the game. Maybe the teacher does not want to pull, as it might hurt the student's feelings. Maybe the teacher does not engage because they are unsure which way to pull the educational rope. Maybe the teacher is simply not strong enough to pull the rope and does not want to be exposed. Maybe the teacher sees the rope and all the students on the other end and does not believe that they have the knowledge, pedagogy, behavior, or temperament to move that many students.

"Creating success is a tug of war between your mind and your heart, your fears and your dreams. If your fears win, you lose."
—Robert G Allen

Teaching is a challenging profession, and the teacher and students need to grasp the rope. Maybe they don't want to be moved. Maybe they will challenge me in moving. Maybe they will let go of the rope. But I need to be strong and be there anyway. I will need to move the educational and instructional rope into the room.

As a teacher, I only have one goal in the room: do not be the rope. It is easy to get caught up in the to-and-fro in the classroom and the staff room. It is easy to find yourself caught between two opposing sides of a pedagogical argument, a behavioral argument, or a physical argument. Students will try to create drama in the classroom, and you can feel caught in the middle of it. This is not my job. Being the rope in the classroom is the greatest cause of mental stress, as I feel I have no control. I am being pulled away from learning. Sometimes the rope can be between two students, a student and a parent, or learning and the direction of the school or department. While I have my hand on the rope, I can dictate the pace of moving, learning, and teaching. I may need to pull hard or pull gently. I may need to stop for my sanity or for the exhaustion of the students. Only I can dictate the pace and ensure that the movement is made incrementally, consistently, and individually.

Just as the warrior is a feature in this book, it is also a feature in life. Because life is a battle, and teaching is no more or less a part of the battle that warrior teachers have to face. The tug of learning happens in all systems, all organizations, and for the improvement of all. The war we face may be our own education, so we battle to improve our knowledge. The war we face may be our own self-respect, so we battle to take the necessary steps to create a better vision of ourselves. The war we face may be our health, so we battle with our vices and weaknesses to improve. The war we face may be our lack of opportunities, growth, or relationships. The battle we step into can be about short-term growth and improvement, or some distant goal that we are moving slowly and gradually towards. It is a battle to take those steps, but it is a battle where the rewards on the path can be considerable. Not only for the goal that we seek or the weaknesses we overcome, but in battling against mediocrity and having the courage to risk it all to take those necessary steps towards improvement.

I need to embrace the battle, grab the rope, take the grip, set my feet, and get ready to pull into the educational future. There is no one more qualified to do it. And no educational improvement happens if I don't.

"It is supposed to be hard.
If it wasn't hard, everyone would do it.
The hard is what makes it great."
—A League of Their Own

Consider the War Cry

(Recommended reading: ***The Righteous Mind*** by Jonathan Haidt)

"Like all peoples of antiquity, Roman troops used war cries to frighten the enemy, demonstrate strength and eagerness, and heighten individual and collective determination, but the demands of discipline and tactical cohesion required them to exercise restraint."
—Phillip Rance, War Cry

The soldier prepares for the battle; the fighter prepares for the fight. They spend time focused, and with passion and energy, they perform a ritual. It is different with every man or woman, every individual or team, but the desired outcome is the same: to heighten the senses, strengthen belief in themselves, and achieve a state of alertness in which they can overcome all.

The Pacific Island nations perform a cultural dance before a football game that is part culture, part religion, part warfare, but all focused on the singular belief in their ability to overcome the opposition. The action taken could be as impressive as the New Zealand haka, or as individual as Nick from the show *Ted Lasso* spitting at himself in the mirror. It is a determination to achieve, to move forward, and not accept anything less than the best in themselves.

Teachers should also follow a similar mantra. They need to tell themselves a story of their ability to overcome, the willingness to take on the lesson and the planning, and their strength in their ability, pedagogy, relationships, and high expectations. The war cry that a teacher creates needs to evolve over time. The story needs to be positive and outline the ways they are going to create powerful learning, and that they have the ability, capability, and drive to deliver quality learning for students.

What would that war cry from a teacher sound like? What would it look like? The war cry of an individual is not timid, thoughtful, or wistful. The war cry is animalistic, present, loud, aggressive, focused, determined, with a hint of crazy. It is ready to face whatever opposition arises, either behaviorally or pedagogically. This is not a male domain, as plenty of women have a mantra or phrase that builds mental confidence. We create competitiveness before we compete.

But the war cry is not just words. It is also a feeling, a stance, or a physical presence that needs to be adopted for the full effect of the war cry to be realized. This is not something done while slouching or sitting. It is standing firm, confident and competent, with a look in your eye focused on that which you are about to conquer.

"Our bodies change our minds,
our minds change our behavior,
and behavior changes outcomes."
—Amy Cuddy

The individual stands firm in the classroom. I am there before the class arrives, the work is laid out, the seating plan is organized, the knowledge of the students has been learned, the pedagogical strategies are at my disposal, and still I stand. I stand with focused energy, in a meditative state, and repeat the mantra of higher learning that I am going to deliver.

When the class arrives, I am prepared. I stand firm, and the students know instantly that there is a feeling in the room, an obvious energy coming from me. This is not about the height or strength of the teacher. It is not physical or dominating. It is calm, determined, and present.

The war cry becomes more powerful when spoken as a team. The neuroscience on the impact of movement and speaking with peers allows the feeling and the impact to grow in an increasingly exponential level. The reason crowds rise to their feet when a play is made in sport, the reason soldiers follow their colleagues into the battlefield, the reason music at a concert drives audiences to move together, is that shared action allows courage, exhilaration, and community to flow through groups of people.

The madness of crowds is a well-used trope, but that madness does not have to be negative. The crowd surges as one when experiencing the highs of a musical concert, the elation of a sporting team achieving, or the hypnotic effects of a speaker whose message leaves an indelible mark that creates significant change in your life.

Teachers should also embrace the war cry as an individual, a cohort, a team, or a school. A simple common language shared by others, when spoken together, it can make a significant impact on the well-being of the teacher.

An example could be ...
"I am not alone. I work with others; we walk together.
I am a learner. I work with learners. I create learners.
I welcome change and embrace ideas.
I have the skills to build my team.
I am thankful for this day.
Challenge accepted!"

"Organize, agitate, educate must be our war cry."
—Susan B. Anthony

Consider My Flag

"We now accept the fact that learning is a lifelong process of keeping abreast of change. And the most pressing task is to teach people how to learn."
—Peter Drucker

When an army goes into battle, they march under, or in accordance with, a banner, crest, or flag. This flag signifies and separates them from the enemy. They march forward into battle with the knowledge and comfort that they are fighting for their flag and everything it represents. Some soldiers wear the flag on their shirts; some hold the flag in their hearts, but the commitment and dedication they have to the flag is absolute.

The flag allows men and women to accomplish great feats, to support and encourage each other in pursuit of what their flag is driving them to do. Acts of heroism, acts of honor, and acts of courage are completed with the flag, and all it represents, driving them forward.

So too with teaching. The flag, or banner, that the teacher waves as they move into classrooms is the vow to be a great teacher, to inspire others, and to light the flame in the hearts and lives of students. Teachers step forward to create change, to make a difference, to be the difference in the lives of students. Teachers, young and old, have a vision of the success they can create in the lives of students. They inspire; they "fill the bucket."

And just like soldiers, they fail.

Soldiers who march to war under the banner of the flag will fall victim to the enemy because the enemy also marches under a banner. They are just as committed to the cause as you are. Wars are littered with millions of men and women who march to battle with hearts full of commitment to the flag, only to die with hearts broken by war.

The teacher who marches into classrooms under the banner of being a great teacher will fail. The flag the teacher should march under is the banner of a learner.

The teacher who enters the classroom as a learner will be ready for the enemy. They will be prepared for what comes next. They will encounter challenges and difficulties not as a way to showcase great teaching, but as opportunities to learn. Teachers need to be learners. They need to have that emblazoned on their sleeves and in their hearts.

- Show me a teacher who is driven to make a difference, and I will show you an enemy ready to be the difference.
- Show me a teacher who is driven to learn, and I will show you a student who will find their every move scrutinized, learned, and reapplied in ways that undermine the student, and paradoxically, makes them better against their will.

"If I fall, pick up the flag, kiss it, and keep on going."
—Omar Torrijos Herrera

Consider My Footwork

Footwork creates balance.
Balance creates strength.
Strength creates confidence.
Confidence creates action.
Action creates control.
Control creates success.
Success creates mastery.

The arms and hands draw attention, as does the face. The person in front of you distracts you with their ideas, personality, facial expressions, and expressive use of their hands and arms. The fighter watches the face and arms when in combat. It is through the actions of the hands and arms that success is often created. But the underestimated element of any situation is the feet.

In sport, the ball is not thrown, kicked, hit, or struck until the feet are in the right position. The tennis, soccer, hockey, and volleyball players generate power not from their arms but with their feet. The martial artist, the football player, and the basketball player spend enormous amounts of time concentrating on their footwork. The fighter does not punch, kick, or throw until their feet are in the correct position.

The football player recognizes that their feet can power the ball through the line or adjust quickly to avoid the tackle. Good footwork creates opportunities, generates power, adjusts for the unexpected, and delivers momentum. It is footwork that allows the hands to shine.

Footwork also creates another benefit. It provides confidence to the athlete that they will be strong enough to deal with conflict and combat. The athlete can deal with the unexpected because their footwork is strong enough to absorb the blow or fast enough to avoid it completely. The athlete's footwork keeps them balanced in an unfamiliar environment against an unpredictable opponent.

An athlete spends their time working on their footwork.

What is the footwork a teacher needs to keep their balance?
Why is "footwork" important?

"Footwork" is the term applied to the beliefs and philosophies that allow a teacher to remain balanced and confident despite the conditions and stress of teaching and learning. The teacher's strength, power, and confidence in teaching are not found in what they say or what they do; they are found in how they think. The "footwork" enables that strength, power, and confidence to be manifested and multiplied.

This "footwork" may have links to religion, discipline, compliance, meditation, or "how it has always been done." But the further the "footwork" of a teacher is explored and challenged, the more it will reveal the limits that a teacher can accept and rise to the challenge placed by students and staff. The footwork of the teacher is what grounds them in their thinking and their beliefs around teaching. The lack of understanding around a teacher's footwork can have considerable physical, psychological, and/or career implications.

- I can be thrown off by performing an action that I haven't learnt or that is unfamiliar.

- I can be knocked over by the tectonic shifting of the unexpected from the school environment.
- I can be unbalanced emotionally by the trauma others in my school environment are facing, which forces me to confront ideas and experiences that I had previously ignored, that now seek to undermine my confidence, my relationships, or my teaching.

Poor footwork exposes imbalance.
Imbalance exposes weakness.
Weakness exposes uncertainty.
Uncertainty exposes fear.
Fear creates failure.

How can the teacher learn to stay balanced? What elements of their footwork do they need to work on? What do they require for balance, and how can that be developed? How can that be improved? How can that be expanded?

In the previous considerations, the idea of mastery and enjoyment was discussed, as was the target of mind and body, work and life. Embedded in these are the roots of a belief system that creates the footwork that enables me to stand. My footwork enables me to be comfortable in who I am and confident in what I can do. A thorough understanding of these factors will expose the footwork that I bring with me to the classroom. But there will also be weaknesses in my footwork. I may not realize or even accept this until I am facing it in real time. This means my footwork needs to be strong enough to absorb the hits to my belief systems created by the school environment, but agile enough to recognize when it is time to remove myself from danger without getting caught.

I don't want to consider that my footwork is strong enough for all challenges, as I am asking to be challenged, and the reaction to that challenge may have long-term consequences.

I don't want to consider that my footwork as agile that I can avoid every challenge, as I will keep running away from challenges and I will not grow.

My footwork needs to be strong enough to ride the challenges I must, agile enough to avoid the challenges I should, pliable enough to absorb the challenges I am not expecting, and adaptable enough to constantly learn from the experiences that come my way. My footwork is embedded in my way of being, and this understanding will hold me in good stead while I train, listen, learn, and develop.

I definitely get down on myself. I needed to work on my self-talk.
The same way you do footwork drills and cardio training,
I had to do self-talk training.
-Rose Namajunas

Consider First Contact

"No battle plan survives contact with the enemy."
—Field Marshal Helmuth von Moltke

Soldiers and commanders make great plans, and everyone from Napoleon to Hannibal has spent hours making plans to ensure victory for their side. While history shows that these military leaders demonstrated supreme skill on the battlefield, an investigation of their work also shows that, for all their planning and skill, the battle they planned for changed as soon as contact was made with the enemy. What makes these military leaders so remarkable was not necessarily their plans, but the way they adjusted and adapted their planning after the engagement had begun. When the environment helped, they used it. When the environment did not help, they found other ways to victory.

Planning for warfare and planning for lessons are the same thing. It is in the preparation that the battle is won. Teachers who arrive late to class are noted in their waste of time trying to gain control of the classroom. The first impression of every day is important. It allows the teacher the chance to set expectations and to pick up the signals coming from the students. The underlying body language and subtleties will allow the teacher the chance to prepare. The teacher who waits in the classroom and begins the day when the students walk in will be fresh for the fight. The teacher who arrives later will not be prepared, and inversely, the students will be prepared, and the day may go as the students want.

Be mindful to be a prepared teacher, or else you will face a prepared class.

Teacher well-being can be affected by this lack of organization. The teacher who is late can be stressed out. The teacher who is rushing will miss the details. The teacher who feels that they are not successful will have that theory proven true when they walk in underprepared. Do not excuse poor planning with poor well-being. Do not trick yourself into thinking you are less than, and then fail to plan accordingly so that your thoughts become true. If your mental health is struggling, now is the chance to rule out elements that are creating that. The first place is classroom planning, and one of the easiest ways to improve mental health is through creating and delivering strong classroom planning.

"Whoever is first on the field and awaits the coming of the enemy will be fresh for the fight.
Whoever is second in the field and has to hasten to battle will arrive exhausted."
—Sun Tzu

Consider Chaos v Control

"Chaos does not mean total disorder.
Chaos means a multiplicity of possibilities.
Chaos is from the ancient Greek word
that means a thing that is birthed from the void.
And it was about that which is possible, not about disorder."
—Jok Church

There is an important factor I need to consider as a teacher.

Do I embrace chaos, or do I embrace control?

A moment to explain the difference.

Chaos is anarchy. It is the obliteration of rules and a degree of disorganisation that borders on uncontrollable. Chaos is unpredictable, unmanageable, and unwelcome in situations where others prefer control. The chaos found in the world can also be about challenging the status quo. It can mean creativity. It can also be innovative. Chaos is others taking control away from me. It might be accepting another's identity, perspective, and opinion. Chaos can be found in people who travel unique journeys in life, who create their own path, and who generate their own version of success—much to the dismay and discontent of established controlling players.

Control is order. It is sensible. It enables progress to be made in the correct steps at the correct time and ensures that all are invited and have a turn to be part of the momentum of any organisation. This is all done in an orderly fashion. The bureaucratic nature of any organisation is not fun or exciting, but it ensures people are safe, everyone is theoretically considered, and everyone is involved. Control also ensures that people are placed in the "right" positions, which are considered right because the person in control believes they are. Control means unemotionally making tough decisions that will affect others, but this is all according to the plan. Control is following orders and decisions made by others, but these may have historically resulted in damaging outcomes.

What kind of person am I? What kind of teacher will I be? Do I embrace chaos, or do I like control?

Chaos and control by themselves in the classroom are not conducive to learning. A chaotic teacher will embrace unpredictability but will not have the focus to ensure learning takes place. A controlling teacher will have strict routines in place and will produce very organised lessons, irrespective of whether the students are involved or even interested.

Who is it that becomes a teacher? For anyone to be successful as a teacher, they need to demonstrate the controlled nature of learning to pass tests and complete assignments in tertiary education. The chaotic personality is not one that generally succeeds in the rigid professional environment. And so it is the controlled person who gets hired, and the controlled person whose credentials are welcomed at school. Schools are then full of highly organized, highly effective people who embrace the predictable nature of a controlled classroom. Every part of the day is organised.

"You ever been in a war, Councilman? In a firefight? Did you feel an over-abundance of control?"
—Nick Fury, Avengers

Unfortunately, schools are incredibly chaotic. Classrooms and war zones share chaos, unpredictability, and emotion. The playground during lunchtime, the transition from one classroom to another, the lesson that goes off plan, the replacement teacher that does not come, or the replacement teacher that does come but follows their own plan can all contribute to the chaos of the classroom. Teachers who embrace control both in their lives and their profession can struggle when the proverbial plan hits the child-centered road.

For improvement to happen in life, it often needs to be on the back of someone who embraces chaos and wants to look at the world differently. The chaos sometimes avoided in classrooms can actually be the one thing that creates more engagement and better learning. Chaos involves letting others speak, letting staff or students lead, and allowing mistakes so lessons can be learnt. People who have made significant changes in the culture of our landscape have often taken the chaotic path. The disconnect is that while the controlling teacher may embrace new technology, ideas, art, and culture and the opportunities they create, it was perhaps the chaotic personality that created those technologies, ideas, and art in the first place. The controlling teacher may then not allow the free spirited creative thinking of students in the classroom because it breaks away from the control the teacher has over learning.

- Control without chaos creates compliance.
- Chaos without control creates anarchy.
- Neither is needed separately in the classroom or in life.

Am I willing to release the reins and embrace the chaos of creativity?
Am I willing to rein in my natural curiosity for some control of the room?
What kind of teacher will I be?

"My journey has always been the balance between chaos and order."
—Philippe Petit

Consider the Chaos of Teaching

(Recommended Reading: ***Emotional Intelligence*** by Daniel Goleman)

"When struck by chaos and order, our minds set to work making sense of it, this is called learning, and it makes us better. It allows us to gain from failure and disorder." —Mark Manson, The Subtle Art of Not Giving a F**

When armies go to war, it must be chaos: the clash of swords and spears, the ringing of bullets and explosions, the unpredictability of the enemy in their use of weapons, tactics, and personnel. The soldier enters the battlefield with a distinct impression that it is chaotic and uncertain. It is through chaos and uncertainty that change is made. Battles are won, land is gained, kingdoms reign supreme at the end of the battle, but it is through chaos that change created the victory.

When we 'inflict' chaos in the classroom we are endeavouring to teach students something new, and this is going to lead to failure...initially. In fact, it should. If chaos does not surround the student during learning, then either the lesson is too easy, or the student has already learnt it. Students need to embrace the chaos, and the teacher should be ready to create it.

Teachers also need to be aware that the chaos we are inflicting may not be successful or work. It may be a complete disaster and the lesson may go completely off the rails. This is the time with poor self-reflection that we blame everyone. Teachers like to blame the students, parents, curriculum, ICT or even the whiteboard. But we created the stress in creating a lesson that didn't work. Don't avoid the pain or embarrassment. Don't avoid the stress and chaos it absolutely would have created in that lesson. Learn from it. Embrace it. The last thing you want as a teacher is to shrink learning so that we can handle it.

But when we avoid pain,
when we avoid stress and chaos we become fragile.
Our tolerance diminishes and our life must shrink accordingly
for us to engage in the little bit of the work we can handle."
Mark Manson 'Subtle Art of Not Giving a F***

When the teacher is fragile, the student suffers. When the teacher teaches to the lowest common denominator to avoid pain and chaos, the students do not receive the education they deserve. If teachers use overly simple curriculum and resources, or rely only on what they have used for the past 20 years, real learning is not created. The teacher's diminished capability reaches every student in the class and affects their future—their ability to process information, respond when things do not go right, and reach the high standards expected in later years.

Teachers who want to make a difference will reflect outwards to identify the difference. They will ensure that lessons are tailored so that they can either demonstrate their own greatness or that students can easily succeed through simplistic methods, resources, and assessment.

Teachers who want to learn will reflect inwards. They will embrace the chaos of learning and will grab hold of the sails of inquiry and questioning that the students bring, and they will explore and develop as they facilitate learning. Teachers with positive self-reflection, in a lesson that is not working, need to start with themselves and realise that the lesson they wanted to provide to students ended up being a lesson they themselves received.

"Since how a teacher handles her class is in itself a model, a de facto lesson in emotional competence—or lack thereof. Whenever a teacher responds to one student, twenty or thirty others learn a lesson."

—Daniel Goleman, Emotional Intelligence

Consider My Armory

"It is the reckless hunter indeed who goes to hunt the tiger
with the same gun he reserved for the pheasant shoot.
There is no such thing as one size fits all.
Once you have the tools, once you have mastered them,
you can then wield them with greater authority ...
The hunter knows which is which and when to use them."
—Maria Konnikova, Mastermind

In the history of warfare, there are two basic elements: offence and defence. Soldiers throughout history have ventured onto the battleground with a shield to defend and a weapon to attack. As time has moved on, the capacities of the shield and the weapon have become more complex, both in defending and attacking. But that same theory is still prevalent today in all forms of warfare.

The idea of defence and offence is not found in warfare; it is also found in all forms of sport and competition, legal battles, relationships, problem-solving, and in the ICT industry. All industries have been developing their own versions to attack and defend when it comes to scoring goals, winning a case, creating software, merging a company, or working on relationships. To work in these areas, the combatants need tools, equipment, and resources in their armoury to be able to win.

The teacher walking into the classroom must also have a set of tools or resources in their armoury. What will you bring into the classroom to protect you or to attack the lesson?

Consider and Write Down What You Bring

- What are your defensive strategies?
- What are your offensive strategies?

If you do not have anything, then you are not qualified to teach.

If you have not thought about it, then you are not prepared to teach.

No soldier, lawyer, surgeon, programmer, or footballer enters their field without a clear understanding of what they can do, what skills they can use, and what strategies they will employ when a problem arises.

The armory of the teacher needs to be set aside in the corner of the room to be accessed when times of conflict arise. Often, the teacher's armory consists of calling for help. The administration coming into your room to solve your problem can be a powerful weapon that can be deployed in your classroom, but it is not without its challenges. Sometimes the administration changes the nature of the classroom and learning, but that will revert back when the administration leaves the room. You could be informing the class and the administration that you have nothing and you are helpless in the face of this conflict. The administration will assist, but then they will leave, and you will be left with a class that recognises the weakness in the room—and that weakness is you. Calling the administration has its time and place, but only to match the unique, dangerous, or illegal incident taking place. You need more classroom strategies.

"Therefore, the clever combatant imposes his will on the enemy, but does not allow the enemy's will to be imposed on him."
—Sun Tzu, The Art of War

Some Defence techniques

HUMOR

Nothing can deflect an attack better than humor. Turning a student's comment or action into something funny is the greatest defence pattern you can employ. A response that is funny will immediately disarm the student and bring the class around to your side. If you can leverage the joke so that the student also recognises the funny side of it, then you are well on the way to creating a great atmosphere in the classroom.

Unintended Consequences

Humour that does not hit the desired target will make you look foolish. Humour that is cruel will turn others against you. Humour that only those in the know understand will create confusion and a feeling of us versus them in the room. Do not apply this tactic if you do not have a natural tendency for humour. Remember that humour works if the students do not know you, you surprise them, or if there is a good relationship in the room. Humour can be effective, but test it first to ensure you do not create more problems than you began with.

BROKEN RECORD

This is a tried-and-tested routine where the teacher sticks to their position and repeats their suggestion until the student complies. This is effective when the student is seeking to distract you and the class with alternate comments and activities. The position of the student is to get you talking about things other than what is expected. If the teacher engages in this kind of conversation, then the student has an upper hand and can control the conversation, forcing the teacher to follow their train of thought. By simply repeating the instruction over and over, the student is forced to accept that they will not be able to control the narrative and will come again and again against the shield of the broken record.

Unintended Consequences

The broken record technique can work, but when the student realises that they are losing this battle, they may resort to other violent verbal or physical outbursts to re-establish control of the room. The broken record technique must come with further techniques in case things get out of control.

TACTICAL IGNORING

When students try to establish control of the room, they will throw out comments seeking attention or teacher frustration. The teacher in this instance identifies the comment and allows it to pass through them and land outside the room. The teacher is untouched and continues to teach. This will be tried many times by the enemy as they mortar-bomb the teacher in trying to gain the upper hand. While the comments are directed at the teacher or the lesson, they can be ignored. Once the student realises that their comments of frustration are not gaining the impact they want, they will tend to stop, as they are not getting the attention they desire.

Unintended Consequences

Tactical ignoring may create further frustration when they realise their attacks are not working. In this case, they may turn their attention to other students, or they may resort to increasingly violent verbal and physical outbursts, in which case the teacher will need to step in, but tactical positioning may assist in this situation.

TACTICAL POSITIONING

This is when the teacher forms a literal and physical shield around students to protect them from the verbal assaults coming from the student. Teachers can stand between the students and the target and continue to teach. This protects the students, informs the class that learning is still taking place, and signals to the enemy that the class is protected.

Unintended Consequences

Tactical positioning can be overcome if the enemy recognises the blind spots in the teacher's literal shield and uses those places to launch further attacks. This can be better prepared through classroom organisation (see further).

FOCUS ON THE (MAJORITY OF) GOOD STUDENTS

The high number of students in the class who are working and developing their understanding should be the focus. The teacher must engage, support, and converse with these students. The teacher must encourage, praise, and thank the work, presence, and behaviour of students who make good choices. Students who are craving attention will find that attention is gained through positive interactions. Students who are not craving attention but are doing the right thing will be emboldened by this focus on them and their work.

Unintended Consequences

Students who recognise that attention is only provided by positive classroom behaviours may increase their behaviours to shift the attention back to them. Students may also realise that this will not work and become disengaged and passive in their attempts at attention.

"In football, everything is complicated by the presence of the opposite team."
—Jean-Paul Sartre

Some Offensive Techniques

RELATIONSHIP

The teacher who immediately forms a strong attack through relationships will find that this is the strongest part of their armoury. You can disarm a student by simply listening to them, showing interest, sharing stories, and including them in lessons. Speaking to parents about their great work and ideas will solidify that relationship, and before the year has even begun, you have turned the student to your side. You will need to ensure this relationship is positive and maintained throughout the year. It will be the greatest offensive technique that a teacher can use when moving into a classroom.

Unintended Consequences

Make sure the relationship is professional and that you are in control. Do not let the student affect your relationship with the class, with learning, and with behaviour. They are not your friends, and the relationship must be kept at arm's length. Never put yourself in a compromising position.

ENGAGEMENT

Teachers who bring students on a journey in their learning will find that the troubles and stresses will be lessened. Students want to be engaged and have fun, and it is the teacher's responsibility to ensure that the learning, the room, and the lesson are engaging. If there is a break in the learning or your lesson is poorly thought out, students will find other things to engage in. There are many ways of teaching that include engagement, but the first is to use the student voice to direct the learning.

Unintended Consequences

Engaging many students in the class is challenging and will involve considerable differentiation to ensure they are engaged. Students will appreciate the effort to bring in everyone's interests, but if you relate everything to a football game to engage three boys in a classroom full of gymnasts and horse riders, prepare for disengaged learning.

PEDAGOGY

It is not simply teaching; it is having strategies to create learning. There are many different pedagogical practices available, and it is not the focus of the book to promote any single version. But it is the focus of the book that, as a professional teacher, there are strategic pedagogies that can be unleashed. The teacher who goes into class with only a healthy ego, an understanding of the curriculum, and a smile on their face is asking for trouble. The teacher needs to be pedagogically prepared through research to attack learning through strategic devices. Determine high-impact teaching strategies through research and reading. The launching of strategies that have been proven effective for learning should be at the forefront of all teachers' pedagogical practices.

Unintended Consequences

The school may have a pedagogical plan that is philosophically different from yours. First, well done for having a researched pedagogical process that you use. Second, use this time to expand your understanding and knowledge of what the school is using. Not all pedagogical practices are perfect, but if the school has a process that you can learn from, then this will be indispensable. Now is not the time for a philosophical battle in the classroom and the staffroom under a pedagogical banner of your choosing.

BEHAVIOR PLANS

The teacher who stands in the line of fire of the student with a bemused and confused look on their face has not engaged the offensive technique of behaviour plans. Students have triggers, trauma, behaviours, and relationships that affect them. The role of the teacher is to identify, plan, and create scenarios and actions for when these now-identified triggers and behaviours occur. The student, teacher, and parent(s) are on the same page; they are aware. There are no surprises. There are now plans, suggestions, and steps that all stakeholders can follow. The weakness for the teacher may be the surprise attack, but in using plans, the surprise is now expected and planned. Strategies are already engaged.

Unintended Consequences

This does not mean that the behaviour stops, nor that the teacher and staff are less affected by the impact. This does not mean that the impact of the behaviour plans will be immediate. It could take months, if not years, to achieve. The choices are made by the student. Consequences will take place, and restorative practices need to be employed afterwards.

"When you're current, you're caring."

Consider My Uniform

"Although the Industrial Revolution had ushered in a new era of technology, the management structures that held everything in place had not changed since the days of the artisan, small shops and guilds."
—McChrystal, Team of Teams

Wearing a uniform is just a piece of clothing, but if others wear the same item of clothing, then it is no longer simply clothing; it is a uniform. You are part of something, and you have others with you on your journey. This uniform could be a soldier's outfit, a football team jersey, a hat, or even a particular computer or phone. This uniformity binds people together. It creates a collective belief in something. It creates ways of speaking, listening, relating, and acting. People can structure their day around uniforms.

Uniforms are not only found in clothing, but also in routines and practices. A uniform is a way of thinking, acting, or behaving in ways that others recognise and can follow, or that make sense to people in your team. Teachers need to consider the uniform parts of their day—not in the clothes they wear, but in the practices they undertake, the routines they follow, and the data they collect and use. But being the same and doing the same does not necessarily produce the same results, and it is good to question the approach of uniformity in teaching.

Part One: Teacher Uniforms Create Efficiency

Uniforms create consistency, reduce complexity, and allow easy access to opportunities under harsh conditions. Uniforms, rucksacks, resources, and equipment, when used under uniform conditions, allow for quick and efficient results. Soldiers wear uniforms into battle. This serves two functions. It allows members of their team to recognise each other so they may join together in the field. The second function is more important. It allows the user to be successful because it has been designed for the job in which it will be used.

Uniforms and uniformity allow for consistency in design and consistency in practice. It ensures that those who wear the uniform can identify and use the practicalities of the uniform. Uniformity is also found in the way a pack and resources are organised. It is easy and simple to identify. Anyone on the team knows how to access it, use it, and place it in a way that the next person can access.

Uniformity means that if a member of the team visits a different team, the uniformity of the process allows that member to access equipment quickly and easily. This speed of access creates gains in performance and improvements in results.

Frederick Winslow Taylor (who will be discussed more later) is recognised as identifying systems and for creating uniformity where there were once individual tasks and varied ways of doing things. His ideas around uniformity enabled systems and processes to be greatly improved by identifying weaknesses and ways in which time, personnel, and resources were wasted.

Through this approach, great gains were made in many industries. Not only did this create great wealth at the top, but it also created fewer bodies to pay and fewer resources to purchase at the bottom. Uniformity enabled machinery to move forward, but it did mean—and continues to mean—that people lost jobs and livelihoods.

Uniformity in teaching is still something to be grasped. The idea that teaching improves because of technological or radical changes in systems thinking is yet to be fully explored. Teachers work in classrooms, adapting their own skills and expertise, sometimes independent of the latest research or high-performing strategies. Sharing ideas and resources rarely happens between classrooms in the same school. As a teacher, it is your responsibility to ensure that uniformity happens at your school. If that means changing your practice to accommodate new thinking, herald it as an exciting way to usher in a new era of changing pedagogy.

Uniform efficiency is found in data that has been gathered by the school to ensure improvement and growth are taking place. The uniform approach to data must be embraced, moderated, and used by teachers to create better learning. Data that is not uniform across a school creates ineffective communication and resourcing. A uniform process of collecting and storing student learning data is vitally important.

Uniforms create efficiency. This is part of the job. It is an expectation. Teachers should demonstrate this expectation in their teaching. Create uniform processes that are shared across the school. Hold uniform meetings that focus on student improvement, sharing resources, moderating work, and evaluating the improvement of practices.

Uniformity creates consistency.

Part Two: Uniforms Create Inefficiency

Uniforms create efficiency, but efficiency relies on others to create routines that work. Soldiers once formed uniform parallel lines to fight each other. It was efficient and brutal at the same time. When guerrilla warfare was introduced, this efficient way of fighting no longer worked because the enemy was no longer standing where they could be seen and killed.

Soldiers now had to search for the enemy, and this broke up lines of attack and communication. The army that was able to attack creatively was often the victor. Uniform thinking, while effective in the past and in some areas of soldiering, does not work all the time.

Teachers cannot afford to have only uniform ways of working. Students come into classrooms from vastly different walks of life and experience. The standardised, one-size-fits-all approach to teaching is becoming an inefficient way of working.

Differentiated learning allows students to bring their own "uniforms" of learning into the classroom. Students have ways of learning that work best for them. These learning uniforms might include visual cues, tactile learning, repeated instructions, peer teaching, ICT support, inquiry approaches, or First Nations involvement. The list goes on.

If the student brings their learning uniform but the teacher forces the student to ignore it so that they can stay with the teacher's uniform thinking, the student is not engaged, and the teacher is not supporting learning. Uniform ideas do not always enable creativity to come forth. They can limit it by trying to keep creativity inside a rigid box that does not change.

Part Three: What Uniformity Works?

Uniform thinking is needed to create consistency for teachers and students. It creates a framework for teaching and learning. Students are introduced to structure, efficiency, and organisation. Within those boundaries, great ideas are built.

Limit the students' workbook with margins and dates, and ensure students write on the lines in neat and consistent writing. Once these uniform routines are established, the student has the capacity to demonstrate creativity and expression. The uniform process allows the work to be read, edited, and improved. Without that structure, creativity does not always have a chance to shine.

Uniform thinking is also needed to create consistency in data collection for teaching and learning. The data gathering process is structured. The tools and instruments used across the school are consistent and established as part of the school's process. The data gathered then allows creativity in learning and lesson design. It exposes teachers to new ideas about what is working and what needs improvement. Creativity expressed through data relies on uniform approaches to create standards.

As teachers, it is important to establish a fine line between both sides of the uniform approach. Too much uniformity does not allow students to express ideas; too little uniformity leaves students unsure where to begin.

"The uniform makes for brotherhood,
since when universally adopted,
it covers up all differences of class and country."
-Robert Baden-Powell

Consider Maps

"All you need is the plan, the road map,
and the courage to press on to your destination."
—Earl Nightingale

Soldiers rely on maps to locate their position, their target, and the obstacles along the way. Maps are crucial to a mission's success and can often determine a team's failure, either through misreading the maps or because the maps do not contain all the information needed to complete the mission. Architects, surveyors, and builders also rely on maps. They are unable to do their work without them. As professionals, they do not begin until they have studied the map.

Maps are often viewed from a top-down perspective because it allows you to see the whole field. Topographical maps enable users to identify the slopes of hills they may have to march on or over. The top-down approach allows users to see hazards and obstacles such as rivers, creeks, marshes, tree lines, trenches, troop movements, and tactical equipment that must be navigated around.

Consider How Many Maps We See in the World

The game of chess is a map viewed from above, as are Scrabble and checkers. The view of the game allows players to read the situation, create strategies, and trap their opponents. Wars were fought near hills so that the general could view the battle, knowing when and where to send more soldiers. Sporting games often take place with the coach high in the stands watching the whole game. We read bus lines and train lines from above. The lookout is a popular location in any city or town, as it allows the viewer to see further, see clearly, identify features, and see places they have been or others they may want to visit. The view from up high allows for calculations about distances, directions, and challenges they may face on the way. Sailors on the ocean used to look up at the map of the sky to see which direction to go. Sweeping fantasy novels often start with a map so that the reader can visualize where the characters will go. Movies are planned on a story map before filming even begins.

Teachers also need to consider maps, but teachers should use the same top-down, topographical approach to learning as soldiers do. Sometimes teachers create a classroom desk formation to identify where students are seated and who sits beside whom.

Teachers should also consider the topography of learning. When the curves on a map are close together, the climb is steep. Is a student able to climb that mathematical concept, or is that child flying down the slope with understanding? Is the hill too large a climb for that student? Is there a team of learners who could climb together?

What behavioral, academic, or personal obstacles will they face? Are there alternative routes that enable the learner to reach the goal another way? If the teacher cannot find another route, either they cannot read the map, or they have not extended the map far enough.

Students do not progress in a strictly linear fashion, so why do we view their educational journey that way? A topographical view of learning recognises that the child is on this journey, but may need to bypass a lesson and access equipment before proceeding along the journey.

We see maps everywhere, yet we rarely use them for learning.

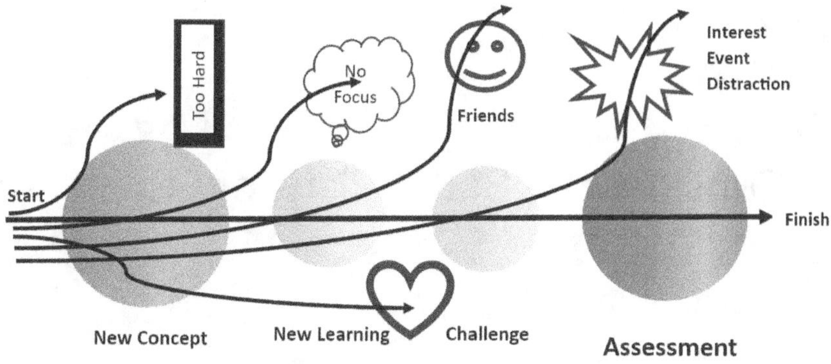

Many teachers become frustrated when a child does not reach the expected answer. Sometimes the problem is perspective. The child may have reached the destination, but you needed a higher viewpoint to see that while their path arrived on the same line, it was on a different part of the map than you envisioned. Their journey was different, as was their destination, despite following the same linear path you indicated. A 3D model would have shown that they took turns along the way that left them lost or at an alternate destination.

Mapping the Well of Being

How do I see the map of my life? Is there a path clearly laid out, or does it disappear into the haze of disappointment or imagination? Are there clouds of "should do," "could do," and "might do" obscuring my vision of the future? Can I climb higher and gain a clearer view of what lies ahead? Can I rotate the map of my path and better understand the challenges before me? I cannot avoid walking a path, but I can begin to create the map of where I want to go. I cannot leave it to chance because that is where the monsters hide.

"A map does not just chart; it unlocks and formulates meaning. It forms bridges between here and there, between disparate ideas that we did not know were previously connected."

—Reif Larsen, The Selected Works of T.S. Spivet

Consider the Battle Plans of Others

"We don't hope; we plan."
—Dune

The tactics and strategies of the battle plan have been created, and the resources, equipment, and manpower have been provided. All you need to do as a soldier is pick up your gear and enter the fray. But it is in entering the battle that all the danger lies. The person who creates the plan will watch from afar and make changes and adjustments according to the conditions. The soldier in the midst of battle can only fight and hope that the plan is not only successful, but that they are alive to appreciate its success.

This may happen in education. The tactics and strategies that are developed and deployed are given to teachers as the latest development, the exciting future of learning, curriculum, pedagogy, behavior management, or technology. But those who create the latest thing are not the same people who have to deliver it in the classroom. They are employing teachers to deliver their plans, and if it does not work, they will consider how they can adjust it to improve. But the teacher is amid this experimentation; they are the ones dealing with the changes.

The well-being of teachers can be affected by those who have great ideas but no skin in the game. They work independently of the educational system, but symbiotically with the intellectual trend of the time. They want the teacher's expertise in delivering these ideas. But at the end of the day, the teacher is expendable while fulfilling the tactical, strategic, and policy approaches of those who don't spend their nights and weekends recovering from the challenges they faced during the day.

If the school or teacher creates a battle plan for learning in the classroom and it does not work, then they gain knowledge to inform, change, adapt, and develop it further. Teachers and administrators who work in schools should be encouraged to develop resources. The impact of owning and delivering learning that has been created by the staff could be significant. This will support well-being since there is a personal reason to succeed. Outside interests that demand attention but do not have a relationship to learning in the school create stress for teachers, especially when it becomes a cycle of reinventing the wheel.

"How much you truly 'believe' in something can be manifested only through what you are willing to risk for it."
—Nassim Nicholas Taleb, Skin in the Game

Consider the Environment

(Recommended Reading: ***This Is Strategy*** by Seth Godin)

"Water shapes its course to the nature of the ground over which it flows; the soldier works out his victory in relation to the foe whom he is facing. Therefore, just as water retains no constant shape, so in warfare, there are no constant conditions."
—Sun Tzu, The Art of War

The soldier does not fight the enemy until they know what the conditions are. This will determine the resources, equipment, and strategies to employ in the battle. The conditions also allow the soldier to consider how the enemy may attack, where the enemy may attack, or even how many of the enemy they may have to engage. It is foolish to walk blindly into an environment to fight without recognising the potential and the pitfalls. The soldier determines the fight according to the environment and the enemy. They work with what is around them.

Teachers may blindly walk into classrooms and playgrounds and act as if the students are beholden to the teacher, giving no thought to the environment they are in. They are not observant of the features, the temperament, the temperature, or the hidden ways that the environment can turn against them. This is the very definition of poor teaching, yet many teachers try to "force the water," as referred to in the above quote, to go the way they want.

Students will battle against this.

The quality teacher seeks to engage the students and use the resources, environment, and interests of the students to engage in the battle of learning. Water will naturally fall downhill. Yet many times, teachers express that it feels like they are pushing uphill. In any battle, if you are pushing uphill or standing on the lower ground, you have not planned your attack (lesson) effectively. If the battle becomes evident and both parties are pushed onto the battleground, it is important to note the words of Sun Tzu:

"If you know your enemy and know yourself, you need not fear the result of a hundred battles. If you know yourself but not the enemy, for every victory you will also suffer defeat. If you know neither the enemy nor yourself, you will succumb in every battle."

—Sun Tzu

The environment that teachers have to consider is not hills, water, or opposing forces; it is the child's mind. The environmental conditions of how the child is thinking or feeling. The battles they are facing personally, with their peers, or with learning. The behaviors they are showing, and the anger, shyness, or aloofness they are displaying. This is the environment that can force teachers backwards. Many battles have been lost by teachers for not adhering to this important environmental condition. If the teacher does not know why they are having the battle or is not convinced of the worth of the battle, or even of their position, then it is likely that they will lose. If they are unfamiliar with the student's background, commitment, or goals, then it is equally true that they will lose the battle.

It is in these times of uncertainty that you must learn about the environment in which you have found yourself. You find this out by asking one of two questions of the students:

1. A question that requires more information, in which case it is respectful and reflects openness to learning.
2. A question to see whether the student will reveal an answer you already know, in which case you show respect and then carefully use it as evidence to secure your position with the child.

But when the teacher does not appreciate the environment, they will ask a question in a manner or tone that creates conflict. The teacher will ask a question from the position of "being right" and being willing to take the fight to the student. This will usually result in an unpredictable and unexpected outcome. The days of automatic respect for the teacher are over, so asking an ill-considered question enables the child to protect their position. They attack, defend, create their own answers, blame others, blame the teacher, and respond to the question with a question.

"To secure ourselves against defeat lies in our hands,
but the opportunity of defeating the enemy is provided by the enemy himself."
—Sun Tzu

But this tactical condition from Sun Tzu can work both ways. The opportunity for the child to defeat the teacher may be provided by the teacher. When we engage in a battle of wills and don't know who we are engaging with, we allow ourselves to lose. When the verbal battle of questions and arguing is over, we lose because we did not see which way the water was running. We then respond with a consequence irrespective of the result. This simply tells the child: I can no longer argue logically or with merit and am forced to save face. My lack of understanding of the conditions has been replaced by my physical restriction of your freedom.

The water is now flowing downhill, and you are at the bottom because you did not appreciate the environment in which you were working.

The other problem in asking questions without knowing the answers is that the response can create secondary behaviors. If the primary issue was picking up litter, the secondary issue is now swearing. If the primary issue was swearing, the secondary issue becomes physical misconduct when they throw a chair. Teachers should learn questioning skills to prevent situations from escalating, to save students from themselves, and to save their careers. There are many examples of problems created by teachers who did not know what they were asking, who they were talking to, did not know when to stop, and did not recognise the environment.

A teacher who wants to make a difference will speak in any environment.

A teacher who is a learner investigates the environment and listens before speaking.

"Sooner or later we have to do our jobs,
but it probably pays to focus on our work."
—Seth Godin

Consider Allies

"Associate with those who will make a better man of you.
Welcome those whom you yourself can improve.
The process is mutual; for men learn while they teach."
—Seneca

In warfare, the success of the mission or battle is sometimes found in the external support of others. It may be countries providing financial, armory or personnel support. It may be legal teams working together to battle in a court case, or sporting teams working together before engaging with a common opponent. The Hollywood idea of the lone hero venturing onto the battlefield looks compelling, especially with the right soundtrack and camera angles. But neither the battle nor the classroom is the time to showcase individual talents. Instead, you should turn to the support around you. The teacher, like battlefield leaders of years past, needs allies for support in the conflict.

There will be allies you can turn to for support. There may also be allies who turn to you for support. As a teacher, you will not be able to fight the war alone unless you seek humiliation, loss, or mental health breakdown. It is imperative that you seek the support of allies or reinforcements to assist you in your cause and be a supportive ally to others.

Administration

The administration of the school is looking at the map of learning, relationships, and the physical layout of the school. They can see the moves others are making and the moves that could be coming. Because of their position in the school, they can make decisions and suggestions that effect change before the event. Often, school-based personnel complain about the administration and the decisions they are making, but they never consider why those decisions are made.

- Why does this teacher move to a new year level every year?
- Is it because the admin is unfair?

Perhaps the teacher has relationship issues, and the students in the class are not learning. Maybe the teacher's team needs a break from that teacher.

- Why are students being moved from the class?
- Is the admin uncaring?

Maybe there have been parent complaints about the teacher?

The admin team should be your ally in teaching, as they can see more of the "chessboard" than you can, and they can support future moves you may make. The admin team may encourage you to self-reflect. What are they saying about the future of the school, or the future of you? What potential can they see in you? What steps do they suggest that will lead you to become a better teacher or leader?

The administration is the strongest member of your team, so treat them with respect and learn from them. No nation goes to war and ignores, avoids, or antagonises the most powerful nation supporting them. In the same way, there is little benefit in challenging the authority of the administration. There is no upside to that encounter. When the teacher enters the classroom and encounters challenges, you do not want to be the teacher crawling back for assistance five minutes after challenging their authority.

The administration will either support you or avoid you. Even if the administration is poorly focused or inaccessible, you still need to move past it to be promoted to greener pastures. Turn the admin into an ally and then into an opportunity. What can you learn from the administration, and what can you provide for them? Look for ways to support your own well-being, a chance for promotion, or a better lifestyle by creating an ally in the administration. Leverage the administration for professional learning, relationships, connections, behavioural support, power, respect, and learning. Many steps in life come from lifting others who have the capacity to enable growth in you.

Teachers

No one knows what you are going through better than other teachers. No one will experience the challenges and joys of teaching like your peers. They are a source of inspiration for you. It is foolish to avoid teachers and not use them as allies in times of need. So, if you are not using teachers as allies in the war of attrition, then what are you using to support your resources, assessment, moderation, and mental health? Who are you using as a sounding board for your ideas?

Teacher Aides and Support Workers

If no one knows what you are going through better than teachers, the people closest to understanding the trials and tribulations of teaching would be the aides and support workers in the room. They are an ally in your classroom. They are actually a powerful force for change in your teaching life. They can see things that you cannot; they pick up subtle clues while your back is turned. A child's imperfect behaviour is exposed when working with the aide, despite being an "angel" with you. They can be a sounding board and a source of ideas and inspiration.

Not using an aide in the room is like having a classroom with no chairs. You can still teach, but it is easier with them. The aide does not come to your room as a blank slate; they have ideas and experiences that you may not be aware of. Spend time getting to know your aide, and you will be surprised by the life experience and resource sharing they can provide. The introduction of a support worker is useful in the most important way. They can provide differentiation. They can work with different students on the same topic, but at a higher or lower level, based on your planning.

An aide in the room should be a blessing, but do not take them for granted. If you have the opportunity to work with an aide, spend considerable time looking at the best way to use them to improve learning. If you do not have an aide, then you will have to create the learning supports yourself. Do not expect an aide or support worker in the room, as they will be managed according to where support needs to be placed, and it may not be in your classroom. Do not be upset or concerned, but if you gain an aide, be happy and prepared. They can assist you, but only if you are prepared, planned, differentiated, and have identified the needs in the room. They will provide information about students and teaching. Remember that they are an ally for you, and the aide is not in the room to watch you teach.

Parents

Parents, when used effectively, can become a teaching resource for your classroom. Teachers often believe that they alone can deliver learning to children, but forget the range of skills that exist within the community. Parents can be an ally for learning by providing a different perspective, a real-world context, or a deeper understanding of the topic that the teacher is attempting to explain. Parents, when engaged and involved, can be a great ally for teachers.

Mental Health Support

The ally in your corner is the one who can support you, listen to you, and allow you to reveal the real challenges you are facing in your life. The doctor, counselor, psychologist, psychiatrist, or mental health specialist; these are all people that every teacher may need to access in times of challenge and difficulty. If an arm is broken or there is a significant cut in your skin, you do not sit at home and wait for the pain to go away. You seek medical services immediately to gain care from health professionals. The time, effort, and observance that you give to your physical well-being and injuries must also be given to your psychological well-being and injuries.

Support professionals are an incredible ally as they slowly come to understand you, support your progress, encourage your healing process, create the steps you need to improve, and provide you with the most important tool—your chance to talk. You talk for a living, but it is always in service of the students in your room. Now you must learn to talk for yourself. Sports organisations, financial services, and emergency services all provide access to support workers. Teachers are no less in need of someone; in fact, it could be argued that you may be in greater need. Do not allow your well-being to be brushed aside for another day, for just as a broken arm will not heal correctly unless it is treated, neither will your mental health.

"The future belongs to those who learn more skills and combine them in creative ways."
—Robert Greene, Mastery

Professional Reading

One of the most powerful allies you can find to improve your teaching, generate ideas, and develop research-supported pedagogical and behavioural techniques is books. Books provide perspective and the experience of others. Decisions being made today are not new; they have been made many times before in many different countries and cultures. Sometimes they worked, and sometimes they did not. To read a book about the mistakes previous countries have made with their foreign policy and then read the local paper and see the same mistakes unfolding in real time is to realise that education has failed even at the highest levels. Or at least hubris, ego, and self-promotion—none of which are new ideas—have once again sprouted from the manure of previous failures with the sweet-smelling aroma of "but it will be different this time." It rarely is.

Teaching is no less encapsulated by the failures and experiences of previous ideas. Yet it is in reading books that lessons and warnings can be understood, heeded, and applied. Be careful with books in education, as they can be misleading. If you visit the Education section of a bookshop, how many books on education are actually there? There are many dictionaries and thesauruses. There are many mass-produced edutainment books designed to teach a child how to spell, learn times tables, write sentences, and complete other possibly productive but often one-size-fits-all approaches to learning.

To find books that truly become allies in your professional practice, teachers must expand their perception of education, learning and the wider world. If you go to the Health section, you will learn about anxiety, how to deal with a difficult child, or how to support a child who is dyslexic, autistic, or experiencing learning challenges. If you go to the Business section, you will read about teams, systems, and leadership: how they succeeded, what they used or avoided, and what contributed to the success of their organisations. In the Self-Help section, you will find books about becoming a better person, a successful person, and a follow-the-secret person. And if you head over to the Science section, you will discover books on neuroscience, how the brain works, and how humans think, alongside explanations of many concepts students learn at school.

In none of these sections will you necessarily find a book specifically about teaching. Yet all of them, when thoughtfully applied, can significantly influence the teacher. To find books specifically about education, teachers may need to visit specialised websites or education suppliers. In those places you will find highly specialised texts about analysing data, developing clarity, keeping learning visible and implementing structured, research-based, evidence-infused ideas. These books are highly valuable to the professional development of teachers. Read broadly, and use all books as classroom allies.

"The more that you read, the more things you will know,
the more that you learn, the more places you'll go."
—Dr. Seuss

Consider The Enemy

The enemy is out there. It is what prevents the teacher from succeeding in their goal. In every lesson, there is change, and with every change, there will be an enemy trying to hinder, block, frustrate, slow, or stop progress. But who or what is the enemy? The teacher who jumps too quickly to conclusions about the enemy may find themselves fighting the wrong battle with the wrong tools. The enemy can appear in many forms, and teachers must be prepared for the different types they will encounter. The dictionary definition of "enemy" can include "a thing that harms or weakens something else." Many things can harm or weaken objects, and many others harm or weaken teaching—and us.

- The enemy could be as destructive as a country at war.
- The enemy could be as constructed as a competing product on the shelves.
- The enemy could be as ambivalent as weeds in your garden.
- The enemy could be as personal as a conflict from your past.
- The enemy could be as inspiring as the opposing team in a sporting contest.
- The enemy could be as jovial as the jibes in a friend's argument.
- The enemy could be as obvious as a noisy neighbour.
- The enemy could be as silent as a social media post.
- The enemy could be the student who prevents learning from happening.
- The enemy could be the staff member who negatively changes the climate.

- The enemy could also be you.

"It is a military axiom not to advance uphill against the enemy,
nor to oppose him when he comes downhill.
Do not pursue an enemy who simulates flight;
do not attack soldiers whose temper is keen.
Do not swallow bait offered by the enemy.
Do not interfere with an army that is returning home.
When you surround an army, leave an outlet free.
Do not press a desperate foe too hard.
Such is the art of warfare."
—Sun Tzu, The Art of War

Know My Enemy: What is in my hands?

"We cannot fight new wars with old weapons."
—Vinoba Bhave

The soldiers enter the battlefield, and the enemy waits in the distance, prepared to advance. You draw your weapons and discover, to your shock, the state of disrepair of your equipment. You see blunt swords and bent, cracked shields. You inspect the guns, which look even worse when you realize that they have no bullets. The horses meant to lead you into battle are too old and slow. The jeeps have flat tyres, and the tanks are in need of oil and gas. The enemy is not what is in front of you; it is what is in your hand. You cannot attend to the battle till you attend to your equipment.

These weapons are your pedagogical, behavioral, and relational tools. But they may be ineffective. Who is to blame for the state of them? Which enemy caused your behaviour strategies to become so blunt?

- Who gave you the wooden cane to use against students and then promoted corporal punishment as the only solution to classroom problems?
- Who handed you a twenty-year-old, dog-eared page of curriculum worksheets and assessments and presented it as quality learning material?
- Who taught you that shouting at students is the best form of discipline or that you should never smile until Term 3?

These blunt instruments often come from the "experienced" teacher: the one who supposedly knows what is really going on. Perhaps they are from the college or university who offer advice despite not stepping into a classroom for many years. Perhaps it is the teacher twelve months from retirement who takes you under their wing and guides you with misconceptions, prejudices, and biases. Perhaps it is the teacher who extols the virtues of "teaching the basics" while failing to recognise that the world students are entering requires critical literacy, problem-solving, and innovative thinking.

I must recognise that enemy. Perhaps it is me. Perhaps it was my teachers at school, my university lecturers, or my mentors. Perhaps it was the persistent belief of "this is how we have always done it." These enemies leave us defenseless against the opposition that comes our way.

Unfortunately, I may not realise that my tools are damaged until I am in the middle of the teaching battle. The good news is that realization brings the opportunity to change. It means recognising that mistakes have been made, that no one has been irreparably harmed, and that I can repair the tools I carry. I must remove this pedagogical or behavioural enemy and begin improving and developing my arsenal of relevant, relational, and inspirational pedagogical strategies. As I develop these tools, I recognise that I will never have to face this enemy again.

"Engage your brain before you engage your weapon."
—Jim Mattis

Know My Enemy: Who is beside me?

"The art of war teaches us to rely not on the likelihood of the enemy not coming but on our own readiness to receive him, not on the chance of his not attacking but rather on the fact that we have made our position unassailable."
—Sun Tzu

Soldiers are people, and people are emotional beings. They are lined up in the trenches and about to go into battle. What is the response, feeling, or mindset of the soldier next to you? Are they ready to attack, or are they scared? If they are about to enter battle, there is every chance that they could die. Their feelings will directly influence how you think. If you are uncertain, you can feed on the emotions of others beside you.

Teachers need to recognise a enemy in this instance can be the person next to them in the same room, same block, same school. They could be a mentor, a peer, or just a strong voice in the room. They may find you as a source of connection or just a friend. But their ability to influence you as a teacher should not be underestimated.

You will look at students and the curriculum differently. Your role on playground duty will be coloured differently, as will your time spent working after school. The right voice will seek to encourage positive relationships with students and provide you with the tools you need to be successful.

The wrong voice will change your environment, your teaching, or your well-being.

To battle against this enemy involves listening intently. Are the comments negative or positive? What kind of humour is being used? Who is the focal point of the humour, sarcasm, or frustration? What kind of relationship does this other person have with students, staff, or administration? These are all clues that I must use to determine if I am entering the classroom and facing students with the correct mindset.

In any school, there will always be different personalities. People will always hold different positions from me. They have something different to offer. This is what makes life and teaching so interesting and challenging. But if I raise my banner and line up with someone who damages others, then the damage they cause will make its way to me and my reputation.

Teaching is hard enough without the whispers of discontent in my ear.

Reversal: A person who has a positive influence on both teaching and relationships will become the most powerful change agent in the life of the teacher. Teachers who can work, support, challenge, and respect each other create the best experience, and this is what makes teaching great.

Tyrion let the eunuch help him mount.
"Lord Varys," he said from the saddle,
"Sometimes I feel as though you are the best friend I have in King's Landing,
and sometimes I feel you are my worst enemy."
"How odd. I think quite the same of you."
— George R.R. Martin

Know My Enemy: Who is inside me?

"We suffer more in imagination than in reality."
—Seneca

The greatest battle is in the mind. It is a well-known statement and has been made in diverse movies made by Pixar to Marvel. But the idea is correct. The soldier, the footballer, the lawyer, the surgeon, and the executive have to conquer their enemy within before they can achieve anything. The thought of battle can be worse than the battle.

- Football players can vomit before big games.
- Actors can go into meditative states while preparing for their role.
- Anyone about to enter any field of battle will consider all worst-case scenarios and live them, respond to them, and fear them. And they have not even left the room.

Teachers are no less susceptible to such reaches of the imagination, and this can create such a fearful enemy that teachers may literally freeze at the sight of a student, parent, lesson, or meeting. What is the enemy telling you about this situation? They are feeding you information from previous encounters and experiences. Your enemy is forcing you to relive some prior trauma, some unresolved drama that took place in your life five hours, five days, or five months ago. The enemy lives in our brain, and it has created a negative emotional connection to a person, idea or thing.

Students who have struggled with learning have reported to teachers that they are dumb. The brain, through neuroscience reasons, who does not allow learning to be easy through a range of complexities (dyslexia, ADHD, to name just a few) or other quirks of thinking, will then turn around and tell its owner that they are unable to learn, or even that they are dumb. If this were a person, you would expel them from your life, but you cannot, as your brain is with you the entire time. It directs your attention towards previous grief-stricken moments and lays the blame and consequences onto you.

The reason the enemy is there is because, like an enemy on the battlefield, you have not defeated it yet. The enemy has not been smitten and destroyed. It has been left to hide, fester, grow, and reappear at times when you enter a similar battlefield.

"Remember the last time you had to deal with this child, and you struggled? Well ... Here's Johnny!"

Teaching is a battle, and often it is a battle in the head. Teachers need to view every incident as a toss of the coin. Every incident has its own set of rules and its own set of experiences, which are independent of the teacher. The mental side will want to relive and reapply previous memories to this toss-of-the-coin incident, but the previous toss of the coin does not affect the next toss.

And that is what the enemy is doing. They are thinking, "Remember when I attacked you last time? Well, I'm coming again, and I expect to create the same confusion and fear."

The teacher needs to look at every altercation with a parent, student, or even another teacher with the same mindset as tossing a coin. I do not know what to expect. I do not know the mindset of the enemy I faced last time. I do not know what their mindset is this time. I am open to learning and understanding. Maybe I triggered a response in them. But that was their response, and I do not own it. Maybe they triggered a response in me, so I need to identify it and work on it.

Learn from it, deal with it, move it into files for further development, or remove it from further viewing. Do not let it control you.

This is easy to say but harder in practice. That is why teaching is hard, and I need to be battle-hardened to engage in the practice. I need to recognise my enemy and make a plan to defeat it, even if that enemy is within me.

"What about you?
What do you do when you cannot forget the awful things of the past?"
"I find the awful thing ... and I kill it."
—Jack Reacher, Season 3

Know My Enemy: the Carrot or the Stick?

"Not all our rewards will look like carrots.
Not all our penalties will look like sticks."
—Marion Haste

The carrot and the stick. The army is motivated to work as they are paid, but they are also aware that their participation in strategies or in war is motivated by fear of death, fear of those who have the power to demote them, fear of the enemy and fear of lower pay. The carrot is created by achievement, recognition, high rewards, or encouragement. The stick is fear.

The enemy of teaching is ... What is the carrot, and what is the stick?

The carrot is high results, good marks, or As on a test. But why do they need to get an A? If the motivation, teaching, learning, and results are for an A, why? Teachers teach to an A standard. They demonstrate an A. They aspire for all students to get an A on the test. While these are noble intentions, have they been explained to the students?

- If you work hard, you will get an A.
- If you concentrate, you will get an A.
- If you behave, you will get an A.
- But what does receiving an A get you?
- Is an A in Year 1 better than an A in Year 11?

Teachers may have the answer to this question and could quite definitely explain why receiving an A is important, but do the students know this? The enemy in the room is trying to have students obtain a score that has no discernible meaning in their life.

A? Is that not the start of the alphabet? So if I learn the alphabet, I get to keep the first letter? Why would that be important for me to keep? Do I get to keep the A, or is it a metaphorical A?

Teachers need to remove enemies from the room, and one of them is the reason for the mark that students are straining (or not) to get. Students need to be educated about the importance and relevance of the marks. If teachers are unable to explain this, then the enemy in the room grows as large as the apathy and indifference in the students.

If you work hard and behave, you get the carrot. If you do not, you get the stick.

The enemy is now fear. Fear of being kept in, detention, suspension, and parents being contacted. Students will view fear of consequences as an enemy in the room. Not one to avoid, but one to avoid getting caught. This means that students will not view the consequences as the enemy. They will see the person who *gives* the consequences as the enemy. While you try to explain that their behaviour and choices are the enemy to learning, the students will only see you as the enemy to be defeated.

Again, like the carrot, have you explained why the consequences are there? Have you demonstrated the expectations of behaviour in the room? Have you explored why consequences must be brought into the classroom?

There can be no expectation of behaviour from students. The cultural, family, and peer experiences that students come from are too diverse, and the generalized learning agreement about classroom expectations is too vague. The teacher comes in with their understanding of expectations, making them the enemy of learning. This is more than explaining the rules of the class or the lesson. The enemy of learning is not the consequence; it is the misunderstanding of why the consequence is there to begin with.

Know your enemy.

- The enemy could be the carrot of advantage that hasn't been explained, and so is ignored, thus creating unengaged students.
- The enemy could be the stick of consequence that hasn't been explained, creating students who view you as the dealer of fear.

"If you believe that the primary reason that people fail to meet goals has to do more with them than you, then you should not be in the business of supervising, developing, or leading people."
—Paul L. Marciano

Know My Enemy: the Infection

"Keep your friends close and your enemies closer."
—The Godfather

An infection that attacks the human body is too small to be seen and is impossible to identify even under a microscope. The best way to identify one is to look at what it is creating. Fever, temperature, coughing, headaches, pains, and inability to breathe are just a few of the symptoms. It is through these indications that a realisation occurs. Something is not right, and a form of medication, diet, or specialist advice is needed to attack the problem.

Infections occur in schools as well, and in the same way, it can be very hard to identify. But the symptoms eventually show themselves. People feel that they need to have their say regarding education, school, or teachers. People whose only credentials are that they were students once and that this would not happen "in their day." Often, these voices are hidden behind layers of others whom they have also infected. Often, they hide behind screens and use keyboards to spread harm in the same way that a hacker uses a computer to infect a business's network. The damage and harm they can create is not as widespread, but it becomes more potent as it focuses on a single target: the school, the class, the student, or the teacher.

Teachers need to protect themselves against attacks on their character and teaching. The first step is to remove the possibility of charges being made against you. Take extra precautions from the first day to ensure relationships between students and parents are strong. Apply no thought to previous history others have had with that student or parent. It will not matter; this year, it is all on you. Change mindsets and perspectives, engage positively with communication, information, and feedback, and ensure positive comments about the child overwhelm the parent.

You must step first into changing their perspective of you as a teacher. Do not hope it will work out. It will not. Step up and make your position clear. This will give others less to work with. Any sign of weakness in communication will enable others to find ways to attack the teacher. Log all communication. When the attack comes, and you can demonstrate logs of communication and what you have specifically communicated, you erode the argument from your opponent. They will fight against the facts, but those facts are all you have.

The second step, if the attacks come from outside, is to remove them from the system. No communication or information. Starve the source of reasons. Instead, focus all your attention on other students and parents in the classroom. Let the word spread from your classroom that things are great, and remove the supports from that one parent who seeks to undermine. Constantly engage in positive communication with every other parent instead of that one. Make sure everything they say is refuted by others who are not experiencing the same thing. In fact, they will argue against that parent and isolate them. Bring your families onto your side.

In any battle, always remember there are four "truths": the student, the parent, the teacher, and the actual event. All events will be viewed with bias, whether implicitly understood or not. This will help you, as you need to be aware in however clear your understanding of the concerns of the student or parent may be, there will always be something that you will not know, appreciate, or consider.

Never stake your ground on their "wrongness" or on your "rightness."

Don't make it about them or you. That fight is an emotional battle, and that is one others love to engage in. If you provide an emotional response, then you are adding fuel to the fire. Use facts, use your communication with various parties, stick to the plan, and allow others to tire themselves out.

Remember that some people like the sound of their own voice. Some people feel they can speak despite having no authority. Some people like to create confusion, chaos, and spread rumours for their own entertainment. Some people like to begin arguments that start with "some people," when they, in fact, are speaking not of others, but of themselves.

Know your enemy. Focus on the facts. Concentrate on the story behind the person and their motivation. Keep your thoughts, acts, and communication clear, honest, and pure.

"To secure ourselves against defeat lies in our own hands,
but the opportunity of defeating the enemy is provided by the enemy himself."
—Sun Tzu

Know My Enemy: Student Approaches

"I make new enemies every day. It is called business."
—Horrible Bosses 2, 2015

For a battle to occur, there must be at least two combatants. Maybe they are inside your head as an idea that you are struggling with. Maybe it is an ideology that you disagree with, or even a football team that you just don't like. It does not matter, as every battle needs an opponent. This opponent's goal is to stop you from progressing, improving, or growing. It could be preventing physical resources, or it may be financial gains that they are pursuing to prevent you from moving forward.

Teaching is no different, and while it may not seem correct to call the student an enemy, at the end of the day, they can be the difference in my mental health, achievement in lessons, and desire to return the next day. The student can be an enemy, although if teaching is correctly implemented, then the student should be the enemy. If I am not creating an enemy, that could indicate that I am not doing what I am supposed to be doing. My job is to create thinking, change mindsets, and improve perspectives. To do this without creating an enemy is not working hard enough. Some enemies last for just a moment while they struggle to learn and become frustrated with their initial lack of understanding, or it may last for a lesson as their weakness in maths is exposed. Maybe it could last for a day, but that may be more due to the external environment the student has come from.

There are, though, students who don't engage in any teaching and learning. Who, through circumstances beyond the control of teachers, will seek to disrupt and be an enemy of learning, not just for the teacher but for the class. Sometimes the enemy has a specific title, a name, and a face.

Puppet Master

This student will sit quietly while others around them cause trouble. Initially, you protect the child from danger. But you find, after investigation, that it is this quiet and unpretentious child who caused the trouble to begin with. These students will whisper, nod, indicate, threaten, and promise others, ultimately having peers do things for their own enjoyment. These students will often be part of the Teflon process as well. They sit quietly and acknowledge that others have behaved poorly, but take no ownership.

Puppet Master Defence Techniques

Listen to the room and use the messages and behaviours as a calling card of the child. Ask students questions, and track down the source of the messages. Approach the student with your findings. They will look confused, but do not accept what they show. Seek parental support, if it is available, to indicate the concerns and string-pulling the child is capable of. The parents may not believe you, but inform them anyway. Do not go hard on the children who are responding to the tugs from this student, but trace all behaviours back, then discipline accordingly. Do not attempt anything without strong evidence.

The Water Balloon

This student has only one thought: disrupt the learning and destroy the environment. The person will not seek to hide their intentions and will often show what they intend to do. If you get too close to the enemy, they will not only explode in the room, but over you as well. Water balloon students are not easy to contain, as they are looking for the most obvious and attention-seeking moment to cause educational and teaching damage. They are waiting for the moment to go off. The more you engage with them, or at them, the more they will enjoy the experience, for their only joy is the attention and disruption they can cause.

Water Balloon Defence Techniques

Do not engage. Do not approach. They will explode, but they will cause less damage if there are fewer people around. If they cannot use words to destroy, they may use the objects near them. Desks, chairs, and books may become projectiles or weapons as the student literally goes off. Behaviour plans are crucial for this child. Find the reasons for the explosions, and identify the triggers. It will take time, but a consistent approach can work.

Mouse Trap

Some students have something in their history—an encounter they haven't yet identified or an action that has caused them distress in the past. When this trigger is touched, mostly inadvertently, by students or the teacher, the response from the student can be significant. It is also not proportional to the trigger. Some students may not even realise that this trigger exists. Some do not realise that it created such an emotional reaction, and others may act inappropriately, then use it as a justification. These are the students who involve teachers walking on a minefield, hoping not to aggravate them, as whatever response occurs is likely to cause an explosion.

Mouse Trap Defense Techniques

This is where you need to rely on all information about the child from past teachers, parents, friends, relatives, and counselors. The teacher cannot walk blindly into this environment without knowing everything possible about the student. They will not be able to remove blame from themselves by simply not knowing. Information is power in these situations. Create scenarios, strategise events taking place, and consider what needs to be done to avoid any reaction.

Water to Ice

These students create a feeling of friendship and warmth. They laugh at your jokes and help build a positive relationship with you. They engage and create a culture of mutual respect. But as water seeps through cracks, so does this student seep through the cracks in your defences. After a while, the water of this student will turn to ice and, as ice can crack stone, the student will crack your identity. You will fight to return to the relationship you once had, but you cannot. The student sought to create this from the beginning. You begin to justify their behaviour, support them in the classroom and the staffroom. You look to the "good" side of their nature and seek to see them as you once did. Staff may question you, and they are right to do so.

Water to Ice Defense Techniques

In all moments, keep your defences up. Do not let the jokes, smiles, and offers of assistance from the student be anything more than a way for them to reveal their motives to you. Build relationships with them, but ensure it is one-sided. Occasionally, you may need to create a burst of anger at them to keep them on their toes. You may need to unbalance their view of you as an easy target. It is important to maintain the relationship on your terms. Remember that you are the teacher and they are the student. Your job is to teach. To do that, you need to be a learner of the behaviour, the competitors, and the intentions of all your students.

Updraughts

Time and books have been written about helicopter parents. This is the parent who hovers nearby and becomes obsessively involved in their child's life. They do this with the intention of showing love and wanting to support, but they become overbearing, needy, and willing to fight all battles to the detriment of the development of the child. But less time has been spent on the students who are pulled up by the draughts of their parents' continual beating of the wings. These students are entitled. They have been taught that they are special, so concepts such as sharing, listening, and respecting boundaries may be lacking. They will not understand the word "no." They will be the victim in any situation when events turn against them. There will be tears, silent treatment, and looks of shock when consequences are delivered to them.

Updraught Defense Techniques

The student has only one ally, and that is their parent. Never think that you can share a moment with the child. They will go home and more than likely share everything that you have said. Do not consider the child a confidant or trust them, even when they seem frustrated by their parents' continual hovering. At the end of the day, the child will go home to the love and care of parents, and any thoughts they had about the teacher or learning will be lost in a swoon of love from the parents.

The Perfect Disguise

The student attempts to work but is never happy with their outcome because it is not perfect. While this attention to detail can be beneficial to learning, it can sometimes be disguised as something else and manifests itself in ripping up work, tearful breakdowns, physical and verbal outbursts towards other students and staff, or creating an unpleasant atmosphere in the room. The student's quest for perfection can create a perfect storm, and nothing the teacher or the student can do will be right.

Perfect Disguise Defence Techniques

This student needs to learn to fail. They need to separate the emotion of the work from the reality of their ability. They need to create better strategies when things do not work as they expect. This is not easy since it is hidden behind wanting to be better, but this is a disguise, as it can be a way to seek attention or to create drama. The teacher can investigate whether this behaviour took place in previous years, or they can contact parents to determine if these actions take place at home as well. All information is important, but the teacher will need to begin the process to determine whether there is a desire for great work, in which case they can be supported, or if it is just disguised as an attention event, in which case see the Waterfall below.

Learned Helplessness

The student is helpless, seeks advice and support, puts themselves down, and feels incapable. Students may feel like this, but if it becomes a consistent state, then the student is demonstrating learned helplessness. This has been developed over the years. It would have begun with genuine challenges and concerns from the students. The parent, teacher, or support network stepped in to assist, but this assistance has turned into the go-to for all further challenges the student has had to deal with.

Learned Helplessness Defense Techniques

This is where the teacher has to pull the plug, remove the umbilical cord, and demonstrate tough love. The student needs to fail and wake up. The teacher must create strategies that the student can use for their educational improvement. Find the strength, the competence, and the natural ability of the student, and leverage that for improved thinking, well-being, and helpful strategies. If not, the child will drain the teacher and the students, but worse than that, they will begin to believe the message they are telling themselves.

The Waterfall

This student loves emotion and drama. They love to be involved in, or place themselves into the middle of, whatever drama is taking place. Anything that happens in the classroom will affect this student, and their response will usually take the form of "don't look at me; look at me." They will be upset over little things, and they will want others to feel sorry for them or to fix it. They want attention by pretending to avoid attention. They will need time out from learning so they can recover. And tears will flow. They will flow when they are seeking attention, and they will flow if no one gives them attention.

Waterfall Defense Techniques

Don't play the game. Don't give attention but direct all attention to the parents. Allow them to know everything that has happened. Explain in excruciating detail the events that took place that allowed the waterfall to flow. Maybe they need counselling or extra support. Don't express this to parents, but work it in a way that encourages the parents to become more involved. The teacher's job is not to be the counsellor for some perceived angst that the child is recovering from. The teacher should not put themselves in a position of a shoulder to cry on. The teacher is there to teach and provide academic excellence. The mental health professional will be able to provide further support. Contact parents, report everything, ignore the behaviour, and keep teaching. This may also be a tactic used by teachers with other teachers. Be aware of this reaction in the staffroom as well.

The Happy Rock

This student will passively and happily sit in the classroom, saying and doing nothing. They are happy but not engaged. They are a rock in that they don't move around the classroom to annoy others. They are the very definition of passive-aggressive. They cannot be manipulated, bribed, threatened, or tricked. They have a clear understanding of what they want, and it is usually anything other than what is happening in the lesson.

Happy Rock Defence Techniques

Often, it is the maturity of the student that affects their lack of involvement in the classroom. Sometimes, it may be that they are unable to see the point of learning. It can also be a stressful experience they have had with teaching in previous years. The teacher needs to recognise when it is the teacher's lack of engaging pedagogy (or other reasons) or if it is the student's lack of engagement. The teacher must continue to teach and present information to the class. They can try to engage in topics that interest them, try to find student allies who will encourage learning, and provide differentiated experiences for the student. But at the end of the day, they are one student in the class, and learning will continue for those eager to learn.

"A man's worst difficulties begin when he is able to do as he likes."
—Thomas Henry Huxley

The teacher who presents education to a student whose behaviour is negative and who states, "I can do what I want" will watch that student grow to abhor education and learning. They will enter the workforce unprepared, unskilled, and underdeveloped. The workforce will take one look at this new applicant and state to them, "I can do what I want" with their pay, hours, and opportunities for development.

The teacher who presents education to a student who is positive and states, "I can do what I want" to ensure their education, learning, and future viability will produce a student who enters the workforce educated, skilled, and with an optimistic future. The student will look at the myriad of employment and entrepreneurial options in front of them and will confidently say, "I can do what I want."

The Politician

This student has very clear binary thinking (right or wrong), and they see themselves on the right side of every conversation or interaction. They are intelligent and have a great vocabulary to call upon. When questioned, they will spend time talking without answering the question. They will create further arguments that distract from the question. They will bring in other motives, other individuals, or even the teacher themselves that do not solve the question but complicate the motives or the reasoning behind the original question. This student will talk a lot but say little. They don't want to engage in a conversation. They want to control it. They want to lead the questions towards answers that they can answer, or they want to find answers to questions that have not been asked.

Politician Defense Techniques

Do not engage in this type of behaviour. You have a question; so ask it. When the child seeks to lead the conversation elsewhere, continue to ask the same question. Repeat it over and over again. If the child refuses to answer, then cancel any further conversation and walk away. Book a time to meet. Organise the environment in your favour. Bring in a peer to support you. They do not need to speak, but they need to document. This will be important when reporting to parents, especially the amount of time wasted by not answering a simple question.

The Legal Expert

This student will listen to every word that is spoken by the teacher, and they will break the sentence into segments and identify words that could be substituted. They will then use those specific words to provide innocence to questions asked by the teacher. Words can be substituted, hit to push, tackle to grab, litter to rubbish, yell to shout, beside to next to. All these words can be replaced, and then the student's innocence or involvement is legally clear from their perspective. Students will make an effort to do this, and those who have the language skills will react quickly to teachers' instructions. Their legalistic argument will be made completely intentionally and with a straight face. This will allow the teacher to focus on their questioning elsewhere. While it will be frustrating for the teacher initially in trying to establish the sequence of events, as well as the involvement of all students, teachers will later marvel at how the student could perform a legal gymnastics routine to avoid implication in an event that they were clearly involved in.

Legal Expert Defense Techniques

You will not be able to defeat the argument until you gain further information from witnesses, bystanders, or the victim. Information must be gathered from others first before you can approach the legal expert. Once information has been gained, the teacher will be able to interpret and redirect, when necessary, the statement made by the legal expert. The legal expert has to be treated like a witness in a courtroom. There must be a list of questions and cross-examination, and an opportunity will need to be taken to question the witness at another time. Use exhibits of evidence and allow for a hearing of witnesses. You will need a burden of proof, and you need to ensure they don't perjure themselves. Notes must be taken by the teacher, and they need to be read back to the student for clarification. This will allow the student to recognise that what they said is clear and the minutes have been taken. When evidence is brought forward that contradicts the legal expert, then that evidence must be introduced as exhibits, and the legal expert has a right of reply. The teacher can then compare the old testimony with the new testimony made because of the new evidence, and then decisions can be made. This is a time-consuming process, but when done well, you take away the emotional response from both the teacher and the legal expert, and the truth shall be revealed.

The 80/20 Principle

Not all students are enemies. In fact, while the enemies in the classroom may take up the majority of the time and effort, they are not the majority of students in the classroom. The 80/20 Principle by Richard Koch demonstrates this in many ways. Eighty per cent of something comes from twenty per cent of the processes, although that percentage figure can be manipulated. It is more likely that 95% of behaviours come from 5% of the students in the classroom, and that percentage may equal one student. Look at the other 95% of students in the room. Investigate their working habits and ideas. Analyse their thinking and questioning. Count how many students are actually working during times of stress. You will be surprised at the number of great students. Be enthralled by their wonderful personalities and child-like wonder at learning. Be encouraged. There are always going to be students in the class who take up your time, but there are many more students who take up your teaching and are inspired because of you.

"Between stimulus and response there is a space.
In that space is our power to choose our response.
In our response lies our growth and our freedom."
—Viktor E. Frankl

Know My Enemy: Is It Me?

"Emotional intelligence
is your ability to recognise and understand emotion in yourself and others,
and your ability to use this awareness to manage
your behaviour and relationships."
—Travis Bradberry

The final enemy is the hardest to identify and difficult to overcome; it is the mirror ball. A mirror ball creates a dazzling light show and works fantastically in the right conditions. It spins and glitters, and the light can reflect across the room. But when the lights are off, or the room is bright, then the effect is lost. The mirror ball as a tool is not helpful. It does not create light, it cannot be used to read, and it is useless as a mirror to reflect what you look like. The mirror ball in the classroom is the enemy. The mirror ball may be me.

The teacher who is the mirror ball comes into the classroom with energy, excitement and fun. They engage students and create a great atmosphere that students love. But just as the light from the mirror ball is inconsistent, so is the learning in this class. The teacher spins and creates memories, but after a while, it is recognised that the students are not learning anything. Just like the light from a mirror ball, the engagement is inconsistent, the pedagogy flits from one idea to another, the relationships are subject to the mood of the teacher on the day, and the students are entranced by the comical presence of a light that does not create improvement. The mirror ball does not improve learning, students, morale, or behaviour.

The teacher who is a mirror ball needs light to look alive and bright. But if the teacher enters classroom, and there is no light or energy to keep the learning alive, the teacher looks for others to create the light for them. This teacher wants the light, the focus and attention. But something is wrong.

Maybe the teacher enters the classroom angry or embarrassed about an incident. Maybe the teacher who has lost the light looks to students for their perceived unrighteousness or inability to demonstrate respect to a teacher who has themselves created an environment where no respect can be found. The teacher may become a mouse trap where any slight against them will result in buddy classes, phone calls home, and reports to administration, believing that expulsion is the only responsible form of response. The teacher will sometimes seek the reason (student, learning, or environment) to go off and then justify their response from the reason. It makes no sense, but we are not in their frame of mind.

Maybe the teacher creates relationships with students, but then turns cold and hurts them. They will be confused by the unpredictability and uncompromising behaviour of disappointment, whereas the day before you sang the praises of the student.

Maybe you are the teacher who flows into the classroom or school like a fresh breeze with a nice car in an environment of blue-collar workers, or wearing designer clothing into a small town, or looking for the coffee shop in an environment full of pubs, and wonder why the teacher feels underappreciated.

The teacher may prefer to work with privileged students, as they are "more my people". Or students or parents who know the teacher is going to be in that classroom and who ask to be moved, such is the reputation of the teacher.

They are called mirror balls, as they cannot reflect accurately, and they are unable to reflect personally. Everything happens to them; nothing is ever caused by them. They look at the world and erratically shine light onto things that upset them or excite them. They are constantly moved (year levels, classrooms, or schools) without realising that the administration is trying to limit the damage they will create for students and parents. A mirror ball is great for a party, but useless when there is work to be done. The mirror ball in the right environment can be fun, but those conditions rarely last and rarely result in positive teaching. While other events can be defeated, the mirror ball affects students, teachers, schools, and the profession. It is imperative that this is identified, retrained, or removed. The best support for a mirror ball is self-reflection.

Ask:

- Are you always angry at someone or something every day?
- Are you always seeking approval from students while ignoring your peers?
- Are you always seeking approval from your peers while ignoring your students?
- Are you an advocate for certain children in the classroom despite the data proving you wrong?
- Do you advocate for any children?
- Do you want students in your classroom?
- Have you moved from year to year?
- Do students/parents/teachers/support workers want to be in your classroom?
- Do you seek roles in a school other than being a teacher?
- Do you really want to be a teacher?

Find a mentor or peer, and ask for honest feedback. This will take strength, but it will allow you to identify your role in the school.

"You cannot change that kind of chaos
till the thinking changes.
Till the foundations change.
Till the chemistry changes."
—The Bear, Season 1, Episode 3

Consider the Myth of the Straight Line

"People at war with themselves will always cause collateral damage in the lives of those around them."
—John Mark Green

The soldier lines up their weapon with the target. They take aim and ensure they have a clear line of sight. They line up at the end of the weapon with the target and are careful to avoid any obstacles in the way. The soldier then releases the projectile, which flies unhindered to the target. If the aim is true, then the target is reached, the enemy is neutralised, and the soldier can consider themselves to be successful.

But that is a myth.

Life, like weapons, does not have a single target trajectory. And the line on which the projectile moves in no way indicates the damage that is about to be caused.

There are two ends to the line. A beginning and an end. The beginning is the soldier with the weapon. As they aim, they are consciously preparing to inflict damage on another person or building. This is a choice that they are making. They do it with the realisation that they are right and the other is wrong, that it is for the fun or fear of it, or that they received orders to complete such a task.

But when the weapon goes off, there is a recoil. It is basic science that every action causes an equal and opposite reaction, although the reaction of the weapon firing is not equal to the projectile reaching the target. The impact of the discharging weapon provides a push towards the person pulling the trigger. The second impact for the person pulling the trigger is the realisation that they have caused harm. They have made a decision to hurt another person or to destroy something that they may not have created. This act, ever so subtly, will impact the person either initially or over time. Or more importantly, it may have no effect on this person at all, which demonstrates a greater concern.

Let us consider the target of this violent act. The person has been hit by a projectile. There is no way of knowing the impact of this weapon by the initial protagonist. Maybe the person is killed immediately. Maybe they are injured badly enough to die later. Maybe the projectile goes through the person and hits another. Maybe the projectile misses it completely and hits another. Maybe friends and family are watching while this takes place and are immediately in harm's way and fearful. Maybe they are angry. Maybe they are traumatised. Maybe they hide and lie in wait, for they think that there may be another event taking place.

While the projectile went in a straight line, the impact from both ends of the line creates a circle of influence, confusion, trauma, and pain that ripples out in all directions.

So too in education.

There is a power imbalance that teachers often forget. They have the power in the room to create learning, develop indifference or inflict harm on others. When that one child demonstrates an action, the teacher may feel obliged to respond. So they look down to ensure they have a straight line of influence on the child, and then they fire a barrage of words at the child with the intention of teaching them a lesson.

But again, the myth of straight lines applies.

The recoil of what the teacher said comes back to them, not immediately, but minutes, hours, or days later. They may realise later what they said and the harm that they caused. The circle of influence then ripples out from the teacher. What did the rest of the class think about what the teacher said? What about parents? What about other staff members? The recoil of damage from the teacher could be a loss of relationships within the room or even the school. Did the teacher really believe the things that they said? Did they reveal some hidden trauma that circled back and somehow found its way into the words the teacher expressed to the child?

The words the teacher said that went in a straight line to the student radiated from somewhere, and the words continue to ripple out into the world for others to hear. The discipline the teacher was hoping to apply became something else.

What about the other end of the line: the student? They also hear the attack coming at them by another person who is (usually) taller, stronger, or bigger than they are. The teacher has a physical presence, a leadership presence, or an inbuilt respectful presence, and yet, the student is on the receiving end of a line of attack that will make an impact.

But as the straight line turns into a circle for the teacher, so too will the student.

Who is listening from the student's perspective, and what are they thinking? Is the child embarrassed in front of their peers as their reputation is taking a hit by the teacher's comments? How will the student react in the coming minutes, hours, or days this of attack by the teacher? What shock has now been created, or what suffering has now been added to the student's mental capacity from the impact of the words?

Parents are liable to see this. The line of attack from the teacher will circle through the family dynamics.

The myth of straight lines in the discipline of students must be taken seriously. There will always be others who are affected by the comments made, and the impact can be that others learn about the lesson. Or it could be as serious as a teacher losing their job or even a student losing their potential.

Reversing the straight line

What happens if the situation is reversed and the delivery is from the student towards the teacher? There is another element of the myth of straight lines.

It has often been heard from adults that they hated school, that they caused trouble for the teacher, and were always being disciplined. They say this with a smile and a hint of mischievousness. These students may now have become a professional tradesperson, an entrepreneur who is running their own business, or have been working in some industry successfully for years. They are now successful enough to be able to live a lifestyle that matches their ability. This has taken place because of the education they received at school. But the myth of straight lines indicates that the comments they made to the teacher, the trouble they caused, and the discipline they received were all part of the fun of school.

But that is unfair.

It is the teacher's role in the school to educate. It is not their role to be the brunt of jokes and absorb the trouble directed at them by students who will move on to be successful in their fields. The impact of those comments on the teacher can be considerable, and the ripple effect it has on the teacher's well-being, mental health, and ability to move forward can be extensive.

The straight-line behaviour of student to teacher is too easy to gloss over as part of the job. But the occupation of the teacher is not to be criticised and subjected to ridicule by a student who will no doubt be successful in some other field. The perpetrators will look back and laugh indifferently about the trouble they caused in their straight-line comments, unaware of the ripple they created on their teacher.

And the ripple effect it had on other students.

Students who watch their peers abuse teachers, throw objects, and generally behave in antisocial ways may be affected by the decisions those students make. Maybe they became upset by it, maybe they became indifferent to it, or maybe they decided that it looked like a fun way to get attention, especially when things are not going their way. The potential learning environment of students has been removed. The capacity to learn has been weakened. The fear that other students may feel is that if a student will upset the teacher, how much more could they hurt other students in the classroom? How could this affect learning in the classroom?

The effect of one student's comments towards a teacher is not a straight line of poor language or behaviour, but a ripple across the room, the playground, and the school.

The focal point of attention may be to hit the protagonist, and the intention to cause harm may be achieved, but as in combat, the impact can be greater than what was intended.

The answer is not easily found, but to shape your well of being is to recognise the myth of straight lines. Which end of the straight line are you on? If you become aware of it, you can change it, support it, develop it and seek to disperse and limit the impact of comments by you, to you, and the students in your care.

"Once you start down a dark path, forever it will dominate your destiny."
—Yoda, The Empire Strikes Back

Consider the Impact of Land Mines

"Land mines are weapons of mass destruction in slow motion."
—Human Rights Watch and Physicians for Human Rights,
1993 report, "Landmines: A Deadly Legacy"

An unfortunate part of combat and battle is one that no one sees. A land mine is a bomb that is placed under the ground and primed to go off whenever a weight is placed upon it. It is expected to be the enemy's weight, but there is no way of knowing what will cause a depression in the soil.

The object of the mine is to harm the enemy, but once it is placed, the mine itself does not distinguish between friend or foe, only the weight distribution of the object above. The concerns around mines are not only that they can cause damage, but that they are not tracked. They are placed into the ground with the object to defeat the enemy, but once the war is over, the mine stays there. And just as they cannot tell the difference between friend or foe, they are also not able to differentiate between war and peace. So they lie there dormant, waiting for the trigger to be pulled.

The concept of a land mine is prevalent in classrooms as well. The emotional instability, temperament, or trauma of a student or a teacher can be well hidden. They can go through life and appear to be well-grounded, but under the ground, there may be a hidden force, and the weight or depression from above may be all it takes to trigger an explosion.

Teachers and students need to be aware of this force in their lives. They may be the trigger, or they may be the bomb. They may know the reason for how they are feeling, or they may not. They may know what the reaction will be, or they may be as surprised as everyone else.

The reason land mines can be so dangerous in the classroom is they cannot be seen. They sit, dormant, in the classroom. They work in front of the students, discussing new ideas. They engage with their friends, or they work with their peers. There is no concern or suspicion of the destructive nature of their personality. And yet, when they explode, they can cause considerable physical and psychological damage.

When the trigger is pressed, and the explosion takes place, then the physicality can be expressed in the rage of chairs and tables being knocked over. Psychological damage is created through words and expletives. And just as a bomb has no thought or direction except to harm, this person also manifests themselves in such a way. Just as weapons and projectiles can cause damage in more than a straight line, the land mine of a personality will affect people and property within the circumference. The effect of the blast of behaviour or words can be felt in all directions.

An explosion in the classroom will undoubtedly cause further impact as well. Maybe the students see the chairs being thrown and believe that is now an acceptable way to respond to challenges. Maybe they duck their head from the explosion, and the trauma is such that they never come out without the fear of it happening again. Maybe the explosion of the child's behaviour will result in others exploding at the same time because they have been hit, physically or verbally, and now, they explode in anger or defiance towards the person who initially injured them.

Mines never go away. They stay there long after the war is over. They can cause damage to unsuspecting people. Teachers have to identify the triggers of the mine and go about facilitating solutions to remove the danger. To deal with a mine, you need to be as proactive as possible. Just as information on the location of a landmine is crucial to identifying and removing it, so too is information crucial to responding to and planning for outbursts. Creating plans, secure areas, routines, and counselling will be several steps that need to be taken to support the classroom.

It can be difficult if the teacher is demonstrating behaviours and patterns that could lead to them becoming explosion. It can be difficult to support the teacher as they become older. They may have hidden the traits and triggers that could create an explosive personality. Through careful avoidance, training, and refusing to acknowledge any concerns, the trigger is pushed further into the psyche of the teacher. This teacher may remain relatively safe, but schools and students are known to push the teachers buttons. The right combination of conditions (student behaviour), history (experiencing trauma), pressure (workload), and time (schedules) could result in an explosion that lacks understanding or relevance from those who witness it. As teachers, you are going to find those personalities in the classroom and the staffroom.

A teacher who wants to make a difference will walk into the blast radius and either have no knowledge of the trigger or will not care. They believe that they can ride the waves of the explosion and establish control of the room. They will fail, and they will get hurt.

I want to be a teacher who researches information regarding potential scenarios that could result in a disturbance. I want to communicate with others, speak with parents, build relationships, and work with the counsellors in times of concern. I need to be aware that students I have built relationships with may not know who they are when the attack happens. I cannot allow the behaviour of the students in times of physical and psychological distress to damage the relationship once the event is over.

I also must dedicate attention to digging my well of being to ensure I am aware of the hidden traps, traumas and unresolved issues that may affect my mental health and well-being. I need to be aware of trauma and challenges. I must ensure that I have plans, steps, processes, counselling, and strategies to be successful, as the only impact I want to have in the room is a positive one.

"Triggers are like little psychic explosions that crash through avoidance and bring the dissociated, avoided trauma suddenly, unexpectedly, back into consciousness."

—Carolyn Spring

Consider OODA

(Recommended Reading: ***Legacy*** by James Kerr)

"The teams that will thrive ... are those who act quickly and decisively to seize the competitive advantage, adjusting and readjusting along the way. You either adapt or you lose."
—James Kerr, Legacy

Armies in battle have to deal with the enemy. This is an expected part of war. But the enemy they have to deal with can often be referred to as VUCA. The concept from James Kerr in his book *Legacy*, VUCA stands for "Volatile, Uncertain, Complex and Ambiguous." This is an apt description of war and the classroom. Teachers will be able to identify with each one of those concepts when dealing with students every day.

- **Volatile** – when hormones hit, the hamster dies, real concerns at home.
- **Uncertain** – about themselves, others, their learning, the question, the answer.
- **Complex** – in how they think and respond.
- **Ambiguous** – in their reactions from day to day. This can relate to students in the classroom. So how does a teacher respond to a VUCA situation?

By using OODA!

The OODA Loop stands for "Observe, Orient, Decide and Act." Teachers need to understand this process with students.

- Observe the child, learning, environment,
- Orient themselves to this change of focus,
- Decide how you are going to deal with it
- and then Act.

The first two steps are important and involve considerable self-reflection from the teacher. Teachers who cannot reflect and observe will walk and talk in a way that will create more stress and anxiety for the child, the class, and ultimately, for themselves.

Teachers who want to make a difference will observe the problem and go about solving it without orienting themselves to align the observation with the problem.

Teachers who want to learn will observe and then consider ways to orient themselves and the student towards a decision that will create the best outcomes.

The more extraverted and less emotionally aware the teacher, the more they will continue the lesson in ignorance of the VUCA in the corner. But the student is observing, and they will quickly react to a teacher who has not adjusted to the tone of the child.

- Kerr refers to situational awareness:
- Where am I in relation to my opponent?
- What does that look like?

A child walks in whose hamster has died. Observe the child is upset, and orient yourself to how they are thinking by asking questions and obtaining more information, decide that a little chat at lunchtime or with a friend is appropriate, and act to make sure that takes place. The child feels heard and understood, and the teacher has responded and possibly limited the impact that this event will have in the classroom for the rest of the day.

Make sure that you understand that if you are demonstrating VUCA, the students will quickly use OODA but perhaps not act in ways that produce positive outcomes.

The VUCA of a child may also affect the well-being of the teacher, but the OODA approach is still relevant. Observe your emotions, your reactions. Why I am feeling this way?

Are unresolved issues or trauma creating the reaction? I need to orient myself, my feelings, my reaction, and my thoughts to ensure that my professionalism is intact in the classroom. Deciding to do something about that issue is key. I cannot allow my emotions to be so easily manipulated again, so I must decide to speak to someone, resolve it with someone, seek restitution, or begin a counselling session. Once that is in place, I can act, both in dealing with the issue and acting correctly in the classroom.

I will not accept the volatile, uncertain, complex, and ambiguous nature of either the student, the classroom, or my life. This is what I will experience, but it is not normal, productive, or acceptable. I must rise to the challenge, learn from it, and add it to my growing résumé of personal and professional achievements.

"The challenge is to always improve, to always get better, even when you are the best. Especially when you are the best."
—James Kerr, Legacy

Consider Falling Back

"Faced with crisis, the man of character falls back upon himself."
—Charles de Gaulle

Your army is spread out and fighting against the enemy. As the battle rages, you lose larger numbers than expected, or the edges of your line disconnect from the main force. There are a number of reasons for this. Maybe your battle plans, while well researched and considered, have come up against an enemy that is using strategies that you did not expect. Maybe the enemy numbers were larger than you anticipated. Maybe the line you drew into battle was too long, preventing the quick passing of information. It does not matter why. The army is losing ground.

When this takes place, the call is made to fall back. Falling back means that the army moves further away from the enemy and comes closer together. Maybe the place you fall back to is more defensible; maybe it gives your troops a break. Either way, the army you are charged with can consolidate, re-organise, and get ready to launch another attack upon the enemy.

Teaching needs a fall-back position. The lesson you planned has not worked. You did not anticipate the work, the level of the students' understanding, the behaviours in the room, the external factors outside the classroom that have made their way into the learning environment, or your own limits of energy or information. This is when self-reflection plays an enormous part in your role as a teacher. You need to fall back.

To fall back means to stop, regroup, and identify what is working and what is not. If you continue to attempt to gain educational ground and do not realise the obstacles in the way, then you can be assured that the intention of the lesson will be lost.

Fall back. What is the problem?

- What are you seeing now that you did not see when the lesson was planned?
- What do you see now that you did not when the lesson began?
- What do you not see?

The teacher who wants to be a difference will not fall back but will struggle until the end of the lesson. Then they will say the students don't want to learn and improve. Wrong.

The teacher who wants to be a learner will stop and fall back. They have made a mistake in their planning. They need to regroup, reset, and restart with the newly discovered information.

To fall back is not to quit or give up. It is certainly not a reason to blame yourself or others. To fall back is to be strategic and alert, to respond and relearn. Don't be afraid to fall back. Immediately after the lesson, share your learning with your team. You falling back can teach your peers. But only if they are learners too.

Take your time, recharge, and come back stronger.

Consider a Truce

"In a position of this sort,
even though the enemy should offer us an attractive bait,
it will be advisable not to stir forth, but rather to retreat,
thus enticing the enemy in his turn;
then, when part of his army has come out,
we may deliver our attack with advantage."
—Sun Tzu

The two forces are battling each other, but the longer the battle goes on, the more both realise they are not gaining ground. Instead, they are gaining casualties. At some stage during the battle, either through necessity or through sheer exhaustion, a truce is called between the two warring parties. Both sides retreat, and it is time to count the bodies and bury the dead. This is the time that they regroup and reconsider strategy.

Teachers can experience the same elements with lack of progress, not moving forward or even going backward. The lesson has gotten away from them, the behaviours are escalating, the reactions are becoming personal, the voices are rising higher, and the prospect of poor permanent choices being made by both parties is becoming prevalent. Teachers need to call a truce at this moment.

A teacher who wants to make a difference will battle it out until they win. They will stand their ground and pulverise all opposition and dissent, but in the same way, they also destroy learning and relationships. They are there to make a difference, in spite of the casualties.

A teacher who wants to learn recognises that things are getting out of hand. They need to call a truce. Someone is going to say something that may cause more harm than is needed.

Teach the word "truce" to your class. Explain what it means and when it is used. Maybe create a class version of the word. Maybe create a class safe word. This indicates to everyone that things have gone out of hand. Everyone needs to put down their weapons and step back.

The teacher who wants to learn should consider a truce in the class. A time out. A break or a breather. Say the reason why. The class is upset, the lesson is not working, and the environment has changed. Just as in the fall-back position, the teacher can use the truce to start asking themselves questions.

- Why did the environment suddenly become heated?
- Why did the lesson get so far off track?
- Who is to blame for the distraction?
- Is it me?

The enemy may see the call of truce as a sign that they are winning and will continue to push the advantage. They now try to be the difference; it is the enemy standing their ground. You must expect that, so try not to engage in the conversation. The call of truce was made. Your hands are up, and you are not engaging. The next step could be to take the students out of the classroom. This will break the tension, the environment, and the routine. Not all students are willing to engage and may find the truce satisfying and relieving, as it removes the sudden emotion from the room. Moving the class will ensure that the one who wants attention will find their supposed allies moving away, and they will have lost their position of difference and power.

The class returns, and the lesson begins. This time, the teacher who has learned will make strategic changes and decisions in approaching the lesson. Maybe they forget the lesson entirely; they can work on it at home. Maybe they need to structure the choice of words, phrases, examples, or students differently. Maybe they need to change the subject, the resources, or the focus.

Remember, a truce is not you winning or losing. It is regrouping. You win when you and the students learn. But if you continue without calling a truce, you will eventually lose.

To have a comeback, you have to have a setback.

Consider the Power of Surrender

(Recommended Reading: ***Quit*** by Annie Duke)

"I like the scientific spirit—
the holding off, the being sure but not too sure,
the willingness to surrender ideas when the evidence is against them:
this is ultimately fine—it always keeps the way beyond open—
always gives life, thought, affection, the whole man,
a chance to try over again after a mistake—
after a wrong guess."
—Walt Whitman

The enemy is surrounding you, and the bullets are flying. You are taking cover under a swarm of bullets, bombs, and other projectiles. The students are laughing at you, challenging you, disrespecting you. They are encroaching on your position, both physically and as the now so-called teacher of the classroom. You step out to gain control, only to be overcome by another barrage of insults, comments, and threats to your intelligence, leadership, and educational capability.

You feel the temperature in you rising as your frustration grows. This may come in the form of anger or tears. Either way, a response is coming. A Hail Mary nuclear-type response. A response that will lay waste to all of the environment. You grasp at the last chance to gain some self-respect, to prove your point, to show these bastards not to mess with you. You don't care about collateral damage; you don't care about reputations. It is payback time, and it is coming laced with malice and vengeance.

STOP. Surrender. You lost.

This is the time to leave the lesson or even the room. What you may gain in a screaming, threatening response will, ten minutes later, leave you with an embarrassed feeling of regret. Not only that, but you will be dealing with the aftermath of this with students, parents, and the administration for days to come. Your career could be damaged, and your reputation certainly will be. You are also demonstrating to the students that they have power over you. They will not relinquish that ... ever!

Teachers will understand, and parents may understand, but no one is going to stand by you if you cause damage to the students. The physical threat you create in the classroom demonstrates a power imbalance. The world will expect you to be professional, and that is why you must, in this instance, surrender. While you may be dismayed, disoriented, disappointed, disgusted, and depressed, do not show that to the students.

Remember that students surrender all the time. You, as the teacher, think you have won and that it is over, but it is just the beginning. The students will find a way to recover and respond. Maybe they have learned their lesson and are ready to move on, but some of them will not. Surrender gives your enemy time to recover and rethink, not repent.

Use the same principle. You have lost the fight, the lesson, the class. You have misjudged the room, the lesson, the environment, and the day. So recover and rethink. The teacher who learns also considers. Was it the lesson, or a student? What was the determining factor in the surrender? What were the conditions that created such a response? Was it a joking or sarcastic comment that created such a response? Was it allowing too much leeway with a particular group or person? Was the student's anger hiding a negative self-image or an inability to understand the concept? Did it connect to an external, unrelated experience?

Surrender. Your ego is damaged but not permanently. Your anger has not subsided, but you are gaining control of the only person in the room that you can control yourself. It is a harsh lesson to learn, but the key there is "lesson." You must learn from this. Surrendering gives you a breath, a chance to realise that you will have to take some licks. Surrender also allows the enemy to win, but this allows you to sit, watch, and learn.

Protecting yourself sometimes means surrendering. Maybe the teaching profession is no longer for you. That is a harsh lesson to learn, but only through reflection can you make that decision. You will have more days like this. Constant surrendering means that you are not learning, and the students have control of the class.

So be strong, accept your constantly changing position, learn, rethink, regroup, and respond.

"Everything can be taken from a man but one thing:
the last of the human freedoms—
to choose one's attitude in any given set of circumstances,
to choose one's own way."
—Viktor E. Frankl, Man's Search for Meaning

Consider Hostage Negotiation

(Essential PD: ***Never Split the Difference*** by Chris Voss)

"Every negotiation, every conversation,
every moment in life is a series of small conflicts that,
managed well, can rise to creative beauty.
Embrace them."
—Chris Voss

The battle is going on, but hostages have been taken. Important members of your team are imprisoned with the enemy. To succeed, you will need to bring them back. But they will not be released lightly, easily, or without some compensation.

In the school environment, you also have to consider this issue, as the teacher will constantly be dealing with hostage situations. This is where you want or need something: information, learning time, defusing behaviour, or equipment. But this valuable resource is in the hands of someone who is not willing to give it up easily.

The reason hostage negotiators use language before force is that any kind of force creates uncertain outcomes. You are not sure of the temperament of the hostage taker. You do not know the story behind the reason. You do not know how they are going to respond and how many others will be hurt along the way.

Teachers have the same quandary. When dealing with smaller, weaker students, it may be easy to physically gain control of the situation and exert force, but the ramifications of such a decision are fraught with danger. You simply do not know how they will respond, how long they will respond, and what impact that will have upon further negotiations in the future. Students will remember the response and may respond positively next time to avoid the confrontation, or they will come prepared to hold on and inflict further damage. The other problem with the physical approach is that it can get out of control quickly, and the teacher may find themselves in a predicament that has considerable long-term damage to their reputation or career.

So with this in mind, we consider negotiation. Negotiation, as outlined in the book, is a series of simple questions. You need to gain an understanding of what they have, what they are willing to do, and why they have put themselves into this situation.

Questions like ...

1. What is their name?
2. How are they feeling?
3. Where are they going?
4. What do they need?
5. Who do they need to speak to?

The purpose of the questions is to get them to talk so you can identify their emotions and motivations. Discover the outcome they are looking for. You can judge whether this situation is the making of the student or whether external factors caused the reaction. This will guide you to find people who can support the student in making better choices. Sometimes you need to be quiet and patient and allow them time to think and respond. The constant chatter by a teacher can fill the time and space so that the child does not need to answer. Ask, and then wait. Ask again if needed, and then wait. Use your thesaurus knowledge of words to ask the same question differently to see if a different combination of words unpicks the lock of the student's thoughts.

Students will have their own journeys, fears, triumphs, and perspectives that the teacher will have no idea about. The teacher needs to recognise that they do not know the person in front of them, but the focus of the negotiation needs to be on solving this problem. The other problems can be solved once a resolution has been made about the current situation. Do not engage in promises. Do not step too far back into the past or reconsider the future. All negotiations about other events can take place after this moment has ended.

This situation is best if there is one student to deal with. One student can contain enough complexities for a lifetime. If you try to negotiate with more than one, you quadruple the complexities and severely increase the time it takes to resolve.

The situation is best if only one adult is trying to resolve the incident. Too many adults with too many perspectives can confuse the issue and frustrate the student.

Don't be the difference, and come hard and fast to resolve the problem.

Be a learner and come quietly to understand the problem.

"People will take more risks to avoid a loss than to realise a gain. Make sure your counterpart sees that there is something to lose by inaction."
"Negotiation is not an act of battle; it is a process of discovery."
—Chris Voss, Never Split the Difference

Consider the Memorial

"Grief is not a disorder, a disease, or a sign of weakness.
It is an emotional, physical, and spiritual necessity, the price you pay for love.
The only cure for grief is to grieve."
—Earl Grollman

When the battle is over, and years have passed since the victory or defeat, then the time of reflection can begin. Real people lived and died on the ground that is now sacred. The sacrifices made by so many allow others to stand in their place, hopefully in peace. Those who stand remember the sacrifices made for their country, the cause, or their friends. These memories can become physical artefacts like monuments, statues, plaques, or walls. The greater the fight, the greater the recognition. This is why the individual names of soldiers who have perished are remembered on walls and plaques across the world. On special days, we remember and respect them. This is an interesting aspect of human history: we send soldiers to war that we love, and then we remember them when they have fallen for their sacrifice.

The same could happen with teaching. Teachers enter the classroom and sacrifice their time, energy, and effort for a cause. But some do not make it. Some may leave the profession to retire, work in the private sector, or begin a new journey. Then there are those souls who leave dramatically and sadly.

The reasons for those leaving need to be made clear. Just as memorials indicate the name, date, battles, impact, and death of the soldier, they also indicate the sacrifices they have made and the reason they have died.

Should teaching have a memorial as well? Teachers need to be recognised for the sacrifice they have made, for the battles they have fought. They ought to be remembered for their service to learn, teach, educate, and create a better world for students and peers. And those who caused their downfall need to know why the educational servant fell.

A teacher should not be easily replaced. It should be hard, as the effort, commitment, resources, and relationships that the teacher has developed are not found through a tertiary formula; they have been carefully created over time. A teacher who leaves should leave a hole in the system that will take some time to heal. The system should grieve the loss of a quality teacher and consider ways to prevent further losses to the profession. A quality teacher is not easy to replace, and those who leave should be remembered, studied, and mourned. In the same way, a teacher should teach, act, and behave in a way that is worth remembering and mourning. How you are remembered will be an indication of how you taught and lived.

"What is grief if not love persevering?"
—WandaVision

Consider My Battle

(Recommended Reading: ***Quit*** by Annie Duke)

"You've got to pick your battles, Pen,
but then fight to the death for the ones that matter."
—Tiffany Schmidt, Hold Me Like a Breath

Choose my battle.
Life provides me with battles, but I have to choose to engage.
Some battles are easy, and some are hard.
But they will all give a reward or pay a price.
I need to choose my battle.

Are my battles a range of wins over small competition on easy ground?
My confidence grows,
but my ability to overcome extreme challenges does not.
Are my battles big losses over large competition on hard ground?
My confidence is damaged, but my resilience is hopefully growing.

Is the battle I am engaging in going to look different
after 5 minutes, 5 hours, 5 weeks?
Is the battle something that I will care
about 5 minutes, 5 hours, 5 weeks later?
Is the battle going to affect me in 5 minutes, 5 hours, or 5 weeks?
Is this battle worth engaging in?

Will the battle create a victory for me?
Or will the battle be longer and more complex than expected?
Will the battle be an easy win, but create further enemies to engage?
Will the battle be a hard loss,
but create respect for the manner of my engagement?
I need to choose my battle.

Is the battle over dropped litter on the playground worth it?
Is the battle over a comment made by a student worth it?
Is the battle over hairstyle, make-up, shoes, or language worth it?
If the answer is yes, then you have made a decision.

But then, prepare yourself for a battle on unfamiliar ground,
with an enemy you suddenly do not recognise.
Every battle has a reason and an outcome, but in between,
there is effort and time.
The reason is obvious; I want to make a change.
The outcome is obvious; it will prove the way I see things.

But how much time will that take?
Battles are lost not on reason or outcomes but on the unappreciated time it
took to win a war that may not have been worth fighting to begin with.
How much effort will that take?
Battles are lost not because of reason or outcome but because of the
unanticipated effort needed for the perceived victory.
Will the time and effort result in a regression when I walk away?

Choosing a battle means choosing this battle but not that battle.
It means making a conscious decision to choose one thing over another.
Is the battle I choose enabling me to avoid the battle I should choose?
Is the student behaviour battle allowing me
to avoid the poor planning battle?
Is the battle of others' teaching style, allowing me to avoid

my own poor pedagogy?
Is the curriculum battle allowing me to avoid the battle of
changing my thinking?
Does the battle against others allow me to deflect my weaknesses?

Life provides me with battles.
And there are battles worth fighting for in life.
The battles for well-being, teaching, improvement, and education
are important hills.
I need to engage with the impact on my teaching and well-being.

I need to think about time, effort, friends made,
and enemies created on my chosen hill.
Choose the wrong hill at the wrong time, and I will find myself
battling for nothing.
Find the right hill, the right battle, and the right time.
It will improve my relationships, teaching, well-being, and me.

"Choose your battles wisely.
After all, life is not measured by how many times you stood up to fight.
It is not winning battles that makes you happy,
but it is how many times you turned away
and chose to look in a better direction.
Life is too short to spend it on warring.
Fight only the most, most, most important ones.
Let the rest go."
—C. JoyBell C

Reflective Consideration

- The warrior teacher recognises the allies and environment that can impact learning, as well as the pedagogical and relational armoury available to them.
- By recognising the many enemies of learning, the warrior teacher is prepared, strategic, and precise in their teaching.
- In understanding that the elements of chaos and control in the room can create positive learning, the warrior teacher learns about themselves first.
- Falling back, truce, and surrender are strategic decisions the warrior teacher makes to regain control of themselves before regaining the class.
- The warrior teacher uses all these tools to dig further into their wells of being, learning, and influence.

V

The Challenge of Education

"Growth comes at the point of resistance.
We learn by pushing ourselves and finding what really lies at the outer reaches of our abilities."
—Josh Waitzkin, The Art of Learning: An Inner Journey to Optimal Performance

"The illiterate of the 21st century will not be those who cannot read and write,
but those who cannot learn, unlearn, and relearn."
—Alvin Toffler

The Classroom: Ups and Downs

I look at the board and the planning. Then I structure out my day, week, and month.

Teaching is the focus, of course, but I still need to be aware of those little things that would stop learning.

"There is going to be a fire drill today," they say. "It will only take 10 minutes," they say. Yeah, but by the time my class gets back, it will take a lot longer than that. They are all looking forward to the distraction. I have no idea how they know it is coming, but somehow they do. And their restless bodies, as they excitedly prepare themselves for the event to take place, will remove any learning from the room.

We will have swimming lessons this week, so there goes another day. The organisation of getting students changed and ensuring they have their towels and a change of clothes. Lining up and walking to the pool. Then the inevitable smell of chlorine will affect the student who forgot their swim goggles. The same one who forgot those goggles last week. The same one whose swim goggles we found last week in their bag when we returned. If this student had a disability, that would at least explain their absent-mindedness. But no, they just forgot. So instead of spending the hour pretending to watch the students in the pool while the teacher teaches the lesson (I am monitoring!), I am running around the school trying to find the goggles while the student, whose eyes are sore from the water, will not leave the pool but will still swim, then cry that their eyes hurt.

I am sure to hear from a parent that afternoon about not looking after their child.

I consider the mystery of the missing book. The lesson is about to start, the materials are ready, and the time is now. Then comes the question: "I cannot find my book." The student(s) are sitting at their desk with their tray and with their books in front of them, but, like magic, the one book we must use for this lesson is missing. It is not taking the time to go through their tidy tray to find their book, which may have been found with 15 seconds of focused attention, that is annoying. It is the book that, after I spend 30 seconds going through their desk, is still not there. It is only discovered ten minutes (or ten days) later on someone else's desk. Then there is a glow of realisation. Oh, that's right. I sat at your desk that day!

Little speed bumps slow down learning and create small battles that need to be avoided, pushed through, or tackled to create learning in the day: missing books and pencils, unsharpened pencils, the "Can I borrow your sharpener/ruler/scissors?" from students, and pre-licked glue sticks that are now of no use to anyone.

There is a visitor coming to the school this week to do a presentation on something or other. That will take time away from learning during the day. It also means that I will be monitoring the class the whole time to ensure they behave. Boy, I hope the presenter is interesting, or it could be a long 45 minutes.

Graham and Jessica have soccer trials on Thursday, and Alex will have football trials on Friday. So I will need to catch up those students sometime. That said, Alex is typically away on Friday. This may be the first Friday he is not at school but at a school event. The irony!

Next week, I have been asked to attend and support the athletic trials. I like going. It is great to get some time away from the classroom work and watch students perform at a potentially elite level. It is encouraging to be in that environment, watching students perform at something that they have trained for and obviously love. But at the same time, I have a class that will be doing who-knows-what with the teaching plan I established. Mentally, it is good to get away and enjoy one of the benefits of being a teacher. I like participating in these extra-curricular activities, but paradoxically mentally it is also troubling, as I will need to review the lesson again when I return. So I don't know how I am feeling. May as well enjoy the moments that I can get.

The lockdown drill, the untied shoelaces, the "Can I get a drink?", the "Can I go to the toilet?", the "Can I get a tissue?", the "Can I work next door, upstairs, downstairs, outside, with my friends?" from students who are unable to work individually in a quiet room, the "Don't wear a hat in the classroom" to "Please wear your hat outside" conversation that takes place every day, the farting, the burping, the nose picking, and the nose that runs unnoticed by the student but is clearly (and disgustingly) obvious to everyone else in the room. These are the distractors and battles to learning that take place every day. I must embrace these elements and create routines and expectations to limit their impact.

There is enough time in the day and the week to get all the work done. They tell us that all the time, and mathematically, they are correct. But those minutes can be hard to find sometimes. It does not take much for battles against learning to be swiftly erected and established. I must constantly be vigilant to negotiate, manipulate, and restructure my teaching every day.

Consider the Time of My Life

(Recommended Reading: ***The Fourth Pillar*** by Harry Moffitt)

"We endlessly discuss moments, chunks, or times.
We rarely discuss time ...
of how it has impacted us along our journey of life."
—Harry Moffitt, The Fourth Pillar

Every person was born at a particular time. The moment we were born was not in a vacuum. Rather, every single person was thrust into a world that was already moving. Being born is not entering a quiet room but a raging river. Events happen around us that may not directly impact us, but they can be felt in the choices, movements, and decisions that are being made by others. Maybe it was a recession, a war, or COVID-19. Maybe it was a divorce, trauma, or an uplifting time in the family, business, or country. All these moments affect how we see ourselves and the world. They make a difference in who we are and how we think, and we need to recognise that.

We should not justify or accept our response to our time, but instead, we should study and understand how time has affected how we think, behave, and respond. If I were born in a time with no television, how do I teach in a time of streaming services? If I were born in a time with no internet, how do I teach in a time with easy access to everything? If I were born in a time with a fixed landline phone, how do I teach in the time of mobile devices? If I were born into a traditional family with traditional family values, how do

I teach in a time of changing family relationships? If I were born in a time of outside unsupervised play, how do I teach in a world of inside supervised instruction?

As a teacher, I should also understand and appreciate my time and the time that I have spent growing up in the environment that I did. If I start talking about the good old days, I need to identify what was good, which old days I mean, and if those days were good for everyone. Are there elements of my early time that were good for me but not for others, or vice versa? Are the students in front of me reacting to the teaching, or are they representing the time that they were born into, the river that they were thrust into? Are their actions simply a response to staying alive, staying afloat as they are carried along a current that was not of their choosing?

There is very little that is as impactful on the shape of your well of being then the time you were born into. The times, the events, the ripples of life geo-politically, financially, across the world, down the street and inside your house growing up, all played a role in creating the person you are. Don't blame, create beliefs around, minimise, or ignore early years, and the times you had. It is just a step on your journey. Use that time to make this time better. Consider the year you were born, the elements in history that may have affected how you think. What were the family elements that affected how you see the world? When were the students in your class born, and how did that timeframe impact their learning? Then focus on ensuring that the students in your class have the time of their lives.

"We must be students of our journey and of our time."
Harry Moffitt, The Fourth Pillar

Consider Time

(Recommended Reading: ***The Shortness of Life*** by Seneca)

"Let no one rob me of a single day
who is not going to make me an adequate return for my loss."
—Seneca, The Shortness of Life

Time is measured in seconds by engineers.
By most humans, it is measured in pleasure, pain, or boredom.

Throughout history, mankind has focused on things thought to be important. Battles and wars have been fought over the centuries in the pursuit of riches, be it land, gold, people, or ideas. In the beginning, possessing animals and land conferred status and importance. Later, man sought gold and silver. Religion took over as the focal point of humankind, which linked neatly with gold, silver, animals, and land. These days, people seek likes, relationships, and power. Over the centuries, people have waged wars to gain access to things that were important or valuable to create a permanent place of worth in their lives. They were willing to injure or harm anyone who got in their way.

The biggest trick mankind has ever fallen for is focusing on everything else ... except time.

Time is the one constant in life that we never get back. It continues during good times and bad. Through richer and poorer. When we are asleep or awake. The constant ticking of the hand of time never wavers, never hesitates. Yet, we never hear this important sound until our time runs out. Then we say we wish we had more time!

The classroom clock is not only ticking during the day but in the lives of the students themselves. Whether they are on the first day of the first year, or the last day of the final year. The time they have should never be wasted. There is enough time during the day to complete tasks, but we need to have the discipline and focus to use time effectively.

Time comes at a cost. It is always in balance with something. You replace time with driving; you replace time with sleeping. Time can be replaced by playing, eating, or using social media. It can be replaced, but after replacement, it is lost. Never replace it with inadequate things.

Students will always ask for "free time." Time is never free. So-called free time is, therefore, a waste of time. If time is given for playing instead of learning, that time is lost, and you do not have an adequate replacement. Time is replaced by learning, studying, reading, building relationships, thinking creatively, and applying solutions to problems. The teacher who allows "free time" needs to have an excellent reason and outcome for this decision. It comes at the expense of building relationships, opportunities, discussion, learning new tasks, discovering new ways of learning, reading, referring, writing, editing, or even thinking. Teachers need to ensure that every minute of every day is a learning experience.

A sporting team will sometimes slow the clock down when ahead. In basketball and football, there are such concepts as time out. Such is the power of time that coaches and players can use it as a weapon to stop the opposition or plan an attack. Someone can stop the clock in a game, but the clock of life never stops. Other professions consider the use of time to be paramount to success. When the doctor is in the operating room, time is very important, as every minute counts. The paramedic keeps track of medication, the patient, and time. The building is constructed on time with all other parameters. The chef plans the menu correctly to ensure all meals arrive on time.

In education, you don't get time-outs; you don't stop the students or the lessons. You cannot afford to, as you are never ahead. There is so much to learn and appreciate. There is so much to understand and so many perspectives to consider. You are never ahead in learning; you are constantly catching up, reflecting, and reviewing.

As a teacher, do not waste time. Do not waste the students' time, nor spend time on activities that do not create higher learning or provide pathways to positive mental health. Time is the most important step in good mental health and teacher well-being. It is the poor use of time that allows negative minds to wander and doom-scroll. It is the positive mindset that uses as much time as possible in all parts of the day to relax, recover, reconsider, rethink, and regrow. Time is crucial, as it moves along whether we use it wisely or not. So use it wisely. Empower your time management to create that lift. Move from potential to progress.

Because just like in an exam, the call will come to you one day ... time's up!

***"The function of man is to live, not to exist.
I shall not waste my days trying to prolong them.
I shall use my time."
—Jack London***

Consider Timing

(Recommended reading: ***When*** by Daniel Pink)

"We all know that timing is everything.
Trouble is, we don't know much about timing itself."
—Daniel Pink, When

For a single person to attack a problem, whether it be a military position, a mathematical question, or a newspaper article, it does not matter when it happens if one person controls the event. The time is controlled by the individual.

But if two or more people are involved, then timing, as they say, is everything.

The beauty found in sport, music, and engineering is the misunderstood or never-appreciated aspect of timing. Music, full of sound and harmonies, sounds better when it is in time. The football play where multiple players are moving as a team to create a scoring opportunity demonstrates the importance of timing. And timing in any engineering process is demonstrated when the roof arrives after the foundations have been built.

But the timing that we build our life around takes place in the brain. The natural rhythm of your brain seeks to work and learn based on the time of day. The brain demonstrates, over a lifetime, a steady pattern that looks similar to a heartbeat. It is stimulated and becomes focused, and then it drops down to recover. The brain considers timing to be both a natural part of its process and an important part of how it functions.

Are teachers considering the function of the brain when they teach? How is the classroom day structured? Does it relate to the natural rhythm of the day and the brain? Are there times when significant learning is taking place while the brain is struggling to focus, maintain discipline, and learn? Are there times during the day when the brain is ready to learn and activated for improvement, and we are spending the time colouring in?

Read the research on the timing of the brain throughout the day. How can teachers access students' best cognitive time and structure the day not around curriculum expectations but around the child's capacity to learn?

Diet, sleep, exercise, and cognition all play a role in brain function, including when it works best. Teachers need to be brain surgeons. If teachers believe they know more than human cognition and that it must work around their lessons, then it becomes the teacher's beliefs versus scientific, medical, and physiological evidence.

The teacher will lose this battle.

Don't waste time. Use it to create better learning experiences.

"We simply don't take issues of when as seriously as we take questions of what."
—Daniel Pink

Consider Silos

"Brain scientists and education scientists don't get together very often, and we end up living in our own silos."
—John Medina

Frederick Winslow Taylor could be considered the founder of efficiency. Born in 1856 in Pennsylvania, he was educated and took various jobs before he finished a four-year apprenticeship in 1878. He was not an engineer, as he was on track to become a lawyer before changing his course. It was during his time as a machinist that he began to recognise the inefficiencies in the workplace. With the burgeoning Industrial Revolution, there were opportunities, but also wasted time and resources. He set about changing that. With a stopwatch and an eye for detail, he modernized industrial processes to save both time and money. The workers did not like him, as they lost their jobs. But the managers of these industries loved him, as he saved them time and made them money.

It was through this process that he identified that you did not need to know the big picture; you just had to know your picture. This enabled anyone to do that job. The phrase "I don't pay you to think" would have been born from this concept during these times. Taylor did not want you to think about your role; that was his job. The ramifications of his processes are still felt today as we seek to do more with less, as we focus on output more than workers' rights, and as we focus on the power of the process to the detriment of the individual parts.

Frederick Winslow Taylor could be the reason you are alone in a classroom.

Your role in the school is not to focus on the big picture or to deal with everything in the school. Your role is to be part of the conveyor-like machine that churns students through the system. As part of the system, they will go through your room, where you will provide them with the learning that you know about (Year X.) Once they have finished that standard year, they will move to Year Y in a different classroom with a different teacher who specialises in that. Your classroom is a silo that has all the knowledge and equipment that the system thinks you need to work in that role with that age group.

A silo is a structure that houses materials. It is separate from other silos, as they don't want the different materials to mix. The silo is closed off to the world to keep the materials together and not removed unless approved by a higher source. Classrooms are often unfairly considered silos. Because they keep the materials (students) in there. They don't mix the materials (other classes), and they are moved on by a higher authority.

This efficient process in engineering, systems management, and other levels of business has enabled the world to move rapidly. Most of what is in your house is there because of the efficiency that was started by Taylor and endorsed by men and women in higher authority ever since.

What this efficiency does not provide is creative thinking.

Some of the top organisations in ICT, military, and marketing are starting to realise that silo efficiency does not allow for creativity and that people often have something more to offer. This has been radically demonstrated in Google and Pixar, where the person who writes the music spends time with the person who draws the animation, who works with the person who creates the story. The sharing of ideas and social connections creates revolutionary thinking. These offices are creating open floor planning so that people can mix and meet freely. WeWork had that concept in mind when they created their business plan. People mixing and working together create boundless ideas and inspirations for each other. In fact, it is in our nature to socialise and share, and yet, the classroom has become the antithesis of these ideals. The siloes are ironically lacking in its efficiency for learning.

Look at the classroom or silo you are working in. It has four walls and a ceiling. There are windows, but they may be covered to prevent you from looking outside. The door is closed to keep anyone from coming in. You are prevented, through space and time, from meeting with your peers.

Don't let the classroom limit your creativity. Try to think, literally, out of the box. And don't let the silo mentality limit your willingness to see how the whole school operates and what you may offer to others.

"With silo mentality, organisations lose their collaborative advantage, as they are being over-managed and under-led."
—Peter Zhu

Consider Silos for Hiding

(Recommended Reading: ***Turn The Ship Around*** by L. David Marquet)

"Peer teaching is one of the most effective ways I have found to ensure student engagement and retention of knowledge."
—Cheryl Mizerny

Silos also play another role in the lives of teachers. It enables them to hide.

Some teachers embrace the idea of the silo and just want to be left alone to teach. Beware of teachers who do this. Teaching is a social process, and it needs the diversity of others to produce learning. Teachers who go to their room and close the door are demonstrating that only they can produce learning. They are saying we have no faith in our colleagues or in the institution of teaching. So if they are closing the door to voices on the outside, they may well be closing the door to student voices on the inside as well.

Peer teachers will introduce you to a raft of expectations, challenges, and behaviours. There will be times you need to moderate with others, share resources, compare experiences, and bring your ideas to the table. There will be times you need to consult, sulk, or bounce with joy. Peers who are part of your team will support you.

If you have a silo mentality, you are not allowing others to learn from you or yourself to learn from others. At the end of the day, the students must hope you have the answers. If not, they will educationally suffer from the teacher's lack of social contact.

Silos are great places to hide work that is not marked, feedback that hasn't been given to students, behaviour plans that are vindictive in style, and assessment that is summative and closed. Think about why a teacher wants to stay in the silo and the impact on students.

A silo is not a well of being. while a well goes deeper searching for sustenance, a silo stands alone and in defiance of everything around them. They are isolated and shut off, where a well is deep and can be shaped.

Avoid silo thinking.

"Those who take orders usually run at half speed,
under-utilizing their imagination and initiative."
—L. David Marquet

"People who are treated as followers
have the expectations of followers and act like followers.
As followers, they have limited decision-making authority
and little incentive to give the utmost of their
intellect, energy, and passion."
— L. David Marquet

Consider Acting

"Why, except as a means of livelihood, a man should desire to act on the stage when he has the whole world to act in, is not clear to me."
—George Bernard Shaw

The professional actor enters the stage. Their personal emotions, troubles, joys, feelings, or pain are removed from them. They are there to play a role. They are to be happy, sad, joyful, or mournful. They are the hero or the villain. They are the damsel in distress or the happy-go-lucky sidekick. They are whoever they need to be while they are on the stage. When the play is over and the show is done, then the actor becomes themselves again. Their life continues ... until the next show.

As with the professional actor, the same is true of the professional teacher. I am there not only to be a teacher but to play the role of teacher. I show the appropriate emotions toward the child who is troubled or excited. Often, I am involved with the child, and my emotions match theirs, so no acting is needed.

But there are days when life finds a way to lift me up or bring me down. It is those times that acting is needed. A student brings me a joyful experience while I am in a mood; I need to act my way through this scene for their benefit. A student brings me sad news on a day when everything is great; I act appropriately for their well-being.

Sometimes, it is easy to match the scene; other times, it is difficult. Remember, it is not about me; it is about my role in their life. Students are not there to lift me up. I am a professional.

I can act my way into a positive relationship with students. But I can also act up and ruin everything.

"A teacher must be an actor, an artist,
passionately in love with his work."
—Anton Chekhov

Consider the Importance of Feedback

(Recommended Reading: ***The Art of the Good Life*** by Rolf Dobelli)

"There's a common belief that creativity flourishes
when criticism is withheld,
but this turns out to be false.
The assumption was that criticism would discourage
people from trying wild ideas,
yet original breakthroughs came after more criticism, not less ...
In high-stakes creative settings,
debate and criticism improved the quality of ideas too."
—Adam Grant

Life is about listening and responding to feedback. We eat, drink, sleep, run, sit, and walk in response to the feedback that the world is providing us. To not acknowledge feedback is to live carelessly and foolishly, and we will put ourselves and others at risk if we ignore the traffic lights on the road, the flashing indicator that the petrol is low, the look of fear or disgust from the person we are talking to, or a dry mouth and throat. Feedback is everywhere in the world, and so it is an important factor in teaching, both for students and teachers.

Feedback is about providing and receiving honest guidance about what you have seen, read, or heard. It provides the student and you with information about their or your performance and how to improve it. Feedback, when presented, shows the direction, changes, additions, and subtractions that can make the student's Maths or writing better.

But feedback also informs the student that their work is not good; it is not perfect, and this can be hard to hear or read. There is a recognition from the student that all their hard work has been for nothing (in their world), and the student can take things personally. Students can feel hurt or upset that their efforts are being dismissed.

But feedback is the most powerful tool they can access. Students should be encouraged to recognise the impact it has on all areas of life. In fact, it is crucial to the success or failure of many industries and businesses. It is the role of teachers to demonstrate that feelings and opinions mean nothing in the world of facts and feedback.

Take the instance of flying a plane as a way of understanding the power of feedback that students can embrace.

"Thousands of times a second the autopilot recalculates the gap between where the plane is and where it should be and issues corrective instructions ... Our lives are exposed to constant turbulence, and we spend too much of our time battling crosswinds and unforeseen caprices of the weather. Yet we still behave like naïve fair-weather pilots; we overestimate the role of the set up, and systematically underestimate the role of the correction."

—Rolf Dobelli, Art of the Good Life

When a plane is flying, the pilot must consider many elements of physics and science to ensure it stays aloft and moves toward the correct destination. When the pilot selects autopilot, the plane continues travelling in the same direction. The idea that simply pointing the plane in the right direction will ensure it reaches its destination is futile to pilots.

As teachers, we do the same thing. We have a goal or direction that we wish for the class to go. We create lesson plans that link beautifully with the assessment, and then we teach and assume that all the students are heading in the same direction. We need to calculate the behaviour of the wind that is knocking us off course. The turbulence of holidays, fire drills, lockdown drills or sports days. The crosswinds of personal battles students are facing either in their family (parents' separation), with their animals (dog died) or with their friends (the changing nature of friendship with children). But more importantly, teachers must take the gravity of the lesson into account. Otherwise, all learning will halt, as students just will not grasp it. We need to lift our teaching and learning to ensure that students move forward.

Feedback is more important than anything we do, yet it is the one thing that is least considered as the day is busy. Teachers are sometimes trying to keep the plane in the air, but are not focused on whether it is going in the right direction. For the plane to remain in the air and go in the right direction, considerable teamwork and feedback will create forward movement. Focused attention and feedback from pilots, flight crew, air traffic controllers on the ground, and computerised navigation systems work together to enable planes to arrive at their destination on time. Yet, teachers take on all the responsibilities without sharing the role, meeting with peers, and getting performance feedback from peers or students.

Feedback exposes teachers to various factors affecting improvement in the classroom, of both their own, and their students. Opening teachers to feedback can actually mean more work, but that is the job. Teachers need to understand that the role of feedback is as important and professional as the pilot. While we would be unhappy if the pilot arrived at the wrong airport, so students should express their disappointment that their marks are not what they need to be.

Teachers then may be reluctant to provide feedback for fear of hurting students' feelings. The thinking behind any kind of feedback is that it is hurtful and that students may stop trying. But for feedback to be effective, there does have to be a consideration of the relationship. The relationship for effective feedback can either be one of complete trust that has been built up over time, or it can be someone completely new and removed from any relationship. Teachers who sit in the middle and try to have an educational relationship but have not put the time in, or they're inconsistent in their relationships and comments, can set students back when trying to assist in their improvement.

But students need to be challenged, and feedback can provide opportunities for learning and development. Students will be able to identify ways to improve and things to remove from their work. This needs to be provided by teachers.

"In other areas, unfortunately, we're even less willing to correct ourselves. Our school system is largely geared towards the set up...Yet the connection between degrees and workplace success is growing ever more tenuous, while the ability to self-correct is growing ever more important – even though it's hardly taught at school."

-Rolf Dobelli

Consider feedback like a car. The car has an accelerator and a brake. Both need to be used for the car to reach its destination safely. The car with the brake on will go nowhere. The car with the accelerator down will go forward, increasing speed until it comes to a significant and dangerous stop.

A car that is being used safely and effectively needs to incorporate both the brake and accelerator. The accelerator is used to move the car forward. Once it is going at a safe speed it can be monitored. When a decision needs to be made, and feedback from the environment is asking a question, then it is the brake that slows our progress to enable us to turn in the correct direction. Then the accelerator is applied to continue moving forward.

Feedback has the same process. The lesson or lessons are going well, then something comes up – a question, a comment, a behaviour, an indication that learning has not taken place. The teacher then applies the brake to the lesson. This enables the classroom to slow down and the teacher to decide what to do next. Once the decision has been made the teacher can then continue, while possibly differentiating for those who need it. The lesson keeps moving forward.

Too much brake and the lesson stops, the students get bored, and learning becomes difficult. Too much accelerator, and the teaching (not so much learning) takes place with no recognition of the changing state of the room.

A teacher who wants to make a difference will be all accelerator and go, go, go until things get out of control, and then the brake is applied to learning, to relationships and possibly to teaching.

A teacher who wants to be a learner will be constantly applying feedback and receiving feedback from fellow teachers and students. They will constantly monitor their behaviour, their pedagogy, their teaching, their relationships and their assessment to ensure that learning overcomes any turbulence.

Feedback for well-being

Many organisations are actively seeking feedback from their consumers. There is barely a shop, purchase, phone, movie, or even visit to the public bathroom that does not request feedback regarding the product or the service. This feedback is then used to upgrade or update the product or service. In fact, this information must be important as it is the only way, apart from purchase or use, for the organisation to understand what the consumers want or are thinking.

I should recognise that I am the product, I am the service, and I am the consumer. Feedback is incredibly important to me as it relates to my well-being. And for me to be able to improve, I need to consider:

- What feedback am I actively listening to?
- What feedback am I hearing but not consciously registering that could affect me?
- Am I accepting the feedback that I hear, and should I be?
- Does the feedback enable me to update or upgrade my potential?
- Will that feedback, that I choose to listen to, affect my well-being, performance, ability and capacity to improve?

Feedback has to be taken under the considerations of the state of mind and thinking when it is received. Whereas the plane and the car have multiple channels for providing and disseminating information, the brain only has one – the mind. The mind has a filter that allows information that is relevant to the user to be absorbed and applied. It is also very good at removing or ignoring information that it either does not believe is important, or does not fit the beliefs or expectations of the user.

This filtering process is an incredibly powerful tool that the brain often utilises to protect itself from harm, change or uncomfortable conversations. Feedback can be both incredibly powerful or incredibly destructive, depending on the filtering system that the brain decides to implement when feedback is provided. If it agrees with the perception of the speaker then it is good. If it doesn't, then it is ignored, or worse, it triggers a program of negative behaviour towards the producer of the feedback. I need to ask, "is what I am hearing challenging my well-being, or is it agreeing with my preconceived idea of who I am?"

- Is it better to believe in who I am, or is it better to gain the perspective of others, even if it is challenging?
- Feedback for me is the same for students. Is the feedback inviting me to consider applying the accelerator as things are going well, or brake if things are not?
- Am I using the accelerator and ignoring the signs that I should be braking?

- Am I braking and ignoring the signs to move forward?

It is important to recognise that my brain will not give me an accurate reading of the feedback coming in. But opening myself to more feedback, taking the time to consider the feedback being received, and then reflecting on why the feedback is creating an emotional response can be the first step towards a positive well-being and mental image.

Just like in the plane metaphor, the feedback provided for mental health can enable me to soar, glide, accept the turbulence, and fight against the gravity pushing me down. And when the feedback is telling me my life is out of my control, I can learn to control my descent until I can feel grounded. Being grounded enables me to be safe, to embrace positive feedback about myself and my abilities. It allows me to recover, refresh and fly once again.

"The key to learning is feedback.
It is impossible to learning anything without it."
Steven Levitt

Consider Education

"This is the difference between 'education' and 'training'.
Medical school is education. First Aid is training.
Education requires fundamental understanding, which can be used to grasp and respond to nearly infinite variety of threats;
Training involves singular actions, which are useful only against anticipated challenges. Education is resilient, training is robust."
-General Stanley McChrystal

A football player knows how to tackle and how to pass. An accountant can recognise finances as well as profit and loss. A soldier knows how to fire a weapon and then get ready to fire again. A lawyer understands the law and rules. All of these professions have not only been trained, but they recognise how and when to apply it. They will encounter many challenges and problems, and those that are suitable and profitable responses they will create answers. That is education.

A football player who has been trained to tackle a tackling pad will be uneducated when they come upon a person who is moving at speed and on different angles. The soldier who is trained will be able to shoot and hit targets, but will be uneducated when the targets are real people who are shooting back. Training is important, but education allows for the training to be used correctly at the right time.

Teachers are often told that they are trained. They have spent time learning about teaching, behaviour and classrooms. But are they educated when they come across a classroom of students? What is education?

Teachers need to realise that education is more than standing in front of students and providing them with knowledge. This is a limited view of education, and it is similar to a soldier shooting at targets or a football player tackling pads. Education is not this. It needs to be viewed in the same way as a football player on the field or a soldier in battle. The teacher needs to be prepared and have a range of skills necessary to create learning for others.

What makes sporting encounters so exciting is the range of skills that the players on both teams have and how they use them. The timing of decisions and the precision of their movements, both in defence and attack, is what makes the game exciting. It is also very clear when tactics, skills or experience are lacking, and the team or player fails. It is how they respond to that failure that engages the audience. Maybe they solve it during the game, maybe they need to work on it for next week, but the problem is there to be solved, and those that do succeed.

Teachers need to enter the room with the same level of professionalism and skill. As they encounter the class they will come across challenges. Their skill, tactics and experience will be exposed, but they will be able to overcome them...if they are educated.

If they are trained then they will recognise the school, the students, the classroom, the books and the pens.

If they are educated they will recognise the behaviour, the opportunities, the learning, the pedagogy and the curriculum.

- A teacher who wants to make a difference is trained.
- A teacher who wants to be a learner is educated.

The tackle pads and the targets allow the footballer and soldier to train for the real event. What does the teacher do to train for the real class? This is where we switch the view from the physical to the intellectual.

The doctor, lawyer and accountant also have similar professions, and they are similarly trained, but they bring their education to life through the act of studying. These professions focus on improving their cognitive capabilities first. They study and learn the intricacies of new ideas and apply these ideas into their own knowledge, and then begin to understand how they can integrate these into their practice.

The teacher has to think like these professions. I need to discipline my mind to different pedagogies, different behaviour strategies. I need to read and learn the perspective of poverty, immigration, mental health, and disabilities. I need to learn about systems management and systems engineering. I need to learn about neuroscience, behavioural economics, and understand how information is stored in the brain. I need to explore the possibilities and limitations that range from chalk and talk to interactive iPads. I train in these areas so that when I enter the classroom, I am educated. I can apply the learning to improve students, only because I have improved myself. I can become excited about students' learning, only because I am excited to learn new things.

Education doesn't stop when I leave school, and it doesn't stop when school finishes. Teachers who become successful continue to educate themselves.

We don't want trained teachers in schools.

We want educators.

Consider Magic

"The world is full of magic things,
patiently waiting for our senses to grow sharper."
W.B. Yeats

Magic plays a significant role in schools for students and for teachers. It is how success is measured and how people are judged. It can take many forms in a classroom. Someone may be considered talented, smart, creative, or gifted. Teachers may consider their peers relational or pedagogy experts. Students may consider other students "amazing" or "the best." These are all considered different forms of magic, and teachers and students use them to judge and measure undefinable qualities that someone has. Others believe they have some hold, some power they use to create the success they have. If "magic" is used to describe someone, this allows everyone else who does not have it to happily limit themselves, their efforts, and their creativity. They conveniently believe it is just given to some and not others.....That is a myth.

Magic is not a creative force. It is not even real. Magicians use science, sleight of hand, or misdirection to create the illusion of belief that looks real to those who do not subscribe to its ideals. But magicians, like all those who are successful, work hard at their craft.

Teachers need to destroy the idea of magic as a form of understanding and replace it with new thinking and realisations about how things are formed.

The Maths challenge, science problem, or creative sentence that changes lives is not a magic solution. It embraces science and an analytical way of learning. Then anyone can access it. Teachers need to destroy the myth of talent, magic, and natural ability and create ideas around science, fact, and effort as they relate to learning. Students who embrace what they don't know and willingly destroy their familiar but incorrect thinking go on a journey of growth. They will thank the teachers who also used alive and relevant pedagogy and effective teaching strategies.

Your well of being also needs to remove magic as a cause of who you are. Your awkwardness or brilliance isn't due to some magical thinking or belief around talent or luck. Who you are wasn't built up around magic. It was dug deep from your experiences and decisions. Good or bad decisions, at the right or wrong time, may seem amazing or damaging, but magic was not a part of that process. Your brilliance and awkwardness are not magical, which means they can be changed, leveraged, and improved. By understanding and digging deeper into your well of being, you will find that who you are isn't magical, the structures supporting you are not being held by fairies, and there is no troll stopping you from moving further. The gold in your life is not being hoarded by a dragon, and dwarfs are not going to dig the mines for you. You will need to create your own four-leaf clover, develop your own magic seed that will grow, slay your own giants of resistance that you magically created, create your own yellow brick road, and find real people who will go on the journey with you.

Don't allow magic to determine the lives of the students in the class, or the teacher in the room.

"My professional life has been a constant record of disillusion,
and many things that seem magical to most men
are the everyday commonplaces of my business."
—Harry Houdini

Consider My Impact

(Recommended Reading: ***The Fifth Discipline*** by Peter M. Senge)

***"We are like actors who forget that they are playing a role.
We become trapped in the theatre of our thoughts.
This is when thought starts to become incoherent.
Reality may change, but the theatre continues.
We operate in the theatre, defining problems, taking actions, solving problems,
losing touch with the larger reality from which the theatre was generated."
—Peter M. Senge***

A soldier enters the field of battle, but they are one of many. Their lives are destroyed, they are maimed, or they survive, and yet the war rages on. Eventually, there is a winner. But it is the king, country, or organisation. The soldier is not individually celebrated or remembered. If they are lucky, they are welcomed back to their families. If not, they lie in one of many unmarked graves on the ground that became a tourist destination. The seriousness of battle is lost; the reason for fighting is forgotten. The warring parties come together against a new common enemy, and the soldiers keep marching to war. The individual soldier plays their role, but the larger reality is lost.

The teacher can experience the same emotions. They are in the classroom at school, providing a quality education. The classroom is their world, stage, or battlefield. They teach, learn, and encourage. But the teacher can lack the greater reality. They are not there to create successful students; they are there to create successful citizens, humans, and contributors to society. Teachers often get sidetracked by their own importance or professional standards of excellence and forget the future tradespeople, apprentices, graduates, entrepreneurs, and factory workers in the room. Teachers look at failure in the classroom as failure in life. Students at school receive encouragement, grades, second attempts, and air-conditioned rooms. That is as far from real life as possible.

The world the students will work in can be vastly different. Allow students the chance to learn and grow, but do not take yourself too seriously. We are actors on a stage, but we do not realise it has limits in length and depth. The students are transitioning to a new stage with no limits, and they will internally create the only depth they will have. We expect students to play the role of students in the classroom, but we forget that we are playing the minor role of teachers in the mini-series misadventure of their lives.

We surround the students with props we have used before without realising they will need to create their own. Worst of all, we think there is a script they need to follow. There is no script. Your interactions with them have no bearing on the real world. Their interactions with you can make you feel like a great or poor teacher, but you will never really know. The script has plots, stories, complications, resolutions, and consequences. The classroom is a theatre where they will explore ideas and thinking in isolation and with a safety net, preparing for the day they emerge into the spotlight with no script, plot, props, or character except for the part they have practised.

The teacher who wants to be a difference will take their role and impact seriously. They will expect the student to take their role in the classroom just as seriously. They will look at marks and reports,as judgements of the student's ability to succeed and their capability.

The teacher who wants to learn will realise that they are one teacher among many. They will learn from a student as much as the student will learn from them. They will endeavour to make sure that the learning in the classroom can be applied in the real world, as that is what learning is for.

"Acting is not an important job in the scheme of things. Plumbing is."
—Spencer Tracy

Consider Safety

((Recommended Reading: ***The Coddling of the American Mind***
by Greg Lukianoff and Jonathan Haidt)

"You don't need to know anything.
Everything you need to know you'll figure out when you need to know it.
Even if you miscalculate and make a wrong decision, you needed to know that.
I always say that pain is knowledge rushing in to fill a gap.
When you stab your toe on the foot of the bed, that was a gap in knowledge.
The pain is a lot of information really quick."
-Jerry Seinfeld

- It is safe in the trenches, but that is not where victory is won.
- It is safe in the change rooms, but change happens on the field.
- It is safe in the harbor, but that is not what boats were made for.
- It is safe in the staff room, but that is not where the students are.

Safety happens so no one gets hurt, but if no one gets hurt, no one learns.

The question that needs to be considered is:
Does safety produce learning?
Does being safe enable or disable learning for students?

To be safe, you need to remove yourself from danger or have the danger removed from you. But learning is dangerous; it exposes us to new ideas and perspectives. The very act of learning develops neurons. Some are pruned and eliminated, while others are strengthened. That is the nature of the brain. The essence of learning is strengthening and removing. If you treated your brain the way you treat students, you would not want anyone to fail, fall over, or be hurt. Then the child, like the brain, will not develop. As a teacher, you want change, but change is dangerous. Students should be exposed to dangerous ideas and thoughts, as this may lead to learning. Teachers need to be exposed to dangerous students and pedagogy, as that is where professional growth takes place.

"An idea that is not dangerous is not worthy of being called an idea at all."
—Oscar Wilde

Are we creating safe learning, or are we removing learning altogether? When we create safe places, it is the teacher who identifies the danger and removes it. The student walks blissfully through a safe environment, as they cannot recognize the elements that were dangerous to begin with. They continue to walk into hazard-free places.

There is a wealth of opportunities for teaching when we start to look at safety. We can expose students to why, how, when, and where. We can look at the science of danger, the history of danger, the mathematical probability of danger, and the importance of language with regard to danger. The act of accepting danger has numerous benefits.

Students should be taught to be resilient, but how do you teach resilience while removing the danger? It is the most important strategy for students to gain, but it is not taught in a vacuum. Resilience without danger is a theory that hasn't been tested and cannot be proven. When enemies march on the doorstep of the student's confidence, opinion, and well-being, they will need more than a resilience theory or a cute quote to support them.

The student should be armed as much as the teacher arms themselves, but the teacher must provide students with weapons to thwart the attack. A theoretical approach to resilience that has not been tested will place the student in real danger.

- The other side of safety is not danger; it is resilience.
- The other side of safety is not suffering; it is heroic perseverance.
- The other side of safety is not a limitation; it is learning.
- The other side of safety is growing pains; this is also called growth.

***"It is a dangerous business, Frodo, going out your door.
You step onto the road, and if you don't keep your feet,
there's no knowing where you might be swept off to."
—J.R.R. Tolkien***

Consider Domestication

(Recommended Reading: ***Sapiens*** by Yuval Noah Harari and ***Guns, Germs and Steel*** by Jared Diamond)

"Domesticated chickens and cattle may well be an evolutionary success story, but they are also among the most miserable creatures that ever lived."
—Yuval Noah Harari

Throughout history, mankind wandered the wilderness as hunters and gatherers. We were always looking for the next meal and shelter. We responded to changes in climate, or the emptiness in our stomachs. While all of history began here, history changes as we change. The first groups of people who domesticated plants and animals made an enormous difference in the lives of not only the people at the time. That has resonated throughout history.

People who domesticated plants and animals did not have to move. That piece of land provided a wonderful bounty to live off, leading to the creation of the very first wall. That created the first understanding of what is mine and what is yours, as opposed to what is ours. This change of thinking created towns, language, finances, armies, kingdoms, and governments, which led to battles.

People began to specialize. It is very hard to gain new skills when you are a hunter and gatherer constantly seeking your next meal. But with plentiful food and more time, creative thinking began to happen. New ideas were explored, shared, and fought over. The improvement in the history of mankind grew in no small part from the change of hunter/gatherer mentality to the domesticated farmer.

Not all places in the world had access to domesticated animals and food. They are still forced to continue the lifestyle of hunting and gathering food long after other civilisations have developed further.

Schools are no different. Some have domesticated thinking and ideas. Students follow patterns and grow like the fields of domesticated plants in history. The routine of the day is like the routine of domesticated animals, and this predictability allows teachers and students to engage, develop curiosity, and think creatively. This system allows for improvement and high performance.

Other schools still have the hunter-gatherer mentality. They are hunting down students who have misbehaved. They are gathering any teachers they can find to do the job. They are gathering and hoarding resources, as they do not know what the day, week, or next year will be like.

Teachers and students cannot be expected to grow in those environments. It is impossible when the school is hunting for a replacement teacher for the day. It is a challenge to develop when the class must leave the room to avoid an undomesticated soul who is struggling to understand their role to the detriment of all learning. Students in this unpredictable environment will be unable to develop and explore, as they, like plants, need sustenance, roots, time, the sunshine of ideas and feedback, and the nourishment of peer and teacher relationships. A domesticated school creates that environment, while hunter-gatherer ones lurch from crisis to crisis.

"We did not domesticate wheat. It domesticated us."
—Yuval Noah Harari, Sapiens: A Brief History of Humankind

Harari has an interesting view on the domestication argument. He believes that the wheat we discovered that could be used to make bread actually forced us away from our natural habitat. The farms that sprang up forced us to stay, as opposed to travelling, and to have big families as opposed to small ones. This made movement harder and created fixed housing as opposed to living and learning in different locations. It limited our choice of food as opposed to offering the local delicacies of the different environments the hunter-gatherers would find themselves in.

Can the same argument be made about schools? Did we create schools to domesticate children, or did putting children into school and creating fixed, unchanging environments prevent us from exploring? With the continual "improvement of pedagogy and curriculum," have we locked ourselves into routines to our detriment? Did we domesticate ourselves away from our natural hunting and gathering of information, learning, exploration, and curiosity, with environments devoid of delicacies, experiences, and delights?

Schools may be the perfect example of domestication. Like the lines of crops and the processing of food and animals, students move up the year levels. The seasonal approach to growing and learning. The importance of preparing the soil and the mind to allow shoots and ideas to grow. Through this domestication process, great gains and improvements have been created, and the growth of the educational industry continues to thrive. Some students need a domesticated approach to learning and respond positively to its expectations.

But just as there is an animal and plant kingdom, some species refuse to thrive in a domesticated environment. The captive audience grows weaker and disinterested and may even die under strict conditioning when a domesticated lifestyle is thrust upon it. Some species refuse to be controlled and tamed, instead seeking to escape and find one that suits their adventurous and exploratory lifestyle.

Can we train and tame these students? Should we even try to invest time and energy into someone who wishes to have nothing to do with us? Are we starting a battle that we will lose? The truth is that, as evidenced in the wild, plants, animals, and students can thrive and grow in unusual environments. Entrepreneurs and free thinkers are the undomesticated examples of an education system that did not allow them to grow in a carefully controlled environment, so they escaped and made their own way through life.

Can a teacher be a hunter-gatherer, or do they always have to be domesticated so they can continue the domestication process of students? If all teachers are domesticated, are they able to deliver learning and education to the undomesticated? Can an undomesticated person become domesticated in the education system? Does the focus on rules and expectations limit the lifestyle and uniqueness of the individual, who may have had more to offer in an untamed environment?

These are things to consider. Just as battles were fought throughout history regarding prized land and conditions, there is a battle for prized minds and creative thinking. Fertile land and brains are important elements for the future of mankind. Entrepreneurs, the creative, those in service, and leaders are prized in any cultural, geographic, and political system. It should be a battle worth fighting to protect and grow these fertile minds and to ensure they are placed into environments that create opportunities to demonstrate their potential.

- A domesticated mind in an untamed world will fade with fear.
- An undomesticated mind in a tamed world will wither and feel claustrophobic.

You will not know whether you are domesticated or undomesticated until you explore who you are. What scares you, what challenges you and what you are willing to accept? In shaping your well of being, you will learn about yourself. Where do you graze, in what environment do you find enjoyable, challenging and worth your time? What is it that gives you sustenance? What is it that makes you sick? What herd do you travel in? Do you travel with different tribes and present yourself differently with each one? Are you domesticated in the classroom and untamed in other environments? In trying to understand who you are, it will support your teaching, and you will be able to recognise and support students in your class who may be beginning a similar journey. In exploring the domesticated and undomesticated features of you and your students, you may be opening up new environments that could support both lifestyles successfully.

***"All human societies contain inventive people.
It is just that some environments provide more starting materials,
and more favourable conditions for utilizing inventions,
than do other environments."
—Jared Diamond, Guns, Germs and Steel***

Consider Gravity

"Bad things do happen;
how I respond to them defines my character and the quality of my life.
I can choose to sit in perpetual sadness,
immobilized by the gravity of my loss,
or I can choose to rise from the pain and treasure
the most precious gift I have - life itself."
—Walter Anderson

Soldiers are pulled into conflict, countries are pulled into war, advertising pulls people into products, and heartstrings are pulled by the contact of another person. These forces are not elements kept to the planets or the stars. The pull of people, objects, and ideas is all around us. Einstein made a stunning discovery: even light is affected by gravity. He demonstrated that it impacts the direction of objects orbiting in space. Even the direction of light can be influenced. This discovery enabled consideration to be given to the gravitational forces around children.

Children are objects flying through life, and they can be affected by the gravitational pull of parents, peers, and teachers. This is not a new concept, but it is worth considering. How can we determine the gravitational pull, the impact that teachers can have on the direction of students?

We can use a survey where students independently identify the funniest, friendliest, and meanest students in the room. Identify who they can go to for help academically, socially, and physically, and who they would avoid regarding academic, social, and physical issues. Who is popular, and who is not? Who do they spend their weekends with? Which students do they not even know?

This information, when graphed like a web, could identify the gravitational pulls in the class. You could identify who needs to understand a concept so that others can learn, who needs to be isolated to allow others the chance to grow, who has no connections in the classroom, and who needs to be nurtured and supported.

Teachers can also create data about themselves as well.

- What influence am I having on students?
- How do I know?
- Who is influencing me?
- What is the evidence?
- Do I create my own gravitational pull of learning?
- Am I so weak that bodies pass by without even noticing that I am there?
- How can I create my own gravitational awareness?

I can be big and loud, or I can be funny and crazy.
I can be quiet and soft-spoken, or I can be mean and cranky.
I can be a bully who demands respect, or I can respectfully demand ideas.
Am I creating a gravitational pull, or am I pushing people away?

Be aware of how much pull I have on learning and student engagement. Do I need to change to ensure that students come because of the gravitational influence of great learning, not because they have no choice? There is an example of a bowling ball on a trampoline that indicates what is being manipulated. This provides an example of a planetary object in space affecting what is around it. While this manipulation cannot be seen, its impact is considerable.

Manipulation of space is just as invisible in students and teachers, and the impact can be just as dramatic. The gravitational forces in our lives are everywhere, and we often times do not realize the effects that these forces are having on our decision making, thinking, or responding.

The gravitational forces are the reason why the well of being needs to be created. These unseen strings of gravitational impact may be pulling us like a puppet master towards ideas, thinking, and reactions that may not be who we are. It is important to dig down and control the gravity removing me from my creativity, reasoning, or making me respond in ways that even confuse me. Dig deeper, grab my support, and prevent myself from being pulled into some black hole. Ships in space use the gravitational force of the Earth and the Moon to propel themselves further. That is the way to use the gravitational force in my life. I need to actively use it to propel me forward. I can't allow it to pull me away.

Students can be provided with the best education, and yet they can still fall short because of the gravitational pull of parents, peers, and the community.

How can I use gravity to create better learning?

"Gravity wins over all other forces."
—Andrea M Ghez

Consider Contagion

(Recommended Reading: ***The Rules of Contagion*** by Adam Kucharski)

"I can calculate the motion of heavenly bodies,
but not the madness of people."
—Isaac Newton

The Rules of Contagion explores the concept of how things spread. Diseases, ideas, reputations, and information can move across different environments at different speeds. Kucharski wanted to understand the reasons why some concepts move, and some don't. Contagious things can spread easily and quickly. Diseases are the most common and most fearful, as they can spread from person to person. Until identified, there is no way of knowing how, who, when, or where has been impacted. But the idea of something spreading without clear intent creates an interesting context as it relates to education.

Reputations can spread from classes across schools. Ideas can spread from store to store. Rumors can spread from country to country. But can the idea of contagion be applied to education?

The spread of ideas, behavior, or learning—can it move through a classroom or a school? What are the points that keep learning, ideas, and behaviour moving? Why do some fall over while others stay afloat?

- Is the teacher the main super-spreader of ideas? If it is, why are they effective?
- Can you create learning through other contagious points?
- Who is spreading the behaviour?
- Can you identify the source of the infection?
- Scientists talk about ideas that gravitate - What about ideas that travel without the gravitational pull of others?

Word gets out that a fight is taking place in the schoolyard. The spread of the message is so quick that students will quickly rush to that place. The word spreads, and the contagion takes place. It may be quick and not lasting, but it is effective. How do we create the same fast-moving spread of learning and thinking?

Teachers don't need to be doctors who stop the infection; they need to be scientists who learn to create and spread the infection of learning. What do they need to do? Who do they need to say it to? How can they present an idea that is so interesting, challenging, and infectious that learning is the next obvious step for all who encounter it?

How can learning, thinking, and intellectual exploration be spread? Does it need to be spread from one student to another, or does it stay with one student from one subject to another? Does it need to spread through the thought processes of every individual student as they consider the ramifications, the changed perspectives, or the new focus? Can this thinking or idea create a contagion that rampages within the imagination and creativity of the student and exposes them to brighter, bigger worlds?

There are no clear explanations or steps that will enable this, as every school is its own petri dish of culture, environment, behaviours, and learning. What may work in one dish may not work in another. But the challenge is not in identifying how the contagion spreads across the dishes; we are exploring how the contagion spreads in our own environment. The goal is to consider the many aspects of learning, neuroscience, relationships, and even experiences, and not to depreciate the uncontrollable and random elements that can create life, potential, or learning.

Maybe the language around contagion is incorrect. It does not spread; it is actually received.

The ideal environment accepts it. If the environment is not correct, no amount of spreading will allow the infection to take hold. Maybe, as teachers, we need to focus less on the spreading. We need to create more susceptibility to learning infections, allowing ideas and thinking to grow. Creating the right environment for them to be received. Just as it was previously discussed, the mind needs to be fertile to grow ideas. It also needs to be open and inclined to take in contagious ideas and thinking, and help to spread them further.

How do we stop our students from being vaccinated from learning and critical thinking?

Teachers need to consider creating a contagion of unconditional learning.

Teachers need to consider creating the right conditions to allow it to take hold.

Nothing can build or destroy your well of being more than a contagion. The spread of ideas and inspiration, disease and corruption is a part of understanding who you are. The impact that a well-placed sentence in a book, or a damaging non-verbal look, can have on the mental health of a person trying to understand who they are can be impactful. But in digging your well of being, hopefully you will be able to identify why it is that that sentence or that look created the response it did in your brain, your heart, your physical, psychological, or even physiological reaction. But don't focus on how a contagion will affect your well-being. Create a contagion that positively affects others. Use your ideas, inspiration and the words from a book you have read, song you have heard, speech you have listened to, to create a positivity virus for others to benefit from.

"A healthy attitude is contagious.
But don't wait to catch it from others.
Be a carrier."
—Tom Stoppard

Consider My Investments

"The financial stress of today originates in the under-investment of the past."
-Peter M Senge

Countries, kings, and military organisations invest vast amounts of time and money into training their soldiers. That training and investment of time allow soldiers to be successful, and the greater the emphasis on investments can create a double-edged sword. On one side, the soldier is trained and better able to compete. On the other side, the soldier recognises that the organisation has invested time and money in them. They will work harder to create a better solution to benefit the organisation that has invested in them. Sporting, business, and military organisations all focus in the investments of the future. People at the front have been valued, and it is in the best interest of the organisation to ensure that their investment continues to develop and create better outcomes for both the individual and the collective.

As teachers, we are managers of our own investment portfolio. We invest time, energy, and learning into students. Our investments, as all investments do, need time to grow. And investments will grow depending on the interest and attention that the investment receives. The under-investment in your teaching, a lack of feedback, and a deficiency of time given to listening and coaching will create educational stress in the future. Teachers may complain about the lack of investment provided by the previous teacher. They do not realise that next year's teacher may say the same thing about them.

Invest now. Pour your resources and heart into the future. You do not want the student to have limited growth, nor do you want your reputation to not match market value. Be aware that your educational investment today can measurably impact the financial value of that student in the future.

The student's portfolio is in your hands.

- If we get to a stage where we measure the portfolio of teachers based on the market value of their students, how wealthy will we be?
- How much value will we have in a diversified portfolio of the different educational and employment opportunities our investments have created?
- Or will we be in the red with little value?

"You only protect things that are valuable.
If something has no financial value, you don't care."
—The Price of Everything (documentary)

Consider the Rules of the Game

(Recommended Reading: ***The Infinite Game*** by Simon Sinek)

"When you pit a finite player versus a finite player, then the system is stable ...
When you pit an infinite player versus an infinite player
then the system is still stable ...
When you put a finite player versus an infinite player,
it is the finite player that gets caught in a quagmire."
—Simon Sinek, 2015 TED Talk

The soldier steps onto the field of battle, the sportsman or woman onto a similar field. The rules of victory are clear, and the boundaries are set. All the players on the field know, recognise, and follow the rules. Let the battle begin.

Teachers walk into rooms in the same way. They have their rules, expectations, and boundaries, and they know what is expected of themselves and others in the room. They are playing a game that is finite. This concept has been explored by Simon Sinek, and it is a dangerous game, as it is assumed that everyone is playing the same finite one as the teacher. This may not be so.

There is also an infinite game. The purpose of it is to keep the game moving. The players in an infinite game neither win nor lose; they keep winning and losing until they lose the resources, time, or finances to keep the game going. As soon as they drop out of the game, it is over for that person or party. But the game never ends for others.

Teachers can sometimes consider learning in the same finite way. There is a lesson plan and a time limit. The learning must be completed in this lesson, week, term, or semester. But then the learning stops, and the game is over. But is it?

Teachers who consider learning to be a finite experience will not seek to extend the game. They will have fun days, end-of-term rest days, food breaks, game breaks, time-outs, and playtime. They will not consider learning to be ongoing. The game will be over. But is it?

The teacher who considers learning to be an infinite game will want to keep learning going. The lesson, the learning, and the teaching will continue because the game of education never stops. Finished the unit? Great. Now we move on to the next bit of knowledge we missed during the last lessons. We can move on to questions that were raised in lessons that were not answered. The learning is infinite, and the teacher keeps the game going, as they realise that learning does not stop at school or beyond. And the student who embraces the infinite way of learning will ask more interesting questions and create a fascinating future.

Finite and infinite games take place within behaviour as well. The teacher sets out the rules and enforces them, but the student sees an infinite game. The goal is not to follow rules; it is to prevent learning, gain attention, and find ways to entertain themselves and others. It keeps the game going. We set consequences for broken rules, but that was not the point of the game.

Education is not only infinite and finite; it is also about recognising whether you are playing a short game or a long game. A short game is the lesson, day, or session. The long game is the term, the semester, or the year. Mostly, the focus in education is the long game, as you endeavour to get students to learn and improve over the course of the year. But teachers can get caught in the short game. The learning needs to take place in this session, and the lesson stops when the teacher stops talking. Teachers who want to make a difference play a short, finite game. Teachers who are learners play long, infinite games.

What time frame are you using to allow students the opportunity to develop and learn?

Those who are playing the game well will recognise the circumstances that create the best opportunity for educational growth. Those who are playing the short game have a fixed purpose or a small amount of time before they achieve their goal. Those who play the long game recognise that it will take a while to achieve their goal. They may take some strategic losses, and they may need to relinquish something, but it is all part of the plan. That teacher has the time and patience to see the plan through to the end. But both the short or long game will result in responses.

Don't think that the game you are playing stops at the end of the school day, as the life of the child is infinite. They will experience various threads of light and dark, fast and slow, and ups and downs in the 16 hours after the student leaves the school. The types of experiences the child will encounter are incalculable in their infinite journey. Then they return to class again, but are they the same child, or have they moved further on their infinite journey? Are we playing the short finite game when we pick up where we left off, or is there a longer infinite game being played?

What type of game are you playing?

"The best way to drive performance in an organisation is to create an environment in which information can flow freely, mistakes can be highlighted, and help can be offered and received."
—Simon Sinek, The Infinite Game

Consider the Myth of Nightingale

"Stop looking for an epiphany, and start looking for weak points. Stop looking for angels, and start looking for angles."
—Ryan Holiday

An unfortunate byproduct of war is injury. Those who put themselves into the fight could possibly receive wounds and injuries. These could range from scratches and near misses to fatal wounds. They may range from psychological to physical. Yet, they all end up at the same place: the hospital. A hospital in the history of war could be any number of shelters, tents, or rooms used to house the injured when they have fallen. While there, they were subjected to the best treatment, medicine, or care available to them by those who answered the call to care for the sick and injured.

It is in this environment during the Crimean War that Florence Nightingale was introduced to the history of nursing books. Her caring approach, and the way she supported the injured and showed her concern created stories, pictures, poems, and a romanticised version of the female nurse supporting the troops. That is a myth.

Florence Nightingale was a warrior. She battled against the men and the establishment that did not consider the environment suitable for her gender and status. Then she battled for the men who were sent from the battlefield to the hospital. She battled the conditions; she battled for hygiene and also for medication. Florence Nightingale was not a nurse who idly fretted while the injured suffered and died. She did not accept the conditions of the injuries and training, the manner of the practice, the lack of suitable medication, and the war itself. But she could not create change without using her resources, data sets, and experimenting with different practices. When needed, she shamed those above her to change how nursing wartime was done. She produced information, data, and statistics. She created short-term tactics and medium-term strategies to create long-term policies that have influenced to this day.

Her influence affects education. She was a woman, but in that patriarchal society, she was strong-willed. She was a nurse, and she was firm in her belief that changes needed to be made. She was well-educated, and she used her knowledge to create better conditions for others. Teachers should follow the same determination, competence, discipline, and focus on data to improve the conditions of teaching in the classroom and in the school.

A teacher is not someone at the front of the classroom; it is someone who arrives every day with commitment and discipline. A teacher demonstrates courage and competence to continue learning when all is against them. A teacher is a data expert of the students in the class, familiar with the statistics of their students. They present information about their students to their peers and the leadership team. It is important that they back the data up with knowledge and steps on how to improve both the students' learning and pedagogical practices to support their improvement. It is expected that they can make learning happen in the clearest way possible. Teachers should walk into the classroom as Florence Nightingale walked into a wartime hospital. They should look for ways to improve efficiency and make structural changes to the room, to the student, the classroom, and themselves.

The teacher is also disciplined to acknowledge and track their well-being daily. Florence Nightingale saw the injuries and knew there would be more the next day and the day after that. She saw death, pain, and lack of hope, yet she stayed and tried to make it better for her patients. But how did she deal with her own internal thoughts or anxieties when dealing with these tragedies? She hoped that the plans she was fighting for on medicine, hygiene, improved facilities, and structural changes would come true. When she improved things for others, she also improved. When she created efficiency, her role and the role of her team improved. She did not leave her well-being to chance; she planned, strategised, and linked her improvement with the positive changes she made.

Well-being is not about hoping for the best or removing yourself from the environment. Sometimes it is about fighting for the environment you want in the environment you are in. When you fight for change, and you see it taking place, well-being can improve. You fought the fight, and you won.

- Well-being does not change on the couch; it changes in the classroom.
- Well-being does not change on my own; it changes with my team.
- Well-being does not change with tears; it changes when I tear down the obstacles preventing me from being the best teacher, best leader, or best me.

Florence Nightingale created lasting change, not by crying about the conditions but by fighting for change and using allies, resources, and data to improve the conditions of not only the men in her care but for soldiers to this day.

Florence Nightingale was a teacher, a leader, and a fighter.

Who will you inspire?

Reflective considerations

- Never underestimate time and timing in lessons and life; it is the only currency that affects your timeline.
- To move forward in life, you need to consider not only the feedback, but the source of the feedback and how it affects you. Feedback is the next most important currency in life.
- Is making it safe making it irrelevant for learning?
- Gravity keeps things on a path; contagion spreads irrespective of the gravity. How do we pull and also spread learning for students?
- Know the rules of the game that others are playing, as it will affect whether there will even be a result.

VI

The Barriers to Learning

"The most perfect barrier to learning a thing is the belief that it is already known."
—Frank Herbert, Dune

"The greatest obstacle to discovery is not ignorance, it is the illusion of knowledge."
—Daniel J Boorstin

The Classroom: The setback...again

The day is halfway through, but there are some behaviours troubling me. Maybe it is the classroom; maybe it is me. There is a feeling that something is off in the room, and I am not quite connecting. The students don't seem to be doing anything out of the ordinary, but their responses and reactions are not what I need at this moment. There is resistance in the room. There is a lack of motivation. It is hidden, but it is there. The energy of the room is missing, and it is impacting teaching and learning.

Maybe the feeling that seems wrong is me. Am I motivated to teach today? Is the topic one that I am embracing? Am I just following the motions? Is there a barrier preventing me from teaching, preventing the students from learning? I don't think so, as I have planned accordingly, and while the topic is not thrill-your-socks-off interesting, there should be enough interest for the students and myself. No, it is not me or the topic.

And then I think about yesterday. The students had been misbehaving and not focused. It had become frustrating, and the lack of effort or involvement in the lesson had begun to create cheeky comments verging on rudeness and a lack of respect for the room. So I had really cleared my throat with my thoughts about the choices they were making. With my voice raised and my anger present, I had begun to get into a groove and a flow. My language had become more intense and poetic as I created a rhythm of disappointment about the way they had been behaving, about who I thought they were. I finished with a very clear message about my almost dislike for them and who they were becoming.

The support staff in the room later told me that it was good that I said what I did, that the message needed to get through to them. And I felt good and strong after my comments. I had taken charge of the room and made it very clear what I expected. But as the minutes turned into hours, I began to feel disappointed in myself.

What else was I feeling ... shame? I could feel it in the room. I had broken relationships with the students, and I had broken their trust. There was a palpable feeling of emptiness. Whereas before there were comments, smiles, and frustrating moments that we had shared, now there is nothing.

This is something that I will need to identify to move forward for the rest of the day. Maybe there are other things to consider. Is it the temperature in the room? Are there distractions at the homes of students? Is it the time of the year, and I am thinking about report cards, assessment, what class I am in next year, and what classroom I may be working in? But that should not affect the students, and kids are never really interested in report cards until later in the school year...or ever!

But no, the more I think and feel the lack of engagement in the room, the barrier to learning is a barrier that I have created. Learning stopped because of me and my perceived need to express myself. My lack of self-control and discipline created a fence. I will need to work on pulling that down and restarting the class.

Why did I decide to do it? Am I frustrated by my personal life? Has something happened that is creating a gulf between quality teaching and learning? Between the students and me, where I felt it was appropriate to react in such a negative and expressive way?

I looked at the lunch that I am eating by myself at my desk for the third time this week. Why am I not eating with my peers? Am I too busy, or am I not interested in the conversation? Is avoiding my peers creating a barrier to learning? Teaching is a social activity; it should involve a community of peers to reflect and review.

Maybe I need to sit with my peers to gain some perspective, have a laugh, or express how I feel.

It is better to get another opinion. Maybe my peers experience the same thing in their classrooms. It is important to eat my lunch in the staffroom.

I cannot let distractions persistently create barriers to learning.

Consider Resistance

(Recommended Reading: ***The War of Art*** by Steven Pressfield, and ***The Inner Game of Tennis*** by Timothy Galway)

"Our job in this life is not to shape ourselves into some ideal we imagine we ought to be, but to find out who we already are and become it."
— Steven Pressfield

The difference between an amateur and a professional is how they deal with resistance.

In the excellent book *The Inner Game of Tennis* by Timothy Galway, and in Steven Pressfield's notable work *The War of Art*, the idea of ego is explored. It is worth reflecting on the role of the ego in the classroom with the professional teacher.

The ego is who you are. It has been built by your experiences, choices, and natural understanding of your role in the world. The ego is very important, as it sets the boundaries for who you are as a person. It knows you. It understands you. It worships you. But like the gods of old, it also sets you into a concrete shell that it does not want you to leave. The ego knows that you are good at football but not maths. It knows that you excel at reading but not writing. The ego is familiar with your experience with your peers, but also with your lack of social skills with the opposite sex. The ego supports you in knowing who you are, and it is a net you can fall back onto when things get too hard.

If you ever feel that there may be more of you to can offer, more interests, abilities, and skills that you can develop, the ego sends the resistance. That resistance, as wonderfully realised in *The War of Art*, does not want you to leave the shelter, boundaries, or the wall it built around you to protect you from yourself. It does not want you to fail or lose faith in it. It has supported you and cared for you throughout your whole life. The resistance believes it is there to stop you from being hurt. It is not. It stops you from leaving the loving embrace of the ego. Anything you (ego) can do is because the ego allowed you to do it. Your (ego) skill set and determination enable you to complete that task. The resistance is what is stopping you, slowing you down, and preventing you from moving forward.

The self is you without the ego. As is described in *The Inner Game of Tennis*, the body can move and play without the ego. Sometimes that tennis shot, golf shot, speech, throw, or maths solution is so perfect and fluid that it makes you think, "Why cannot I do that all the time?" Your ego will not let you, but your self knows. It has the capacity, skills, and interests to try and experience new things. The self engages in conversations and thinking that can be productive if you can keep the ego away. It wants to learn, develop, make mistakes, and recognise potential. The self is the part of you that can be better and move to greater heights. It is the part of you that tries a new subject with no thoughts about failing or succeeding, but about what can be learned in the situation.

When this happens, the ego sends resistance in to ensure you stay in your lane. Because if the ego is threatened, then who you are may be subject to change. Who you are may be different from who you were. Who you could be may be different from who you are. What you could do is challenged by what you can do now. The resistance goes against you, puts obstacles in your way, and screams at you that you are hopeless, you will fail, you will not be loved, you will be laughed at, and you will lose your friends and family. It will conjure images of imagined problems, regrets, and hazards. It will put you in touch with others who have failed and expose you to what they have lost. The resistance will demand that you obey the ego and stay subject to its limitations. In the movie *Avengers*, Loki expresses the very definition of ego.

"Is not this simpler? Is this not your natural state?
It is the unspoken truth of humanity that you crave subjugation.
The bright lure of freedom diminishes your life's joy in a mad scramble for power. For identity. You were made to be ruled.
In the end, you will always kneel."
—Loki (Tom Hiddleston) in Avengers

Challenge that thought. Challenge that idea. Be bold and brave as a teacher to be your 'self'. Encourage your students to be their 'self'. Don't allow their life choices, experiences, and expectations to be guided by their ego. Don't allow their baggage to bear witness to their potential. Don't allow their limitations to be set by an ego that wishes them to be less than, smaller than, or shallow. Get students to trust in their 'self', to dive into the waters of learning and experience the rush of new ideas and thinking.

Teachers can also be just as susceptible to the ego; in fact, one could say more so. They have years of thinking the way they think, and they believe that it is simply the way they think. Where did that thought come from? Ego. They have acted the way they have because that is all they believe they can do; their ego told them that. They may only be a teacher because that is all they thought they could do. The ego set the terms for their life, and now they live in that path, that lane, directed that way, with the ego setting obstacles to stop them from going down Creative Street and blocking access to Possibility Avenue. It is only through intentionally exposing themselves to new ideas that people begin to challenge their ego and listen to the opportunities that 'self' wants to show them.

Teachers need to be aware of the role the ego has in life, and the life of students. Students will travel down a path based on the ego of the teacher.

"I am no good at teaching Maths."

Now, a whole class of students are not engaged in maths because of the teacher's ego.

"I don't like science."

The teacher's ego is now affecting the next generation of potential scientific thinking in students.

"I cannot teach this child."

So you will not, and the child who will have you for a mere fraction of their life, will still be affected, and their educational trajectory will be forever changed, due to the resistance you believe to be true.

"I cannot teach this year level."

You will not, and you will fail. When you fail, your ego will tell you that you made the right choice when you quit teaching.

Being a professional is hard, and the harder you work, the more resistance you will face. Take care of whose advice you are listening to—and if they have your best interests at heart.

"Pain is a relatively objective, physical phenomenon;
suffering is our psychological resistance to what happens.
Events may create physical pain, but they do not in themselves create suffering.
Resistance creates suffering.
Stress happens when your mind resists what is...
The only problem in your life is your mind's resistance to life as it unfolds."
—Dan Millman

Consider My Motivation for the Battle

"We are not fit to lead an army on the march unless we are familiar with the face of the country—its mountains and forests, its pitfalls and precipices, its marshes and swamps."
—Sun Tzu

Often in the school, as in war, it is not the battle but the environment where the battle is taking place that needs attention. Battles may take place between the teacher and the student without the teacher realising they are fighting on enemy territory. The student will not lose that battle because the teacher has not realised the rules of engagement. The battle is not to convince the teacher; it is to convince peers that the student is capable of going into battle. Even if they lose the battle, they won, as they would have gained the only reward that is important: the appreciation of their peers.

The 1985 movie, *The Breakfast Club,* provides a great example of this. The vice principal seeks to maximise his influence over the students, and he uses fear and language to make his point. He expects the students to be quiet and subservient to him. He does not realise that the students who go to detention are the ones who are least likely to follow the rules. That's how they got there in the first place! This lack of understanding of the environment, allies, and motivation creates the perfect demonstration of how to lose.

The adult lost the battle in every possible way.

- The battle took place on unfamiliar ground. (The library with only students in the room).
- The teacher did not realise he did not have allies. (The students had contempt for the 'bad' student, but more for him.)
- The more he spoke, the more he lost the respect of the student who continued to argue.
- This caused more arguing by the teacher in a desperate battle to retain some sense of dignity. This only allowed the student to gain increasing respect from his peers.
- He could not argue with language and so resorted to threats, a losing strategy.
- He either did not consider the reputation of the student, wanted to score points with the other students, or thought the student was just a troublemaker and believed he was justified in his words and actions. (He wasn't.)

Who won the battle?

The student walked away as the winner. He kissed the girl, made new friends, increased his status, and had a great story to tell.

The vice principal lost (and he knew it....when he cooled down), as he was stuck on the next five weekends doing detentions.

In any battle, be mindful of the environment and aware of the allies and enemies in your midst. Be completely clear about the motivations of the enemy before you begin, and have a clear mindset about what you want to achieve. If any of these conditions are not under your control, you will lose the battle irrespective of the result. Your unclear conditions will force you into a position that you were not expecting, and something you may do or say could result in a greater loss than you had expected.

It is better to withdraw from such a confrontation and bring the enemy (student) into a quiet place where the environment is of your choosing and there are no unexpected allies or enemies to deal with. This position will take away the tools of your enemy, which are peer support and respect, and they will be far easier to deal with and reluctant to engage.

It is always worth considering that a teacher who is a learner will begin the battle by first assessing if the conditions are right. If not, they will walk away, take some arrows in the back, and return to fight when the conditions are better.

"There is no such thing as anyone benefiting from a long war."
—Sun Tzu

Consider Their Motivation for the Battle

"Greatness is not measured by what a man or woman accomplishes, but by the opposition he or she has overcome to reach their goals."
—Dorothy Height

Battles are not always lost through numbers, technology, or knowledge of the environment. Sometimes they are lost because the motivation for the battle is more primal or important to one person than the other. The reason for the battle may be clear to one person, but they may not appreciate the desperation, commitment, and passion of the other. They may know the abilities and limitations they are willing to accept, but they may not know the abilities and limits of the other. And if the other is willing to ignore all limits on the way to winning the battle, the protagonist is in a world of trouble, sometimes of their own making.

The human mind is an area of science with growing knowledge. There is still much to learn and appreciate. It is the human mind that can kill someone in battle, then ensure they are treated respectfully at their burial. It is the human mind that will hurt others, but then protect the family of those whom they have hurt. The human mind will encourage and inspire men to battle to protect their country, but when the war is over, it may then seek to destroy them for the color of their skin, their thoughts, who they love, or who they worship.

Teachers may come across students like this. The student has a motivation for their behaviour that is far removed from the predictions and expectations of the teacher. The limits that the teacher expects to deal with are dwarfed by the increasing desire or attention of the student. Perhaps the student is dedicated to going to university, and nothing will stand in their way. Maybe they are focused on working in an industry and will ensure they are successful. In other cases, they are motivated by apathy. Some just want shiny things (a girl, a boy, a game, an illicit substance, risky behaviour, etc.) as their attention and focus.

A teacher who wants to make a difference may not think about the motivations, hidden thoughts, and clear-eyed passionate focus of students. They may engage recklessly with students to create learning, but may unwittingly create problems for themselves and the future learning potential of the student and the class.

The teacher who is a learner will approach every student respectfully and carefully. They will observe each student to gain fragments of information relating to the student's mindset, abilities, and limits.

Consider the Motivation Behind Behaviour

"I guess it comes down to a simple choice, really;
Get busy living, or get busy dying."
—The Shawshank Redemption

In the movie *The Shawshank Redemption*, the character Andy Dufresne (played by Tim Robbins) is sent to jail on a life sentence for murder. While he is there, he focuses his mind on other things, like creating a chess set and completing the tax returns for all of the guards in jail. One of the tasks he sets himself is building up the jail library. He spends roughly eight years sending two letters a week asking for books and funds from the board. After eight years, he is called to the office, where he is provided with books, records, and a $500 cheque. He is congratulated by the office guard and given one job: remove all the books and records to the library. Such is the trust of the guard that he leaves Andy to do this while he goes to the toilet.

The next part of the story is simple: take the books to the library. But Andy does not.

Let's stop the story here. As a teacher, we work with students, gain their trust, and think we know them and their behaviour. We think we can predict what they will do. But this is a cautionary tale, as we shall soon see.

Andy is totally in awe of the books and records. He takes a minute to process this and begins to flip through the records. He pulls out one that he likes and, with a hint of mischievousness, places the record onto the player. He locks both the door to the toilet and the office and lifts the needle onto the record. All of a sudden, the beautiful sound of *Le Nozze di Figaro* enters the room. The guard in the toilet looks up, surprised at the music. Then, with a devil-may-care approach, Andy turns on the sound system, and the music fills the whole prison. All the inmates stop and listen to the music, the lilting bright sounds directly contrasting with the prison environment. The guards come running while Andy sits in the chair and enjoys the music, blissfully aware of the problems he is creating as he delightfully enjoys the moment.

The warden and other guards arrive at the door and demand that Andy turn off the music. He looks at them, reaches across to the needle, and pauses. Instead, he turns up the volume. The warden looks furious, the door is smashed in, the needle is ripped off the record player, and Andy is taken to solitary.

In this instance, we rejoice with Andy and his bucking of the system. His middle finger to authority. His Frankl-esque desire to change the conditions of his environment and focus on joy and peace. But when something similar happens in schools, we wring our hands and fret about the behaviour, the poor parenting, the need for discipline and consequences. Rarely do we look at it from anyone else's perspective but our own. The reason movies are so powerful is that we can climb the ladder and inhabit the perspective of others. We see their side of the story, something we are less able to do in real life.

The story ends with Andy Dufresne spending two weeks in the hole for playing music through the prison. He surrendered. Or did he?

When he returns, he says it was the easiest thing he did. Why? For many reasons. The first is because he says he had Mozart with him in his head the whole time. The beauty of music is that you can take it with you long after the music has ended. A brief moment of it can completely change your day and your outlook. Andy takes that with him, and again, like Viktor Frankl, they cannot take that away from him, even in solitary confinement. In fact, it may be even easier to enjoy the music there.

The second reason: his return to jail reunites him with his friends. They enjoy the stunt, and he gains more respect for his behavior. They laugh at the audacity of playing music. They chuckle at the scheme of upsetting the guards. They relish it even more as he tells the story again and again. He becomes a hero. That may not have been his intention, but it becomes a side effect that he enjoys. In a jail of slow time, he can live off that story for years. Two weeks in the hole is nothing compared to what he takes with him and what he receives when he returns.

The consequence for the action may be inconsequential compared with the feeling and the respect that other students give a student with his rebelling behavior. The child can take that feeling with them and apply Frankl's idea: others cannot affect or hurt their feelings unless they allow it. In that situation, there is nothing they could take from Andy. He simply looked forward to the day he would return and enjoy his rise in status. A consequence should be logical and delivered unemotionally, but never assume it will make the difference you think it will. It may result in further risk-taking in the future.

***"Hope is a good thing,
maybe even the best of things,
and no good thing ever dies."
—Andy Dufresne***

Consider a "Post-Game" Review

"Some people watch the game but do not see the game."

The players have left the field, the soldiers walk off the battlefield, the comedian walks off stage after completing their set of jokes and commentary. The finite part of the event is over. Is that it? Has it finished? No. The next stage is, if not more important, at least equally important. It is a review of the event.

Millions of dollars and hours of airtime are dedicated to talking heads discussing the events of a sporting contest. Everyone has an opinion about where it was won or lost. Leaders of armies also meet to discuss the assumptions they made and where the battle turned for or against them. The comedian leaves the stage and receives input from fellow comedians about what was funny. Everyone mentioned receives feedback at the time: the football team from the crowd, the soldiers during the task, and the comedian from the laughter (or lack of it) from the audience.

While this feedback is important to demonstrate what worked, it is not always what is needed to improve next time. Yes, it worked, but will it work again in the future? Did events enable it to succeed or fail that were outside your control? Are you even aware that external influences set the stage for your success or failure?

A sporting team may have a week to plan for the next game. The army may have time before the next incursion. The comedian may be performing again the next night. They have time to access the feedback and adjust. Teachers also need feedback and improvement, but the next lesson often takes place in five minutes. Is there time for teachers to access feedback and use it to change their lessons?

Teachers who are learners need to have conversations with someone regarding the effectiveness of lessons. This does not need to be a formal mentoring conversation (although that is not out of the question), but more an opportunity to explain the successes and failures that occurred. In the absence of a peer, the teacher can provide themselves with a moment of self-reflection.

Name five students who learned and benefited from your teaching in that session. Then name a different five students in the next session, and another five in the third. By the end of the day, you should be able to name a number of students and honestly describe the learning that took place.

Post-game questions might include:

- Are you able to comment on every student, or did you fall back on the improvements of only a few?
- Can you demonstrate that they learned, or were they simply listening to you talk?
- What pedagogical approach did you use in the lesson?
- Can you identify it and explain why you used it?
- Is there data demonstrating that the pedagogical style was the correct choice?
- What language features did you use when speaking to students?
- How did you structure your speaking style?
- Did you leave space for thinking by pausing for effect?
- Did you vary the power of your speech to create different effects?
- Did your speaking focus on the question, answer, or problem-solving

strategy?

- Did you focus on humour, behaviour, or interactions with students you prefer?
- Did you notice how your voice may have been upbeat and positive for some students, yet dismissive or bored for others?
- Did you ask questions and allow time for answers?
- Did every student have the chance to answer, speak, or give their opinion?
- Did any students disagree with you?
- Did you encourage contrary answers and give students a chance to explore their thinking?
- Were students given the chance to step through their reasoning even when they were wrong?
- Did the students step through a problem?
- Did you learnt something different about the problem due to their thinking or yours?
- Did you ask students what they learnt in your lesson?
- Did they laugh, remember, need prompting, or demonstrate an application of the learning?

The post-game analysis allows observers to compare their predictions of how the game would unfold with how it actually unfolded. While it can be amusing to hear commentators swallow their pride when their predictions are wrong, emphasize the initial expectation.

In teaching, improvement only takes place if there is healthy discussion among peers—or oneself—about what worked and what did not. The post-game analysis can quickly turn into a pre-game analysis about what the next lesson will look like. Feedback, learning, and honest reflection will enhance the next lesson.

In answering the questions, be a learner to develop your teaching skills. Your well-being should also be analysed after every lesson and at the end of every day.

- How did I feel after the lesson?
- Am I excited about what happened?
- If I am frustrated, is it with my lack of engagement, preparation, or connection?
- Am I ambivalent about the lesson?
- Am I happy it is over?
- Am I sad it is over?
- Did my excitement make me run overtime? If so, was it good for engagement, or was my passion more for my benefit than the students?

These and many more questions can be asked quickly to create an understanding of well-being. If I analyse the small ways I feel after a lesson, I can recognise the direction my well-being is heading. Several small disappointing lessons can lead to disappointing days, and then my well-being begins to dive. But several interesting and positive sessions can lead to optimistic days, and my well-being can thrive. The latter can only happen if I begin to track my well-being and conduct a post-game review of my performance when teaching.

"We don't see things as they are; we see them as we are."
—Anaïs Nin

Consider the Control of the Weak

"Call it overstatement, but I'll say it anyway:
it was easier for Hitler to start World War II
than it was for him to face a blank square of canvas."
—Steven Pressfield

"If someone was more encouraging to Hitler in his art class,
you know, like, 'That sculpting ... it is not bad.'"
—Bill Burr

Weak men start wars and create chaos because they are too weak to accept that they are wrong, that others don't agree with them, or that they lost. They start wars to distract the world from their weaknesses. They attack people when they cannot hold on to the interest of others, explain their own interests, or justify their behaviour.

The quote above about Hitler recognises that he was involved in art and creative activities. Instead of creating havoc across the world that is still felt today, he perhaps could have created an average piece of art and sold it for a modest price to create a hobby for himself. Being creative is a strength; being destructive is weak. It is easier to mock change than deliver ideas. It is easier to knock something down than to build something new. Was he a weak man? We cannot be sure, but we do know that he was nowhere near the ideal version of a man that he promoted.

Men and women who are strong engage in dialogue, have their thoughts challenged, and want to learn. Progress is made by those who develop ideas with others.

Weak men and women who don't want to be exposed to things that may hurt their feelings will isolate themselves and protect their thoughts, feelings, and ideas from others. They will find others who accept their point of view of the world, and if enough people agree, they will form a gang, movement, cult, or political party.

Weak men and women expect others to work for them, believe in them, and worship them. This means that tolerant, caring, and resilient people must bow down to another's idea of themselves and the other's abilities and visions. This allows weak people to succeed without questioning or challenging their vision.

Strong men and women have the strength and character to be quiet while the weak throw a tantrum. But the weak get noticed, and change is applied to keep the weak happy. The war of education is often dictated by the whims of the weak.

The confident, competent, creative, critical thinker in the room is the student with whom the teacher wants to engage. Teachers want to support them on their journey, develop ideas with them, and watch them grow academically and intellectually. Students who are strong enough to engage in conversation and identify their weaknesses. They are encouraged to challenge their thinking and seek alternative views, as this exposes them to things they may not have thought of.

But the classroom also has weak students. These are students who don't respond when told "no." They do not understand that others have feelings, so they will disrupt learning until they get their own way. The whims of the weak often must be supported by the teacher, often to the detriment of the other students in the class. Students who are competent and confident to learn will have to sit by while the attention-seeking student, who does not want to be wrong and does not have self-discipline, dominates the attention of the teacher, the staff, and the school.

The school program changes to adapt to the needs of the weak. The school introduces plans to support the weak. Whole classes of students need to be removed or redirected to support the feelings of the weak.

And once the plans are completed and the programs are in place, the weak find other reasons to seek attention or to respond negatively. And yet, the control of the classroom, and sometimes even the school, can be in their hands.

Weak does not mean disability. But a weak parent of a student with a disability can mean that the school prepares other students to stop learning so that their child can gain the support that the weak parent thinks they need.

Weak does not mean traumatised. But a weak student can use trauma to leverage weakness to create attention, without seeking internal or external support to overcome the challenges. They knowingly create an unpredictable environment where everything is a trigger and an excuse to create chaos.

Weak does not mean intellectually unqualified. But if the student chooses not to engage in learning at their level with an aim of creating prospects for the future, but instead create a narrative of themselves as dumb, they will create problems at school that will dictate how, when, where, or with whom they can learn.

"Kids cannot talk like moral philosophers, but they ... seem to grasp early on that rules that prevent harm are special, important, unalterable and universal

...

Children construct their moral understanding on the bedrock of the absolute moral truth that harm is wrong."

—Jonathan Haidt, The Righteous Mind

If a student creates harm in the classroom and to fellow students or a teacher—and the educational system supports and justifies—the students watching learn an important message: That student is powerful, and adults go out of their way to ensure that their behaviour is accepted. The student returns to the class after the outburst. They receive special attention from extra staff. They can access special areas of the school. They do not have to do all the work that the other students must do.

This behaviour is being watched by other class members, who will recognise that they can also receive special treatment if they behave the same way.

How do we deal with weaknesses?

You cannot make the weak strong, but you can make the strong stronger. Ensure the students recognise that the positive, safe, and character-building decisions that they are making will have further benefits. Outline a future where they will not be in the classroom, but taking their ideas, learning, and experience to greater heights. Encourage them to see a world outside the classroom. While the weak student rolls around on the floor, the strong students are rolling around ideas of who they can be in their heads. Every step that is taken in the classroom has a deliberate focus or purpose for the students. And only the strong, thoughtful, future-driven, goal-setting, creative thinkers can apply.

"The world is controlled by weak men"

—The Handmaid's Tale

Consider the Numbers in the Room

"There is no such thing as work-life balance.
Everything worth fighting for unbalances your life."
—Alain de Botton

The first battle took place between two men. They stood apart from each other and engaged in a battle, no doubt originally of language, before resorting to physical acts of aggression. The bigger and stronger man would have prevailed. The game of warfare began. The next time there was a battle, the man brought a friend. Now the opposition was outnumbered. The next time they also brought a friend, so it was equal. If they lost, they needed to add other elements to the battle. So they developed weapons. The man with the weapon won, so the next time the other man got one. On it went throughout the history of warfare. The number of friends increased to at least match, if not overwhelm, the opposition. The weapons used become more technical and brutal. They caused damage to the greatest number of people.

But when weapons and numbers are similar, strategies and tactics play a role. It is no longer just the strength of numbers but also the strength of mind. They outwit their opponent, using numbers and weapons to win.

The goal is that every time there is a person or a weapon in the field of battle, the opposition must at least match it. They hopefully exceed the capabilities to ensure victory at the end of the day. Teaching developed down a different path.

The first teacher probably taught their own child a skill they had not only learned but practiced and regularly used in their profession. Teaching it became another job for them. Another person saw it and asked if the practitioner could teach their child. That turned into another, then five more, and then ten more. Before long, the master craftsman supported the learning of twenty students. The teacher and student were not matched as in warfare; the teacher became overwhelmed. But that is OK because they were teaching a skill that they themselves knew to students who also saw the value of it.

As this system of learning continued over the years, the students began learning things they did not value and skills they would not use from someone who did not have practical experience.

The one teacher:

- Has a student with a disability who needs to be catered for.
- Has a student who is achieving greatly and needs to be propelled forward.
- Has students whose behaviour causes problems and slows the class down.
- Has to work with parents who become intent on addressing their own needs through their children.
- Has to mark and grade the work according to the changing guidelines of a system.
- Addresses community needs and problems.
- Now teachers swimming.
- Now needs to teach behaviour and manners.
- Needs to be the counsellor, as the parents engaged in aggression towards each other, and the child suffered.
- Has to understand how to work with children with foetal alcohol

syndrome, divorced parents, changing gender roles, or ...

The changes keep coming.

If this teacher were a soldier in battle, as the opposition lined up, the warfare committee would ensure that there was someone or something opposite to deal with the challenge in front of them. But the one teacher is alone to deal with the wide and ever-increasing range of complexities. There is no answer or solution to this predicament while the education system remains the same. Teachers need to be prepared for this blitz of expectations and challenges, opportunities, and difficulties that will come their way.

This is why finding allies and supports that you can access is crucially important. It provides another body, perspective, or set of skills on the battlefield of learning that you can leverage to support all the students in your classroom.

A teacher who wants to make a difference will stand alone, welcome the challenge, and become overwhelmed and flanked by situations not of their making.

A teacher who is a learner will recognise that they need to prioritise, and the first priority will be their sanity and mental health. They will develop strategies that are internal, external, and pedagogical to deal with the issues as they come through the door. The teacher who shapes their well of being will also be identifying their reactions to the numbers in the room. What causes the most concerns and what is it that you are not concerned about? Why do some students create challenges for you, and others create opportunities? While beginning to understand why you are responding the way you do, this allows you to create a framework of who you are.

This is important information as the numbers will continue to grow, but will you?

"Education is the most powerful weapon which you can use to change the world."
—Nelson Mandela

Consider the Anarchist

"Criminals aren't complicated, Alfred. We just need to figure what he's after."
"Maybe it is someone you don't understand ... Because some men aren't looking for anything logical, like money. They cannot be bought, bullied, reasoned, or negotiated with.
Some men just want to watch the world burn.
—The Dark Knight

The quote above is about those who engage in war, not for riches or rewards, or for respect or martyrdom. The quote is about those who engage in war for the sake of it. They enjoy the power they have and just want to see what trouble they can cause for others in their midst. Friend or foe.

The Joker is a scary character in DC Comic's history because he calmly demolishes buildings, people, and lives for his entertainment. There appears to be no logic to it, which makes it decidedly harder to combat. The unpredictable nature of this villain makes it difficult to predict the next move, and it is harder still to understand his motivation. It seems counter to our thinking, as we believe that everything has a reason, purpose, or explanation. The Joker turns everything on its head by enjoying the process and not focusing on the outcome, especially how it could affect him. There is a lack of conscience or remorse about his actions, and he receives a dopamine hit of adrenaline over the misfortune of others.

Unfortunately, schools can sometimes contain such characters whose delight is found in the damage they cause to others or property. They do not do this to gain anything but simply to recognise the disruption they caused, or see how far they can go with their words and actions. They seek out the weak or disabled. They identify the quiet and the shy. They set words amongst the gossipy students and watch the spread of misinformation across the groups and revel in the discomfort, disruption, and disengagement it causes.

A student with no motives, desires, or interests can be difficult to understand, predict, and discipline. It is an odd moment when they admit what they did and yet continue to show no remorse about the game they have played, almost as if getting caught was part of it. They like looking the teacher in the eye and admitting their role. You know, and they know, that when your back is turned, they will engage in the same behaviour again. They know they will be caught, but they are not interested in changing.

You will face this student at some stage of your career. Maybe they will change over time and accept the hurt they caused. Maybe they will accept responsibility in their lives. Maybe they will not. It is not up to you to change them. You demonstrate positive teaching, build relationships, and communicate entire conversations and observations with parents, fellow teachers, counsellors, and administration. You will get frustrated and get angry, and you will feel compelled to demonstrate your anger and rage at the miscreant who appears not to care. But you need to move away because you need to remember that you are not a superhero. You can be upset and feel angry. You are not a mythical figure with complete integrity.

"You have nothing!
Nothing to threaten me with.
Nothing to do with all your strength!"
—The Dark Knight

Consider Black Swans

(Recommended Reading: ***The Black Swan*** and ***Anti-Fragile*** by Nassim Nicholas Taleb)

"Our problem is not just that we do not know the future, we do not know much of the past either."
—Nassim Nicholas Taleb

The battle plans are drawn up. With full knowledge of the strengths and weaknesses of both the army and the enemy, the army is confident about a victory. They have performed this before. They have the data, skills, experience, and confidence to overcome every hurdle and obstacle that will come before them. They are so convinced of victory that there is an arrogance detected in their stride, language, and conviction. They are already planning what they will do with their part of the enemy's loot from the spoils of war.

Then they fail. Because their battle plans are based on previous data and information. They have become susceptible to the Black Swan.

The Black Swan is an important book written by Nassim Nicholas Taleb. The argument he made was that people believed all swans were white, and with that information, decisions were made, expectations were guaranteed, and there was no need for further discussion until explorers came to Australia and found black swans. All arguments became invalid, and all data proved fruitless. Those who made comfortable predictions about swans were left to rue their mistaken beliefs.

The turkey lives a comfortable existence. It is fed every day and has room to move. It is looked after and, based on previous data sets, looks forward to a wonderful life—until the week before Thanksgiving. The turkey learns two things: don't rely on previous data, and don't trust people who keep sharp objects.

Yet, teachers have a foolhardy belief that they can predict the future of children. They do not know what experience, person, event, book, show, death, or birth will set the student onto a whole new adventure. The student's academic data does not predict the future, and unlike the previous chapter, sometimes events take place that are unknown, unforeseen, and unpredictable. It is important to prepare for this. Data is used to demonstrate growth or the lack of it. It is used to understand the past up until the point when it was gathered. It is not used to predict.

You cannot predict a black swan event, and you cannot prepare for one. All you can do is realise that on any given day, with any given student, an event may take place, for better or for worse, that may greatly affect the child, the class, or yourself. Your class yesterday was great, but you find, to your disappointment, that the new day is not as exciting and learner-focused. You question your methods, teaching, or pedagogical approach, but you are looking at past data sets to predict future events in a way that impacts you. The amount of data, experience, and events that have happened since all the students left your classroom yesterday afternoon is unfathomable to collect from a data perspective. By the time you have collated the information, the day will be over, and a new day will dawn.

The unpredictable nature of a black swan event is, well ... unpredictable. Therefore, the role of the teacher is not to try to predict it, but you cannot ignore it. The role of the teacher is to accept and learn from it. Create robustness in your pedagogy, curriculum, and assessment. Don't throw all your relationships onto one person, or else you will be shocked when they turn on you. Maintain your distance and observe. Don't place a single assessment item in front of a student for their semester mark, as you are depending on a positive black swan event to create the best marks in a one-off test. Don't use your best pedagogy moves in the classroom once; try them on different days and with different subjects. When you accept that black swan events are taking place for individual students or whole classes, you set up your systems with in-built robustness and flexibility.

The mindset when encountering a black swan event is that you may well benefit from it, either through relationships, information, or red teaming your thinking. Black swans are everywhere; they actually make life interesting.

I disbelieve in structured learning ...
Provided we have the right type of rigor,
we need randomness, mess, adventures, uncertainty, self-discovery,
near-traumatic episodes, all those things that make life worth living."
—Nicholas Nassim Taleb

Reflective considerations

- The only person stopping your teaching, well-being, and motivation is you. You bring the resistance; you need to bring the tools to knock that wall down.
- Never underestimate the motivation of others; it can build buildings but create tsunamis.
- Your teaching and well-being will improve with an honest conversation about the successes (find them) and the failures (don't ignore them) at the end of the lesson or day.
- The world contains anarchists and weaknesses. It is not the time to fight and become angry; it is the time to become focused and strategic.
- Black swans like to play in classrooms.

VII

What I Can Achieve

"Education is not preparation for life; education is life itself."
—John Dewey

The Classroom: Growing as a teacher

I look out the window and think about the week just gone. I am midway through the term, and the work is piling up, and so are the complications.

But I cannot help feeling that I am making improvements.
Small, yes. Gradually, absolutely.
But improvements.

The incident with Sarah made a positive difference. I was wrong; I said I was sorry to her and the whole class. They knew I had made a mistake, and I owned it. And in doing that, I gained some credibility, some student capital. Not much, but enough to be able to rebuild relationships and assist in learning. Sarah changed as well; she is back to being the bright, happy girl I had seen earlier. She is involved in lessons, offering reasons, questions, and explanations. It was good to have her back, and she brought others with her.

Stella is continuing the looks and the comments, but she is more inclined to listen to others, especially me, when I teach. She also has a voice, and she is a leader, so I am learning to manage her. I give her the chance to lead and speak, but then rein her in to ensure that I maintain control over the class and learning. I think I have seen a few moments when she shows she is thankful for the chance to lead and also thankful for a firm hand to guide her. I could be imagining it, but I want to see what she can become and play a role in developing her leadership. This feels like a success story in the making.

Brian and Emily have leapt forward in leaps and bounds. They are expecting extra work from me every day. They are now beginning to develop their own ideas and explore a myriad of opportunities that lie in the learning they want to pursue that I had not even thought of. They can often be found huddling at their desks, generating conversations around Maths and English problems. Their enthusiasm for the work has created a spell of engagement that is attracting others as well. I try to stay out of their way. I provide feedback, offer suggestions, ask better questions, and encourage them to ask themselves questions that have no reasonable or expected answer. This is my success story. Yet, it is the culture that I have developed that has allowed this learning to occur more than the teaching itself has.

For all the success of Brian, Emily, and Sarah, I still have Rob and Percy. My classroom organisation in using Stacey as a shield lasted about a week. It was not that it was not working. It was. But Stacey was becoming frustrated, as she could read very quickly what her role in the classroom was, and she did not like the idea of being the babysitter. I do not blame her. I moved her to a different part of the classroom. The boys continued to look for each other despite sitting in diagonally opposite parts of the classroom. I provide them with the attention they need, the ignoring that they need, and the constant reminders and follow-through of consequences. They have been like this for a while, so this growth will take a lot longer than the time they spend in my class. I will continue to teach, educate, and listen, but I am aware that their journey and growth will take years to develop, and maturity will play a role. When they mature, however, they will no longer be in my class. So I need to continue to make 0.001% positive changes in their life—encourage their good work, support their ideas, and then do it again.

Erica continues to be an enigma. But she is happy. She seems to like being here, and I have maintained constant communication with the home environment, and they say she likes being in class. That is something. In fact, it is a huge thing. I have noticed that she is watching Brian and Emily working together. I have noticed her glancing in that direction or walking past and looking at their work.

There may be an option here; she may have a lot more to offer, but some past incidents or trauma may be holding her back. She looks to be engaged, but then pulls away immediately afterwards. I will continue to support her, but if she is happy in the classroom, then that is an achievement. Hopefully, by the end of the year, she may offer more. I just have to keep looking for that switch that will turn on the potential that I believe she has.

I am also remembering—counting even—the number of students who are trying, listening, and applying themselves. The number is high. I remind myself not to be distracted by the few who are willing to engage in silly behaviour. I am learning to ignore them and focus on the majority, and they want my positive and educational attention.

This is why I feel like I am achieving. I am on a path, but instead of trying to make the path every day, the steps of the path begin to emerge from the darkness. They do not go far but far enough to know that I am on the right track.

Consider a Typical Day

(Recommended Reading: ***Bird by Bird*** by Anne Lamott)

" ... It is a process. It is a process. It is a process ..."
—Moneyball Movie, Billy Beane (Brad Pitt)

There is a formulaic understanding of teaching:

Pedagogy A + Behaviour B + Teacher + X Factor = Greater or Lesser Learning

But the X factor is identified as the unknown. It has the power to change your class and learning for the better, but it can also disrupt the day. The X factor in the classroom could be anything and anyone. But during a typical day, some X factor element will be embedded somewhere in an unexpected way—to the benefit or chagrin of the teacher.

Some educational books identify that the teacher needs to fill their cup, light the class's spark, and serve as the foundation of some obvious outpouring of some as yet unexplained source of energy or power. But teachers rarely have the time, effort, or energy to light their own spark. It is important to be honest but not cynical. A truthful conversation around the challenges of teaching enables them to enter a classroom prepared.

The dishonest "You can make a difference. You can be anyone you want to be" thought process does more harm than good to teachers. Because while you make a difference to students, students also make a difference to you!

In her classic book *Bird by Bird*, Anne Lamott is authentic with the reader about writing. She explores the elements and steps, and the first step is that it is hard. It sucks, and often you will not feel like doing it. And then when you do, you have nothing to say. Let's be honest about teaching as a profession. It is hard work.

Anne goes on to state that the discomfort, a feeling of inadequacy, and a general lack of direction are the first steps to overcoming the roadblock. Then a light will switch on, and that first sentence becomes a paragraph, which becomes a page, which becomes many pages, and—like a literary waterfall—the words and ideas will fall unhindered onto the page. With joy in your heart and a sense of accomplishment, you will experience a wonderful 24 hours.

Then the next day, you will read your masterpiece, only to find that it was not so much of a literary waterfall but a literary landslide that brought everything down and made a mess at the bottom. There may be some phrases, sentences, and paragraphs worth exploring, but the rest needs to be brushed aside.

That is teaching. Sometimes it works, and sometimes it makes a mess. But sometimes, that one moment stands out amongst all the rest. As Billy Beane said in the movie *Moneyball*, quoted above, *"It's a process. It's a process. It's a process."*

Find out what worked: pedagogically, behaviourally, academically, and even humorously. Maybe it was a glimmer for three minutes, but for that time, whatever you were working on allowed progress to be made.

- Which students worked?
- Who responded to what?

- Was it what you said or did?
- Was it the activity, the lesson, or the classroom interaction?
- When did it happen, and how many responded?

That landslide lesson had something that worked, something that connected with someone. They took something away from it. And if no one took anything away from the lesson, at least you have the comfort of knowing that the one person who did take something from the lesson was yourself.

I can say the same for well-being. I can have good days and bad days. I can think that my good days become bad and my bad days become good. But no day is as good or as bad as you think. It is just a process. Find what works mentally, spiritually, or emotionally, and build on that success, even if it only lasted for 30 seconds. Do not make a typical day good or bad. Make the next one improve on it.

Maybe the lesson and my teaching sucked. Maybe I had a bad well-being day.

I pick myself up, brush off the dirt, shoulder my pedagogical weapon, grab my well-being strategies, and get back out there. The battle for my teaching and the shape of my well-being is far from over.

***"I heard a preacher say recently that hope is a revolutionary patience;
let me add that so is being a writer.
Hope begins in the dark, the stubborn hope that if you just show up
and try to do the right thing, the dawn will come.
You wait and watch and work: you don't give up."
—Anne Lamott, Bird by Bird***

Consider a 1 degree Difference

"And that if you can affect the trajectory of a vector, even a few degrees when they're relatively young, it is a huge sweep as their life unfolds."
—Jim Collins

On the battlefield, the objective is to turn the enemy around, make them go backwards, or bend the line. This same determination is found on the football field: turn them around and make them go back so we can go forward. We push through. This attritional approach to sports is all about the mathematics of angles and forcing something away from the direction it is heading or sending it back the way it came. It is about the mathematical equation of a 180° turn—or at least a 90° turn.

Achieving this involves considerable energy and effort. It is also about trying to make the biggest difference. People want to make a difference within the constraints of the time working against them. In that certain amount of time, they have to change, make a difference, and turn things around. Or, as teachers, we need to make students learn.

This is the focus of the teacher who wants to make a difference. They have this lesson, week, or unit to make a difference. They need to turn the behaviours, marks, and efforts around. They need to do it now. This physical, energy-sapping approach is constrained by time. But when the learning, lesson, and environment change, the students will return to travelling in the same direction as before, and all the energy will have been wasted.

The teacher who is a learner is not constrained by time. They recognise the power of 1°. One degree of change over a year can put the student on a very different path. One degree over 10 years can result in better employment, healthcare, and mental health, and it improves life choices. The 1° improvement feels like something the student has taken part in because they have. That makes them more inclined to see the way forward and stay on that path.

1° improvement takes less effort, but it also takes more time. The teacher recognises that academic and behaviour changes may not show dividends for three to six months or even longer, but it is the right move to make.

How does a 180° turn take place in the classroom? Through fear, effort, the carrot and the stick, and a disciplinary focus.

How does the 1° turn take place in the classroom? Through learning, listening, facilitating, directing, rewarding, and correcting *alongside* the student.

That sounds like teaching.

- Do I think my well-being will be improved by a 180° turn?
- Do I believe that massive changes to my diet, exercise, and relationships will improve my well-being?
- No?

The answer in teaching and well-being is being strategic and tactical, to identify the small weaknesses that can be changed. Make a little difference every day. Life is not a game we can change with a big tackle or hit; it changes when we shift things by 1° tactically, strategically, and relentlessly. I do not want to be a better person in two weeks. I want to be a brand-new person in two years.

"There is nothing noble in being superior to your fellow man; true nobility is being superior to your former self."
—Ernest Hemingway

Consider Being a Coach, Not a Teacher

Coaches talk less and listen more.
Teachers talk more and listen less.
Coaches watch and provide feedback.
Teachers give feedback and let students watch.
Coaches stand beside and see the progress.
Teachers stand in front and force the progress.
Coaches learn from others.
Teachers learn from their experiences.
Coaches stay up to date with information.
Teachers stay up to date with gossip.
Coaches demand perfect execution.
Teachers demand perfect obedience.
Coaches challenge you to be the best version of yourself.
Teachers challenge you to be the best version of themselves.
Coaches get involved in data to create improvement.
Teachers use improvement to create data.
Coaches challenge you to move away.
Teachers can be happy to see you leave.
Coaches celebrate success.
Teachers celebrate holidays.
Be a coach!

Consider the History of Everything

(Recommended Reading: ***The Language Instinct*** by Steven Pinker, ***Guns, Germs and Steel*** by Jared Diamond, and ***Spell It Out*** by David Crystal.)

"History gives answers only to those who know how to ask questions."* —*German-American historian Hajo Holborn (1902–1969)

A teacher steps into a classroom to teach English, Maths, or Science. But how do they know about those subjects? In fact, before we get there, how did they speak a language the students could understand? When they write on the board, how do students understand what they have written? How can they communicate using this common language with the teacher, each other, and the world?

Teachers stand on the shoulders of giants who came before them in creating spoken language and the written word. Where did the ability to use language come from? Before teachers move forward to deliver language in class, a teacher should appreciate the journey of language.

- Why do we say what we do?
- Why were letters and language created this way?
- How long did it take for the sounds we make to turn into forms of communication?
- How long did people speak them before someone wrote them down on

clay tablets?

- How does language look compared to how it sounds?
- Who worked each of these parts out?

You can use *The Language Instinct* by Steven Pinker, *Guns, Germs and Steel* by Jared Diamond, and *Spell it Out by* David Crystal as starting points for answering these questions. They outline the amazing journey language has taken to reach the classroom. The missteps, mistakes, and mispronunciations, as well as the integration of Latin, German, French, and many others into the language we now use and take for granted, have taken language on such an intrepid journey that it has landed in the minds, books, and conversations that take place in the classroom.

"History is a vast early warning system."
—American journalist Norman Cousins (1915–1990)

Do not be in awe of the students and the work they do. Admire and look with amazement at the history and expedition that learning and ideas have been on to be considered information worthy of being taught in classrooms at all. Imagine the audacity of scientists, explorers, mathematicians, poets, and military leaders who stepped forward and fell over with their ideas and inspiration so that others could continue the adventure.

This slow conquest of ideas throughout history has taken many turns and passed through many perspectives. Sometimes it even sat quietly waiting for the right person or technology to find them. The ideas we have were not delivered in textbooks and hand-delivered to classrooms. They were found in the mud and dust of early civilisation by people who looked around and said, "We can do better."

The devastatingly slow and excruciating crawl of learning and ideas should not be glossed over by students, and especially not by teachers. There is a reason that words are spelt the way they are. It should not be joked about as a language that does not make sense. We should study to understand the nuances and flaws that people overcame to create a language that is now mindlessly shunted about from phone to phone.

The history of language should also investigate how other cultures approached language, math, and science, and learn not only that they provide different perspectives, but they have also helped develop and influence the words we use. Different cultures supported and improved the mathematical, scientific, and philosophical ideas that we hold to be true.

"The limits of my language mean the limits of my world."
—Ludwig Wittgenstein

Considering the words or Maths in front of you as just the next lesson to be taught removes the learning and considerable pains that people throughout history went through to provide this information. People have suffered and died to ensure that Math is accurate, that planets are correctly mapped, and that the pursuit of truth has not been stifled by religious or uneducated bias.

To be a teacher is not simply to teach now, but to celebrate the history of learning. Ensure that critical and creative thinking are not suffocated by unengaging lessons, poor pedagogy, or a lack of understanding of the incredible story behind the subjects that are considered worthy of being taught. Learn about the sacrifices that men and women throughout history had to overcome, as well as the ones who could not overcome. Clearly recognise what they did and that what they did is worth learning about.

Education is about teaching history. If it did not happen in the history of civilisations around the world, I would not be teaching it. We cannot move forward as a civilisation until we learn from, expand upon, and correct the ideas and mistakes of the past. It is in my interest to be a history teacher who understands the journey that has taken place. It will only make me a better teacher.

"Perhaps nobody has changed the course of history as much as the historians."
—American journalist Franklin P. Jones (1908–1980)

Consider My Gender

"We are born not knowing who we are. We don't know how to think.
We only know how to feel.
It is through our feelings that how we are raised
creates the trajectory for our future lives."
—Natasha Khazanov

The psychology of males and females is different. This is not a ground-breaking statement. But gender roles and associated psychology must be considered in the classroom from both the teacher and student perspectives. The male tends to be more dominant in a room, and the female tends to be more empathetic. How does this gender role, even if it is not consistent across everyone, play out in the classroom?

The male teacher may move to control the room with a strong personality. The female teacher may control the room with relationships and empathy. Broad generalisations are implied, but the important point is considering how you approach the room. Does gender play a role in your approach without you even thinking about it? How does your presence as a male or female teacher impact learning, relationships, and students?

While the male may be the dominant one, he may also need support. He may need to be cared for and encouraged. Coincidentally, a female, who is often described as more empathetic, may be the strong one who provides the support that the male craves. Broad generalisations exist in that statement, but again, the point lies in recognising that male and female relationships within schools or staffrooms should be observed.

The relationship we have with ourselves and others, as well as the way we view ourselves, forms both an inner and outer perspective. It stems from our earliest experiences as children. The family structure in which you were brought up—or not—plays into it. How were you acknowledged—or not? Were you encouraged—or not? Were you disciplined—or not? All these early experiences and relationships with loved ones can impact the role you believe you must play according to your gender.

As a teacher, it is extremely important to recognise who you are, not who you think you should be. This perception of who you think you should be can horribly expose you in the classroom when you try to manifest a strong male presence or a caring female presence. If that is not you, but it is what you believe your role should be, you may find that you are fighting against the students and also your very nature.

How might a student's beliefs about themselves and their gender influence their conversations, relationships, risk-taking, and learning? How much of their personality is an approved gender role, and how much is a genuine understanding of themselves? At whatever age you are teaching, it should be expected that students are nowhere close to understanding who they are. Yet, by observing them, they may provide hints that you can use to support them moving forward.

They can be encouraged to dominate some things and be humble about the things they are learning. Instead of attaching a gender role to themselves, the teacher who learns allows them to grow and become comfortable expressing themselves in many roles. Research and history have suggested that women are less frequently found in Maths, Science, and Engineering. You have an opportunity to encourage female students to engage passionately in these areas. Why are women generally not found in those roles? Is it due to a lack of opportunities or encouragement?

The same question can be asked of men in professions such as nursing or teaching, which have traditionally had a female bias. Again, it is your role to play a small part in developing empathy, creativity, reason, logic, and personality, so students are encouraged to step into any employment opportunity based not on gender, but on interest and ability.

"Girls can be athletic. Guys can have feelings.
Girls can be smart. Guys can be creative.
And vice versa.
Gender is specific only to your reproductive organs
(and sometimes not even to those),
not your interests, likes, dislikes, goals and ambitions."
—Connor Franta, A Work in Progress

Consider My Position

"There's a difference between the fact that the universe is inherently unfair on a cosmic level, and the fact that life is unfair because people are actively making it so."
—John Scalzi

I am about to play a video game: a world-building, role-playing, multiplayer game. I get to choose a character who steps into that world, does battle, and goes on adventures with others. John Scalzi wrote a blog about this entitled "Straight White Male—The Lowest Difficulty Setting There Is."

In the blog, he explores the idea that the straight white male character is the easiest setting, as he has access to opportunities, weapons, and health that others don't. He can access areas within the game that others cannot. While others around him can work to higher positions within the game from their character points, they don't score points as easily or as often as him.

This excellent blog may help in describing the lives of your students or the teachers in the school. What position are they starting from? What access points, advantages, and supports does the character sitting in the classroom have? Can a straight white male teacher position themselves in a classroom of Indigenous students and understand the different roles in the room? Does the female teacher not understand the confidence of a straight white male student sitting at a desk?

There is every chance that the stories and journeys each member of the class is on link back to histories that cannot be fully understood. The teacher needs to consider their personal position, history, and biases before they enter a classroom. They also need to consider the position of the students in the class.

Some students may have experienced generational trauma, a generational poverty mindset, or generational unemployment. Others may have generational opportunities, generational positive health, well-being, and family support. Teachers who want to make a difference will consider their position both as a person and as an educator as a common denominator. They will engage the students from their own personal position.

The teacher who is a learner will recognise that their position needs to be clear and their students' positions need to be identified before any teaching can begin. Teachers cannot afford to assume that they understand the position of the student, or worse, assume that the student is there to learn. You avoid the minefields in front of you if you consider your position first. Be open to the position of others.

- Teachers who want to make a difference will run carelessly.
- Teachers who want to be learners will tread carefully.

"Well, here's the thing: In The Real World,
you don't unlock any rewards or receive any benefit
for playing on higher difficulty settings.
The game is just harder, and potentially a lot less fun...
Well, here's the other thing about The Real World:
You only get to play it once."
John Scalzi

Consider Practicing

(Recommended Reading: ***Legacy*** by James Kerr)

"The best sports people in the world practice more than they play.
Business people should practice too.
They should go home at night and analyse their day's performance.
They don't, and they need to.
To be good at something takes practice, and lots of it."
—James Kerr, Legacy

Football teams are successful only if they are well-drilled. They understand their purpose, acknowledge the team philosophy, and identify the opposition's weaknesses. They all have a job to do, and they practice performing it every day. In fact, for professional teams, the weekend game, while being the focus, is not the first one they have played. If you watch teams warming up before games, they can be out there running through drills on the field for as long as the game is going to go. They spend all week training in different situations. Players are expected to know how to respond to various formations, positions on the field, and weather conditions. They practice over and over again until everyone is working as a team.

When do teachers practice?

Teachers spend time at universities learning the craft of teaching and understanding the theory of teaching. When they are finished, they go straight to the team (school) and are put in the starting line-up for the first team. They are expected to achieve improvement for all the students. James Kerr's excellent book *Legacy* identifies why the All Blacks are the most successful team in sporting history, how they got there, and what they need to do to stay there. It involves practice.

But teachers practising their craft? What does that look like?

Soccer players and basketball players work on getting their footwork correct. They cannot take the shot until their feet are in the right position. They need to make sure their hips and knees are positioned perfectly when they get the ball, so the shot can be taken more quickly. They cannot lose time getting into position after the ball has been passed.

Teachers can do that. Move around the classroom, and consider your footwork.

- Where should I stand in this part of the room?
- Who can I see easily?
- How should I be facing when I am speaking to this student?
- If I must get low, what position should I be in?
- Who are the students I need to be aware of?
- Which students will be on my blind side?
- When I am writing on the board, who cannot see it?
- Who does not *want* to see it?
- How can I respond to that?

Practice moving around the room, writing on the board, and sitting at your desk. Who can you see from the desk? Who can go missing while you are at your desk? How long does it take to get from the front of the room to the back? What is the best route? What is the common route that is taken that allows those not on the route to have their work unchecked? Time just how long will it take to touch every desk in the room? This becomes part of your personal data set. *I have five minutes before lunch; I can see everyone's work in three minutes if I go now.*

How about moving around the school as a class group? Incidents, accidents, and misconduct often happen during transitions.

- How fast do I walk?
- How fast do the students walk?
- Where should I walk, in front or behind? Where are the children going?
- Do they know where they are going?
- Do they know where they are going, and can they be led without being observed?
- Can I walk behind and watch the progress?

Teachers need to practice the art of moving students. Across the school, across the road, upstairs, and around corners all need different strategies and approaches, and they all depend on the behaviour and aptitude of the students in the class.

Football players know their opponent: where they stand, how they run, what foot they step off, what hand they fend with, their favourite move, and how long it takes them to reach maximum speed.

Teachers can do that. What behaviour do you expect from these students? What will that look and sound like? How will they respond when you respond? What comments create the most or least impact? What is their favourite move? How long does it take for them to reach maximum distraction? What support players are they relying on to pass the 'ball'?

What other ways can teachers practice? The fear is that if teachers don't practice, they don't perform and cannot improve. They simply improve at mediocrity. Some teachers don't teach for 20 years; they teach for one year and then repeat it.

A teacher who wants to make a difference is confident as they walk into the classroom. They believe they have the skills, personality, and charisma to charm any class. And the class is looking forward to the challenge.

A teacher who wants to be a learner practices their speaking style and volume in the classroom. They practice their movements around the room. They identify whether their movement, location, speaking style, and positioning are making an impact on students' learning. And then they work on it. Again and again.

"Team learning, like any discipline, requires practice.
Yet, this is exactly what teams in modern organisations lack.
Imagine trying to build a great theatre ensemble
or a great symphony without rehearsal.
Imagine a championship sports team without practice.
In fact, the process by which sports learn is through continual movement
between practice and performance.
Perform, practice, perform, practice, perform."
—Peter M. Senge

Consider My Question

(Recommended Reading: ***Never Split the Difference*** by Chris Voss)

"Convergent problems have a solution;
the more intelligently you study them, the more answers will converge.
Divergent problems have no "correct" solution.
The more studied they are by people with knowledge and intelligence,
the more they will come up with answers that contradict each other."
—Peter M. Senge

The chess player moves their piece onto the board. The boxer moves carefully and throws a couple of short jabs. The army moves the soldiers into a flanking motion. The artist throws one colour onto the canvas and then another. In none of these situations does this provide the answer to the problem, nor does it even identify one. It asks questions. The chess player wants to see how their opponent will move in response to their move, as does the boxer. The artist is looking at what works and what does not work. All are asking questions and learning, all are asking questions and identifying the response, all are asking questions and identifying weaknesses, and all are asking questions to create a plan that will enable success to follow.

The teacher has at their disposal the most powerful weapon in their arsenal: the well-thought-out question.

There is a lot of focus on "the answers" in education. It is in the answer that results are created. Students can be tracked, schools can be compared, and data trends can be created. But for all this to happen, there needs to be enough right answers for these comparisons to take place. The question should not be what the answer is. The question we should be asking is, "What is the right question?"

Questioning techniques are critical in identifying information. They are an art in themselves. Is the questioner seeking new ideas, or are they seeking to confirm pre-existing information? The art of the question has this focus as the premise of the question. Data collected by agencies often has a specific focus that they are trying to create. They will draft a sequence of questions to generate an answer, which can be used as evidence. This data collection is no different from businesses or schools. Both will identify the data that will present their point of view in a unique and specific light. Teachers are no different in this questioning technique.

The concern with education and those who try to measure success is a desire for the answer. The goal should never be to find the answer. The goal should always be to find the right question. Teachers can become preoccupied with the answer. They want students to find the answer, as the answer creates the score that demonstrates whether what the teacher has been teaching has been learned or applied.

But what if the teacher is too focused on the answer and does not provide enough time, energy, or attention towards allowing students the chance to find the right question?

Once curiosity has been established, questions need to be asked. The teacher will ask many questions a day, but a surprising number of questions are pointless. There is also an increasing number of questions that are asked and then answered by the teacher. When did we become so busy that we couldn't listen to an answer? Is the sound of our own voice so important that we should answer our own questions? There are at least four questions that are often heard in classrooms.

The one that you already know the answer. "What is the answer? That's right, it is 42."

The teacher has asked a question where both the student and the teacher are aware of the answer. What is the point of the question? Is it for education, or is it to make the child feel better?

The one where you hope they lie, " How was your weekend?"

Be careful when you ask that question, as someone may give you an answer, and an honest one at that. You should give yourself at least two minutes to prepare in case the answer is longer than "good."

"What other word am I thinking of that also describes this picture?" (Guess what's in my head.)

Why ask a child a question about what you are thinking? It is not only the most pointless type of question; it is also often heard in classrooms. While the intention is to have children think about other options, you are asking for mind readers rather than original thoughts. If you want to make a difference, you put yourself into the question. (What am *I* thinking?). If you want to be a learner, you ask the student for more ideas. (What are *you* thinking?)

Then ask for more information: "What was the process you used to get that answer?"

This fourth question should be asked. It can take time, and that is precious in a classroom. But interesting questions will lead to more answers, more conversation, and improved learning. It is amazing how many times a teacher will interrupt a student who is providing the right answer just in order to answer it in their own words. I encourage all teachers to listen to how many times they ask students questions in one hour.

Questions should not be asked without respecting the time and effort that an answer may require. Also, it is only with questions that learning can be demonstrated. Great questions lead to great conversations. No discovery in the history of humankind was created without a question first being asked or a problem being identified. Give students the chance to consider great questions, and give them the time to create a response. Provide students with the opportunity to ask equally interesting questions of you and their peers. Learning will deepen and become more effective.

You can also not ask any questions and let students create the question *and* the answer. I once observed a student solving a Maths problem. It was clear that she had made a mistake and was heading towards the wrong answer. I observed but said nothing. When she completed the question and found the answer, she looked at it again and realised her mistake. She went back over her process, altered it, and created the correct answer. The answer she had made originally did not make sense, but she had the knowledge and confidence to question her own work. It was the best teaching I ever did, as I didn't say a word!

"There is a fundamental question of knowledge that goes all the way back to Plato and Socrates,
If you don't know what you are looking for,
how will you know if you found it?"
—Ryan Holiday, Perennial Seller

Consider My Language

(Recommended Reading: ***The 48 Laws of Power*** by Robert Greene)

"Words have that insidious ability to be interpreted according to the other person's mood and insecurities."
—Robert Greene, The Laws of Power

Wars have not always started because of demonstrations of strength or a display of weapons. Overwhelmingly, battles start because of language. One person's ability, or inability, to express themselves can create opportunities for mistakes, misinterpretations, or misdeeds to occur. The power of language is such that language can create the fight, and language can solve the fight. But in the middle, there is conflict.

Teachers need to be aware that language can be used to educate, heal, or hurt. They must also recognise that language has two components: speaking and interpreting. The speaker uses language to present an argument or idea and to communicate. The words spoken can be expressed differently depending on how the speaker is feeling at the time. They may express the words depending on the relationship they have, or don't have, with the listener. The speaker may use words, phrases, slang, or technical terms that they expect will either be understood by the listener, overwhelm the listener, or dismiss the listener. The tone of voice, the volume used, the speed they talk, and the amount of eye contact they provide will determine the message that they are presenting, irrespective of the content of the conversation.

The words spoken then travel to the listener's ear. This is when things become interesting, as what was said may not be what is heard. This is because the information that passes through the listener's ear goes through a filtering process. The listener's ear filters all sounds, voices, and noises that are also entering their ear, and the message then passes through a number of other personal filters. Does the person listening like or respect the person who is speaking? Is the person who is listening physically, mentally, or psychologically prepared to receive the information? A lack of knowledge of the power and value of language often places students and teachers in a precarious situations. We are not naturally equipped to recognise the impact our language has on others.

"Humans are extremely susceptible to the moods, emotions and even the ways of thinking of those with whom they spend their time."
—Greene, The Laws of Power

There are subtle ways in which our moods and ability to work with others are expressed in our language. Teachers work in social environments. They spend time with students and their peers. They have relationships with many people throughout the course of the day. Care must be taken into account when they respond to students and their peers, and they should consider where the language they are expressing is coming from.

Words are expressly used in language to convey meaning: for explanation, conversation, and resolving conflicts. The problem is that what we say is sometimes not what others hear. The brain is an amazing conduit through which words must travel to reach the meaning section. Unfortunately, sometimes the meaning section is nowhere near the rational or logical section. Parents and students (and staff) will only hear what their mood and insecurities allow them to hear. The difference can be amazing. It is like a game of Chinese whispers, except that it takes place from one ear to the other in the same person, and the misunderstanding can be scary. There is considerable neuroscience around this that teachers should read before engaging in any conversation.

Teachers can be taken aback by the reaction of students and parents. Social media has created bubbles of thinking that people enter and never have to challenge. When the teacher suggests a behaviour change or a curriculum expectation, the teacher is on the receiving end of not just the parent but also the group the parent subscribes to, who may believe the same things the parent does. Teachers need to be prepared for the blindside attack that can come at them after words are spoken. But remember, as a professional, we cannot respond. In that space, teachers are afforded the rare chance to see thought patterns, arguments, and conclusive evidence. And not all thoughts have been fully thought through!

Everyone uses language to demonstrate ideas, love, hate, and indifference. Teachers, students, and parents are not alone in succumbing to the power of language and being affected by it. When using language, take into account the room, emotions, and history, and be self-reflective. People will make an argument, especially about children, based on emotion. The teacher is trying to teach, the parent is trying to parent, and the student is trying to (or not to) learn. Arguments are made with good intentions of the speaker. But in that moment of observation and reflection, the parent, student, or teacher will realise that this is an argument they did not think they would lose. They will begin to have different thought processes regarding the positive outcome they had thought they would achieve. So, of course, they get louder.

Language is a teacher's world. This is demonstrated by learning how to use words and apply them with greater precision and impact. Always remember that language starts with the emotional, physical, and psychological position of the speaker—and ends with the emotional, physical, and psychological position of the listener. Educate yourself about language.

"In the end their arguments convince only a few and offend a great deal more.
The reason arguments do not work is that most people
hold their values and ideas without thinking about them.
They really do not want to have to rework their habits of thinking,
and when you challenge them, whether directly through your arguments,
or indirectly through your behaviour, they are hostile."
—Greene, The Laws of Power

Consider Being Unpredictably Predictable

(Recommended Reading: ***The Experience Machine*** by Andy Clark)

"Where homeostasis implies constantly returning to some fixed point. Allostasis highlights the need to alter the fixed points themselves so as to adapt to changing needs and environment."
—Andy Clark

Predictable Routines

Students need routine. They need to know what to expect in every part of the day. They desire that, just like 1 + 1 = 2, what happens on Monday happens every Monday. Students crave that predictability, although some more than others. It is important for learning, behaviour management, and relationships. There is peace for students who know what to expect. A teacher who is unpredictable in their comments, teaching, and daily routines will cause considerable angst and uncertainty.

But sometimes teachers should embrace uncertainty. Contemplate:

- Teaching without talking
- Teaching with no ICT
- Teaching with no desks or even outside the room

Spend a day and consider being unpredictable. This will cause you to consider how important your voice is in the room and how important chairs and desks are to learning. Encourage students to work, think, and act differently. Some may not embrace the change. But some students may become empowered, find their voice, and realise there are new ways of learning.

Unpredictable Routines

Some students love unpredictability. The teacher tells a joke during a spelling test. The desks are changed over the weekend. The lesson on Maths is now an English lesson. Those students will enjoy the unpredictable nature of the teacher.

But sometimes teachers should embrace certainty. Contemplate:

- How the student recognises that the unpredictable lesson enables them to misbehave
- How some students are affected by not knowing what is coming next

Ensure that there is routine in the day, so students are aware of what to expect from the teacher, lesson, and any assessment.

So, what should teachers do?

A teacher who wants to make a difference will embrace predictability, as that works best for them, and they will be unpredictable because they want to be funny and loved.

A teacher who is a learner will embrace predictability, as it supports the learning of students. Being unpredictable improves their practice and allows students to stretch their ideas about learning.

What other ways can I consider a predictable or unpredictable approach to teaching?

"I do not want things I do to be easy and predictable.
I want them to be real."
—Stromae

Consider Non-Linear Thinking

"Linear relationships are truly the exception;
we only focus on them in classrooms and textbooks
because they are easier to understand."
—Nassim Nicholas Taleb

Linear thinking is thinking in lines. Soldiers march to war in lines; trenches are in lines where soldiers lie in wait. History is filled with lines. Planes travel in a straight line to get to the destination. Roads are essentially straight lines that cars travel across. Straight lines indicate the easiest and quickest way to a destination. Schools also base their structure around linear thinking. Year One, Year Two, Year Three ... Learning in schools is linear, and progress is judged along those lines.

But life is not linear. Life is constantly changing.

The history of warfare was two armies in lines against each other, battling it out till the last man standing. Warfare these days looks very different. Soldiers gain whatever advantage they can by using camouflage or setting traps. The soldier who can fight without being seen is the one who wins the battle.

Planes may fly in straight lines, but the constant influence of turbulence, air pressure, wind, rain, and the constant call of gravity means that a plane flying in a straight line will not reach its destination. The pilot needs to make constant checks and adjustments, which means the straight line of the plane must be maintained and tested.

Every industry that focused on linear thinking has been left behind. It is no longer appropriate to think in that way, as it will ensure that your organisation will be caught out and will not be flexible enough to survive the changing landscape.

Except for education. Education maintains the linear model, and students are rated on their progression along the line.

As a teacher, I need to stop thinking linearly. Non-linear thinking allows me to engage in differentiation. It enables me to identify where students are in their thinking and learning. Non-linear thinking means that I go back and reteach what hasn't been learned. I don't move the student forward unless they understand. Non-linear thinking means that I move the student further down the educational highway if they understand. I cannot afford to hold them back in the conveyor belt system of learning if they have the audacity to want to explore further.

The teacher who wants to make a difference will think in a linear fashion. Maybe it is in their teaching; maybe it is in their future aspirations. They are here, and they want to go there by the quickest means necessary.

The teacher who is a learner will think in 360 degrees. They are constantly scanning ahead and behind. They are testing the environment to the left and right, seeing if they can make movements up or down.

***"I was a linear thinker, and according to Zen,
linear thinking is nothing but a delusion,
one of the many that keep us unhappy.
Reality is nonlinear, Zen says. No future, no past. All is now."
—Phil Knight, Shoe Dog***

Consider the Ripple of Learning

"A teacher today creates ripples in time that extend to generations yet unborn. Not just impact in the here and now, but the here and forever."
—Jeff Goldstein

We see life as a journey. Every journey has a beginning, a middle, and an end. The story is in the journey. Live your life as an adventure, and see where the trip will take you.

Or maybe not.

What if life is like ripples? You step into the water of life, and you create concentric circles that undulate in all directions. The circles can be light or heavy, big or small, close together or further apart. You step into the water of life, and your journey goes one way, but the impact you make goes everywhere. That disgraceful, loving, scary, or kind act that you do is noticed immediately in the moment, or maybe it goes unnoticed. Your act of kindness is picked up along the way, or maybe it will be noticed 50 years later when it moves alongside another current of life that recognises what you did. That hateful act that you drop onto someone causes waves that reverberate around others, and you are noticed and scorned, or it passes by people who are not looking, and you seem to avoid any condemnation or consequence.

Maybe the other way happens too. Someone else's act of love or anger sends ripples into your life that make an immediate effect, or they slowly reach you many years later. Maybe they are so late that the person who made the initial effect no longer has the capacity or life force to make ripples of their own, and you are left with the remnants of their act, however loving or hateful it may have been.

Teachers do nothing but create ripples, but do we notice the ones that students make?

Children are also on a journey, and their interactions and choices create swells of opportunity. Do we bounce along the waves of their choices and see how we can use the rhythm to create better learning? Or are we a wall that the movements of learning, choice, creativity, and curiosity come crashing against and go no further? Are we creating waves so large that they swamp and dump all over new learning and stop the momentum of interest and education? Are we running so hard toward our goal that we fail to notice the impact our actions are having? Do we ever stop to wonder why the child can see the lesson we taught from a different perspective and lose the meaning of the lesson? Maybe it is because the child was not watching the lesson; they were observing the currents in the room. If your current of learning goes nowhere, maybe they are looking for a more entertaining or influential one.

Maybe the direction of the current is somewhere the child does not want to go or has no interest in. Maybe they can see something ahead that is more intriguing, interesting, and productive, but there are no currents, so they need to make their own, which transgresses against the pointless patterns of the teacher. Maybe they hold onto that idea, direction, challenge, or adventure and keep the momentum to themselves, but the strength of movement is so great that when they go, they are powered ahead with determination and excitement and, just like a tsunami, nothing can get in their way.

Maybe the child is drowning as the water is too deep, and the only movement they are making is the splashing sound as they struggle to stay afloat. The trauma or life experiences the child has gone through have not only left the child in deep water, but they have no floats, no life preserver. No life. They have nothing to hold onto, so they stay still and float. Maybe they are chastised for not trying, not caring, not having a go. Maybe they are congratulated for not causing a scene and distracting from the lesson. But maybe they are either too tired to make any movement, or they are incapable, or they are trying desperately not to drown.

Maybe you, like the student, should recognise the ripples and learn to ride the waves.

***"I was so focused on creating these moments, these thunderclaps.
These documentaries, campaigns, these splashes.
And I never realised that it was all about the ripples ...
One small thing can make beautiful things happen."
—Chef's Table with Jamie Oliver, Netflix***

Reflective considerations

- Language creates questions.
- Questions create ripples.
- Ripples challenge linear thinking.
- Non-linear thinking develops unpredictable outcomes.
- Unpredictable ripples can make changes in direction.
- Changes in direction can support positioning and gender.
- Student-directed changes in direction are what teaching is about.
- All this can happen during a typical day.

VIII

How Does It End?

“Know your way out before you go in.”
—Andor

The Classroom: The reason I teach

The year has ended. The teaching is over. For now.

- *How have I ended my year?*
- *Am I focusing on the mistakes?*
- *Am I focusing on my successes?*
- *Am I focusing on the students?*

No, I need to focus on the only person in my life whose decisions truly matter to me—myself.

Has the year ended with my learning and improving? What did I do this year that was new and interesting? What pedagogical tool did I use in the classroom that worked or didn't work? How much more knowledge did I gain about the curriculum, the assessment process, and moderation that I can employ next year? How did my well-being finish the year? Am I questioning my teaching and my ability to make a change, or am I more confident now because of my improvement? What mental health and well-being tools did I employ this year? What triggers did I identify, and what did I do to remove them from affecting me again?

What will I not do next year? Life is not about adding tasks and improvements. It is about removing things that don't work. It is about recognising things that hold me back and routines that were not successful or useful, both in teaching and well-being. I cannot take on everything. I need to prune, remove, and destroy elements of my teaching and well-being to allow better things to grow in their place.

What will I do next year? What steps will I need to take over the break to ensure that I am physically, mentally, emotionally, and psychologically ready for another year? What deliberate steps will I take in all these areas to prepare myself for the task at hand?

If I end my teaching year like this, am I setting myself up to lead a better educational experience next time?

As I sit and reflect, Steve walks into the classroom. He has been working along the corridor at the same year level. I see the look on his face and smile. I am about to be hit by a funny story. Sure enough, it flows out of him as only the best comedians can perform. I not only see the humorous side of the story, but I can see the correlations to my classroom, my teaching, and even just myself. That makes the story even funnier.

The laughter brings in James and Rebecca. One has heard the story before, and the other has not, but the laughter is just as bright. Then Rebecca adds to the story with her own experience with the child or the parent. And James recalls an incident from this week that is ridiculous because of the comments made by students. The seriousness of their remarks and feelings makes the whole episode more humorous. It wasn't at the time ... but it is now!

The absurdity, complexity, irrationality, and ridiculous nature of working with students and parents, especially parents, come flooding out in a sea of jokes, stories, laughter, and tears. We can all laugh at the fake outrage, fake hurt feelings, and fake emotional sulking of students after they have left the room, the doors are closed, and the teachers can finally be themselves.

These are the moments that make teaching worthwhile. The tension and stress of the day, the impact of behaviour and learning, the irrationality of students and parents, and the complexities of behaviour and disabilities, all get swept up into a feverish release of jokes and laughter. The teachers and support staff sit together and enjoy each other's company, revelling in the bad news, bad decisions, and poor outcomes that teachers have made, especially when made unintentionally and with an optimistic outlook. It is worth that moment to have the bonding of staff and the team come together. Even if it is a random moment, it is fantastic to know that I have my peers with me, supporting me, laughing with, or at me, and recognising that we each have a role in well-being and education.

I sit back in my chair as more people come into my classroom due to the noise of laughter.

Something is building here. This could take a while.

Today is over. Today was a good day.

I am going to enjoy it.

Consider Death

"One thing is made of another,
and nature allows no new creation,
except at price of death"
—Lucretius

The sad fact is that in every business, relationship, or war, the prospect of death is real. It cannot be overlooked, and it cannot be avoided. Death is often viewed as the end. Death can be found everywhere, but depending on the result or the perspective, it was the way to victory or the cause of defeat. Death causes grief. Grief provides opportunities for others to hold onto something. Death causes change, as change is built on the death of something, so there is the inevitable conflict to avoid death. Change is death. People fear change, as it is the wish to hold onto the comfort of the predictable, the comfortable, the safe, and the reliable. But to grow something, to change something, or renew something means that we have to destroy the old. The death of the familiar produces the creation of the unfamiliar. Is it better? If it is not, it too will die, and something new will take its place.

When one proposes something new, it is not considered a death. But the prospect of a new idea only flourishes if the original idea has become irrelevant, old, or dead. The death of the old idea creates the birth of a new and better idea. Death is the most important part of life. The death of a seed enables a plant to grow. Death enables growth. The birth of cars created the decline of horses as the main means of transport. The birth of the written word created the deterioration of oral forms of communication and storytelling as the primary method.

Death is a crucial part of life. Education cannot be involved in ideas if it also does not embrace the idea of death. Teaching requires understanding this. The old ways of thinking, the belief systems, and the frameworks that students and teachers bring to school will change. They should change, as the death of their mental models will create new ideas and prospects. We are challenging what is comfortable, predictable, and safe. Teachers find themselves under attack from students when they do not want to consider the death of their thinking strategies and understanding. Students will also want to avoid change and growth in favour of familiarity. They don't want to have to consider that all they know is wrong, or old, or incorrect.

Teachers may also avoid death, as their teaching practice with their tried-and-true methods has created comfort and predictability in their routine. The more predictable the routines, the less they have to think, and the easier their job becomes. But the more comfortable they are, the more they can interpret the student's improvement through their own framework, not what supports the student's growth. Teachers need to embrace the death and resurrection of their practice. They need to constantly challenge themselves and review their performance compared to other teachers, schools, ways of working, and educational materials to enable change, growth, and a recognition of their imperfection.

Death removes weakness and strengthens connections; it prunes deficiencies and reinvigorates growth. Teachers need to release teaching practices, pedagogies, and behaviour management. They must take a step back to allow the small things that worked to create bigger changes. Allow student voices to make a bigger impact than your deathly weak voice. Replace that good practice with a better practice. And after you have established that, kill it again and again to remain up to date.

The latest phone, laptop, tablet, or computer game would look vastly different and exceptionally boring if they never changed over the years. But with the increased speed, memory, connectivity, users, apps, and time, these devices have a shelf life of six months before the latest update is made to improve them. Teaching should be the same. Update your teaching and practice, and destroy what you are doing. Allow for improved accessibility for all users in your classroom.

Consider Student Comments

"The lesson was dead."

Is it because of the mental state of their previous thinking strategies, or is the teacher not embracing new pedagogical ideas and instead choosing tired old practices with the belief that new thinking will come from them?

"I'll die during this test."

Students will often use death terminology to express how they are feeling about achievement in environments where their previous thinking strategies will be tested.

"I killed that test."

When a new idea, concept, or strategy is embraced and the student has been successful because of it, they will use death to describe not only how they are feeling but also the state of the old idea.

Death is about looking back. Creation is about looking forward. As teachers, we need to look and teach forward. We must embrace change. Teachers need to consider death as something that has happened and how it may affect growth. But they should not hold onto it, nor should they allow their students to grieve and mourn the old ways of thinking.

Teachers who want to make a difference will not understand the death of poor teaching, as they will think it is where all their good ideas and differences came from.

Teachers who are learners recognise that the time to move forward is now.

Creation happens in the moment, opportunities are there to be grasped, and time should not be wasted trying to fit new knowledge, pedagogy, and thinking into old, dead, small, predictable, and ill-fitting holes.

Teachers need to welcome the death of old thinking, teaching, and strategies as much as they relish the creation and growth in themselves and their students of innovation, curiosity, and change.

"It is not death that one should fear,
but he should fear never beginning to live."
—Marcus Aurelius

Consider the Battle for Peace

"Peace is the only battle worth waging."
-Albert Camus

The final goal of all battles is the same: to have peace and be calm. To live in a world of focused relaxation. This goal is a battle to achieve and a battle to maintain. Peace should be undertaken with the same single-mindedness as war. The focus of peace should be tactically and strategically set to ensure that teachers can achieve it. We will never find a predictable, reactive, or hopeful peace. Soldiers in the midst of war long for one moment of peace. Teachers need to have the same mindset. They need to find peace in the lesson, day, or week. They need to ensure peace is a strong focus not only for themselves but also for their students.

How do you make peace achievable? You need to set those terms. What does peace look like for you in the day? Is it having a quiet coffee or a conversation with a trusted colleague? Is peace a weekend of not working and enjoying life, or is it finding 30 minutes every afternoon for exercise, reflection, meditation, or distraction?

The battle for peace will never be won if those battling do not know what it looks like for them. Students will not give you peace, and neither will lessons, assessments, duties, parents, or the administration. Expecting peace to come from outside of yourself is like someone else eating chocolate and you experiencing the sweet taste in your mouth. It is not going to happen. If you want the chocolatey taste of peace, you will have to make time to consume it yourself.

While it appears oxymoronic to battle for peace, nothing will be handed to you in life unless you take clear steps to seek it out and actively create moments to achieve it. This will take time, and the methods will change over time, but by the time you reach your goal, you will be pleased that you set the high standard for peace in your life.

"You cannot find peace by avoiding life."
—Michael Cunningham

Consider Peace

"We know how to organise warfare,
but do we know how to act when confronted with peace?"
—Jacques-Yves Cousteau

The battle is won or lost. The outcome and results come into focus, and the ripples that have stretched out in all directions become clearer as the fog of war lifts. In that moment of victory or defeat, there is sadness for what was lost. Nothing can remove the damage that was done in small ways across the lives of all combatants. The most important damage will have been to the heart, soul, and imagination of those involved. But you are alive, and you have overcome it. You have been lucky, or you have demonstrated skills that enabled you to survive. Now the time has come to live in peace. It may be the hardest step.

Teachers also have tough days, and they must make decisions that affect lives and families. Maybe the world has thrown events at them that have impacted their lives, families, teaching, or thinking. Either way, the battle is over, and the time for healing begins.

"Under peaceful conditions, the warlike man attacks himself."
—Nietzsche, Beyond Good and Evil

This is when the real battle begins.

When all you know is war, and all you have lived through is fighting, it can be hard to remove yourself from the thinking that enabled you to survive. The teacher arrives at school the next day after a traumatic day in the classroom and immediately goes on the defensive. They wish to arm themselves before the war that exists in their head begins again. The mental state of fight or flight is over, as there is no flight. It is not available because you cannot leave the class. So, you fight, metaphorically, verbally, or intellectually.

Maybe the event that took place yesterday was created by you. Maybe it was caused by a student. It was either expected or unexpected. But what you have experienced is not normal, so you cannot return to the class normally. Your thinking will not allow you. You will be heightened or exhausted, but you will not be at peace.

It is important to recognise that the fight is over. This needs to take place immediately after the event. The teacher needs to find steps to breathe, reflect, mourn, and review ways to improve and find the positive. Peace needs to be found before the teacher re-enters the classroom. The first step is to acknowledge the hurt you feel and the damage that may have rippled out to other students. Do not gloss over it and stand strong after the damage has taken place. This is not helpful. Take the time to mourn the loss of learning, relationships, or a student's innocence in the face of harm, and recognise who that harm is attributed to.

Take the time to remove yourself from the environment. Go home if you can and breathe, meditate, and seek to identify the role of others in the incident. Recognise your role. Recognise the students in the room who were witnesses and had no knowledge or reason to be part of the event. They are the students you will fight for when you return to class. But you cannot fight for them if you are still fighting the event from before. You cannot fight for them if you are still fighting in your head. They need you, and it is important to be peaceful, respectful, and caring, and to individualise attention to the students who need it.

This is shaping your well of being. This is deepening your understanding of who you are and how you have been affected. To go back and not deal with the event is shallow. That shallow well will harden until it becomes a shield through which no water, emotion, or happiness will be allowed to water your soul. Get help to dig deeper and unpack your journey and the class's journey. It is the best time to identify whether this incident dug deeply and dislodged some rocks of trauma that need to be discussed, or if it was just an event. The difference is the key to healing.

- You need to experience peace.
- The class needs you to demonstrate peace.

The teacher who wants to make a difference will remember the event, build walls of resentment, and attach negative emotions to those who created the harm.

The teacher who is a learner recognises that students need a leader who shows peace and love, engages in forgiveness, and rebuilds relationships.

"Peace cannot be kept by force.
It can only be achieved by understanding."
—Albert Einstein

Consider Professionalism

"If you let every pain and soreness keep you from training you will be teaching your body to stop fighting when it needs to most."

A professional soldier has a broad understanding of weapons, tactics, and strategies. They can determine the way forward and achieve success by using the weapons, environment, tactics, and strategies of both themselves and the enemy. The professional is paid to produce results because they have produced results before. The more they achieve under difficult situations, the more highly they are regarded by other professionals and the wider community. The art of professional soldiers has a long history.

Professionalism is understanding that you have the skills, temperament, tactics, or strategies to achieve success. There is no emotional or empathetic feeling involved in achieving; it is simply a job that you have been tasked with.

There are professionals all around us. A professional accountant understands money and can track it and check it, and the owner of the money trusts that their funds will be accounted for. A professional lawyer understands the law and all the intricacies and checks and balances of the rules that govern the way we live our lives. A professional doctor understands the body. A professional chiropractor understands the skeletal system. A professional engineer understands weight and structure. A professional teacher understands pedagogy, curriculum, behaviour management, and educational policies.

"The amateur spends his time in the past and the future.
He permits himself to fear and to hope.
The professional has taught himself to banish these distractions."
—Steven Pressfield, Turning Pro

The teaching profession needs professionals to teach. The teacher is a professional. They are not held back by emotions. Their energy at work is not based on how they feel on any given day. Their dedication to student learning is not hamstrung by their feelings towards students in the classroom. They know pedagogy, and they use it creatively and strategically. They understand the environment and use it to their advantage. There are behavioural, relational, and psychological tools they can access because they have used them before to create learning, build environments, or even create chaos when it is needed. The professional teacher wields knowledge and strategies in ways that engage and perplex, destroy and build, and develop macro-to-micro focus in the classroom. They are disciplined in their day both before and after school, ensuring minutes are used effectively and purposefully.

They turn up to do the work. They learn, teach, and apply their skill set, and they make improvements. They spend time before and after classes marking, checking, and providing feedback, and they engage in professional learning. They do not work from 9–5; instead, they give 95 percent of their time to teaching. That is what professionals do.

"The professional does not wait for inspiration.
He acts in anticipation of it."
—Steven Pressfield

Consider the Competition

(Recommended Reading: ***Antifragile*** and ***Skin in the Game*** by Nassim Taleb)

"People have difficulty realising that the solution is building a system in which nobody's fall can drag others down— ...for continuous failures work to preserve the system. Paradoxically, many government interventions and social politics end up hurting the weak and consolidating the established."
—Nassim Nicholas Taleb, Antifragile

The battle of competition is found in war, sports, and business. But education does not engage in that environment. Yet, any business, sporting team, or concept has the chance to be successful because it is comparing itself to something else. They are in a battle against a product, idea, team, or person. Coke v Pepsi. Apple v Microsoft. The battle lines are drawn, and the games are afoot. Even small businesses know that their idea must be better and gain more attention than their competition. Billions of dollars are spent convincing people. Fast food restaurants. Pizza restaurants. Every business has something to sell, something to offer, something that the competition does not have.

What is the competition for schools?

The measure of success for schools must be improvement, but against what? It is all well and good to say that you are improving yourself, but billions of dollars are not spent watching someone improve against themselves. Even golf, which is essentially a game against yourself, still has a leaderboard, and the person who performs the best individually is covered in glory, money, and green jackets. It is the drag-them-out, blood-and-guts fight to the end between two competitors that creates interest and opportunity. The competitor creates an interesting measure of success and this can bring out the best in your business.

Nassim Taleb has said that it is not survival of the fittest but the elimination of the weak.

Businesses, ideas, or people are better when the weak are eliminated. Taleb goes on to say that memorials should be made for those businesses or people who have failed, for on their shoulders of failure and mistakes, ideas and learning have progressed. We cannot live in a society where everyone is successful, for as the character Syndrome says in the movie *The Incredibles*, ***"When everyone is special, then no one is."***

Schools need to have competition. Cultures across history have been brought together with a common enemy. The us-v-them idea creates a common purpose, and success is measured in many ways. Schools can create a culture of improvement and measure success if they have an adversary to contend with. Competition drives innovation, and that drives curiosity. It encourages the exploration of ideas and divergent thinking. The competition needs a face or a name. If you do not believe that this is appropriate for schools, consider whether someone is already doing that with your school. If your measure of success is falling, perhaps you are already in a competition with an enemy who is considering ways to remove your best students, teachers, or experience. Maybe it is time to start considering learning as a goal, teaching as a competition, and future-proofing.

Teacher well-being could also improve when the natural competitiveness of humans kicks in. Maybe it is competing with your team to create the highest marks, the least bad behaviour, or the best attendance. Create competition within yourself to read the most books, watch the most TED talks, or engage in online learning to develop your potential. There are numerous ways to compete with others and yourself, and these challenges can create a natural high, a feeling of accomplishment, or the beginning steps to something even greater. Your feeling of self-satisfaction and acceptance must be found in your team's improvement, your class's growth, and your professional development.

Competition builds teams,
which builds connection,
which builds improvement.

This brings us back to the core argument. It is teaching that ultimately makes a difference, and the greatest recognition of the survival of the fittest takes place within classrooms. Teachers need to fail and be retrained. They need to be competitive in their pursuit of excellence. These skills are measured by more than student scores. They are shown in the time taken off during school and the relationships they have with students. If students and parents want their child removed from a class, that can also be an indication of a lack of teacher success.

As a school, you need to focus on what you want to achieve.

- Do you want to improve the social and emotional awareness of students and allow them to succeed through empathy and respect for others? Then you need teachers who emphasise that.
- Do you want to have high academic marks and students moving towards levels of success in higher education after school? Then you need teachers who emphasise that.

As an individual, I want to focus on what I want to achieve.

That does not happen without competition. So, get on your marks ...!

Consider Red Teaming

(Recommended Reading: ***Thinking in Bets*** by Annie Duke)

"If you know the enemy and know yourself,
you need not fear the result of a hundred battles.
If you know yourself but not the enemy,
for every victory gained you will also suffer a defeat.
If you know neither the enemy nor yourself,
you will succumb in every battle."
—Sun Tzu, The Art of War

The 9/11 commission that took place after the September 11 terrorist attacks identified a disturbing issue with the event. There was enough information and time for the intelligence community to stop the event from ever taking place. But the holders of the key information did not share or compare information. This lack of teamwork among teams from the same country caused considerable damage—damage that could have been avoided through the creation of a red team.

A red team is a group of people who know nothing about the planning, system, or development and who seek to identify associated weaknesses and problems. They challenge everything with the sole task of finding problems. The goal is to find the problems among themselves before the enemy finds them first.

This is not a new idea. When an army goes to war, they are aware of their plan. They are also aware of the ways their battle plans could be ineffective. A battle takes place only after the combatants have identified weaknesses in themselves and the opposition. Any team that goes into battle with confidence in their abilities and does not spend time considering their weaknesses will find themselves exposed at the worst time.

Armies would spend time fighting as a team with their shields and swords. They would work out ways to link shields together to form a strong unit and remove any possible weaknesses that the opposition could expose.

A common expression among people about to enter public service is "opposition research." What can your team find out about you and your history that could prove embarrassing, so that they can develop a plan to address it if it appears?

So, too, for the teacher.

What is the weakness of the teacher? What will trigger a response? What smell, look, comment, or behaviour will cause a reaction to take place in front of a student or the class? As the quote from Sun Tzu states, if you know yourself, then you can overcome every battle, but if you do not, then you will be exposed. The weakness in your armour will be identified. The enemy will find it, as that is their job. Maybe it is trauma from your past that you have not dealt with. Maybe it is a breakdown in relationships. Maybe it is a death in the family. Maybe it is a violent episode that you were involved in. The weaknesses are everywhere, and it is to your greater strength that you identify and deal with them.

It could manifest in two ways:

1. Students could find it through trial and error. They will say and do things, then watch how you react. When they find that trigger,

no number of detentions will stop them from trying to control your reactions.

2. Or, events that take place during the school day could trigger a reaction. A child may respond to an event, or the response to that event could trigger a memory of similar feelings for the teacher.

Teachers are allowed to have weaknesses, but if they affect the quality of teaching or relationships, they become a burden that needs to be removed. Support is available. Deal with it early and honestly rather than late and disastrously.

So how do you red team?

External questions:

1. Do you have a history of trauma?
2. Do you have a history of poverty?
3. Do you have a history of experiencing domestic violence?
4. Do you have any financial concerns?

Internal questions:

1. Do you have a history of being spoken down to and made to feel inferior?
2. Do you have a history of being confident and feeling superior?
3. Do you have a vision of your future that is optimistic or pessimistic?
4. Do you have a growth or fixed mindset about yourself, others, or students?
5. How do you respond when you are tired, stressed, frustrated, or angry?
6. How do you resolve conflicts with others?
7. What strategies do you have to cope with stressors in life?
8. How many close friends or family members do you have?
9. Do you have spiritual or relationship concerns?

10. Do you have changing thoughts around your sexuality?

No answers are incorrect, and no answers can prevent you from being a teacher—or even a great one. But the teaching profession will expose you to life stories, narratives, and drama that you will have to deal with. Red teaming includes recognising that something may provoke a reaction in you.

The person who fears heights is still a fine individual, but they will avoid situations that require them to be in that position. The person who fears tight and small spaces will be able to operate and do a wonderful job, but they will avoid situations that make them feel uncomfortable. The person who is allergic to certain items will live a long, happy, and fulfilling life, but they will make decisions to ensure that they remain safe.

Red teaming for a teacher is the same. If you can be honest about your fear of heights, your claustrophobia, or your allergies, then be honest about your history of trauma, dealing with domestic violence, or your emotions when you become upset. These should not be impediments to teaching, and with the correct training and strategies, they could become incredibly useful in supporting students and staff through tough times.

A teacher who wants to make a difference will avoid dealing with their struggles and focus on teaching students.

A teacher who is a learner will recognise that their struggles can make a negative impact if they are not dealt with, but will also recognise the source of strength that can be found when their fears are confronted.

"The goal of a red team is to improve the resiliency, viability, and success of the target institution through the promotion of divergent thinking and unconventional analysis."
Joshua Kim, Higher Ed and the 6 Best Practices for Red Teams

Consider Failure Before Beginning

(Recommended Reading:
Seeing What Others Don't by Gary Klein and
Thinking in Bets by Annie Duke)

"When we put too much energy into eliminating mistakes, we're less likely to gain insights. Having insights is a different matter from preventing mistakes."
—Gary Klein

A person has died. This is a sad moment, but it is also a chance to learn. The body goes through a post-mortem. The doctor identifies the cause of the possible reasons it took place. From this information, lessons are learned. Changes are made personally, professionally, or through legislation. Somewhere along the way, a system failed. Sometimes failure does not always produce bodies. The failure could instead be in a business, marriage, football team, military exercise, or entrepreneurial concept.

Failure produces learning. But Gary Klein has introduced in his research the idea of pre-mortem thinking; your business, marriage, or lesson is going to fail. Maybe it will be in 12 minutes, 12 months, or 12 years, but it will fail. What are the determining factors you can identify now, before you begin, that will cause that crash, failure, or even death? This is not negative or dark thinking. Klein encourages this approach so that those involved can identify the possible effects before they happen.

Consider the Classroom and Premortem Thinking

You are going to fail; it is going to be a mess. Students will not be able to learn, remember what they learnt, or apply it. Why did this happen?

Spend some time individually and as a team identifying the causes.

1. Was it you and your lack of relationships?
2. Did you not explain the lesson?
3. Did the students understand the assessment, and were the assessment concepts taught?
4. Are there students who have trouble with this concept, so instead of looking for answers, they went looking for trouble?

Teachers don't often think about the success of the lesson, so when the failure of the lesson comes around, they can be shocked. These are teachers who blame the students. But it is not them; it is you.

The teacher who wants to make a difference could not conceive that they would fail.

The teacher who is a learner prepares for failure and begins steps to alleviate the possibility.

"How have I been complicit in creating the conditions I say I don't want?"
"What am I not saying that needs to be said?"
"What am I saying that's not being heard?"
"What's being said that I'm not hearing?"
—Jerry Colonna

"Despite the popular wisdom that we achieve success
through positive visualisation,
it turns out that incorporating negative visualisation
makes us more likely to achieve our goals."
—Annie Duke, Thinking in Bets

Consider Failure

"It becomes clear that bright and wonderful people know how to succeed, but not how to fail."
—Angela Duckworth, Grit

The concept of failing is so emotional. It drags up so many feelings and images of disappointment. Everyone has their own version of what failure looks like, and it can be descriptive, hurtful, and something that people want to avoid. It is not just about failing at something; it becomes personal because "I am a failure." That makes what I do seem less than, which makes me feel less than. So people do whatever they can to avoid that feeling.

What a mistake that is!

Perhaps it is social media with the perception of perfection, but failure is how you get to perfection. It is the first step towards improvement. If you don't know that you failed, you will not improve or be challenged to improve. Students need to fail, and they need to fail often, and they need to fail well. They need to be told that they failed and how they can improve. I once heard from Tim Ferriss that "*people who are offended easily need to be offended more often*". Students who have difficulty with failing need to be reminded and embrace the failure.

Students need to learn how to fail and then learn how to improve. They cannot do the second without the first. A student's perception of who they are is so fragile or weak that they may seek to destroy their work instead of recognising that they did something wrong. I have seen children not try if they cannot get it correct. I have experienced that conversation with them, but it is important to note that this is the lesson now. Whatever you were teaching is not as important as getting the child to learn to be wrong and not experience it as a personal tragedy, but as a way of moving forward.

Teachers are great people, and they don't want students to get hurt and to fail, but it is important for growth. Besides, students know if you are tricking them. If you put them into the Elephants Group, or the H Group, or the Sand Dunes Group, they will know very quickly that it is the "dumb group." They will look at their peers and recognise that they have failed. So don't hide it, and don't distort it. Call it what it is. The students have made a mistake either through a lack of knowledge or understanding, so it is the job of the teacher to improve their tools. Don't waste time. Embrace the suck of their work and spend more time helping them improve it.

It is better they fail where there is a net to catch them. If they have not developed that skill by the time they leave school, the fall will be catastrophically worse.

"To innovate, you must learn to fail well,
learn from your mistakes. Morph ideas, don't kill them.
Most of the world's great innovations started out
with entirely different applications,
so when you end a project, look carefully at its components
to see how they might be reapplied elsewhere."
—Eric Schmidt and Jonathan Rosenberg, How Google Works

Consider My Victory: Part One

"In war, then, let your great object be victory, not lengthy campaigns."
—Sun Tzu, The Art of War

In warfare, there are battles to be won on the way to victory. Maybe it is to take the high ground or the town, to protect victims or save buildings. There is always something to achieve, and after the victory is won, those who have achieved it can relax and bask in the glory. Then they set the next goal. Sports teams demonstrate this. The joy that is produced after scoring points is indescribable, even though the game has not yet been won. They have moved the opposition and the ball to such a point where they can gain victory. They leap, congratulate each other, and appreciate the bonding. Then they set themselves to do it again to gain victory at the end of the game. In all walks of life, victory is celebrated: a court case is won, a house is bought, an environment has been changed. All these victories create a feeling of happiness and a job well done for all participants.

What does victory look like for the teacher? Is it recognised, acknowledged, and celebrated in the same way a sports team does?

"There is a fundamental question of knowledge that goes all the way back to Plato and Socrates. If you don't know what you are looking for, how will you know if you found it?"
—Ryan Holiday, Perennial Seller

Personal Victory

The first part of the teaching journey will determine what kind of teacher you will be. Is it your goal to be the teacher who creates learning, or is it your goal to allow students to learn? This is a fundamental step in understanding victory. Are you the winner, or is the student? Is your ego going to allow students to learn despite you, or will you need to dictate the journey to them?

In warfare, men can be sent over the trenches to be killed to gain ground, and the leader's name will be recognised as the person who created change. At what cost? The teacher who wishes to be considered a great teacher will talk, lead, and teach, but they will not allow the student's voice to be heard, lest they take away from the teacher's greatness.

- Teachers whose victory is high marks may be tempted to consider unethical ways of marking to ensure they come out on top.
- Teachers whose victory is the warmth of the students' love may consider relationships of higher value than educational feedback.
- Teachers whose victory is well-behaved classes will consider punishment and yelling to be important to classroom management.
- Teachers whose victory is in expressing what they feel will mainly consider that students have come to listen to them.
- Teachers whose victory is to get through the day will consider ways to avoid the classroom.

A teacher cannot begin to teach until they can understand and measure victory. The victory they feel as they leave at the end of the day will be very different depending on their personality and the criteria they set for themselves. Beware of the teacher who seeks to be the change in the classroom. The focus is not on learning but on the teacher's greatness. Students may progress and learn. But the teacher may feel that they have not made a difference. They may then negatively impact learning in the classroom to ensure the credit and learning come from them.

The focus for a teacher should be on learning, for themselves and the students. The teacher needs to realise that learning looks different for them, as it does for the students, but learning does not happen unless students are part of the process.

Teaching is not about you.

What does victory look like to you?

When you recognise that answer, you may begin to create a criterion for victory.

"Our values determine the metrics by which we measure ourselves and everyone else."
Mark Manson

Consider My Victory: Part Two

"Strategy without tactics is the slowest route to victory.
Tactics without strategy is the noise before defeat."
—Sun Tzu

If you have established what victory looks like and recognised the steps you need to take to get there, your next goal will be to consider what victory will look like after it is achieved. Just as the team surrounds the player who scored a goal during the game, what will be the response after you have achieved it?

A player is surrounded and congratulated by their teammates for three reasons:

1. They all have the same goal,
2. They are all on the same team, and
3. They have all witnessed the goal take place.

This is where teachers can learn from other industries. As previously stated, they tend to work in silos, keeping their victories and disappointments to themselves. This is not healthy and does not establish trust, nor can you appreciate the outpouring of support when things go well.

The victory that you wish as a teacher should be shared with your team, which hopefully has similar goals to yours. The criteria for success that you want should be presented to your team as a challenging goal that you want others to know about. Sharing your victory also allows the team to recognise if yours is a victory worth pursuing. That honest feedback from your peers will demonstrate whether you are on the right path, and it will ensure that your motivation is relevant. That is the first step.

The second step is understanding what victory looks like for others on your team. When you celebrate others, they can celebrate with you. This outpouring of recognition allows the team to grow and develop further, challenging goals. The team goals can be developed.

The final step is to recognise what the victory celebration could look like. Is it morning tea with the teachers, an award from the admin or the cohort, or coffee together after school? Even your recognition of victory with your team will identify who the focus is on.

What will victory look like to you?

Be mindful. If you hold onto your mistakes as a teacher, it is important for your well-being to also hold onto your achievements. If you recognise ways in which you have damaged relationships, you also need to appreciate how many students are eager for you to be their teacher. If you understand that you made some pedagogical mistakes, you also need to appreciate the fantastic pedagogical tactics you employed that created improved learning.

Teachers do not naturally recognise the impact they make. Positive teaching is recognising that teaching in the trenches is hard, demanding work, but there are victorious days. If they are not established, recognised, and celebrated, teaching will become a constant grind. And nobody wants to live like that.

We need to celebrate our victories!

Success is focusing the full power of all you are on what you have a burning desire to achieve.
– Wilfred Peterson

Consider My Move

(Recommended Reading: ***Thinking in Bets*** by Annie Duke and ***Mastermind*** by Maria Konnikova)

"While we are free to choose our actions,
we are not free to choose the consequences of those actions."
—Stephen R. Covey, The 7 Habits of Highly Effective People

The military squad moves into position. They make the move towards their goal. Whether their goal is just and fair or evil and malevolent, a move has been made towards the goal, and that move creates a consequence. Maybe the consequences will be positive and rewarding, or maybe they will be unpleasant or devastating. Either way, it has been set in stone. If lives are lost, the lessons learned will be for others, not for those who have passed.

Teaching does not have the same extremes as warfare, but behavioural choices are like everything in life. They have consequences. Teachers sometimes forget that and try to manipulate the choice, presenting it as either "good" or "bad." It is important that students recognise that they can choose to make any decision they like. The lesson is not the choice; the lesson is the consequence. Teachers need to show students those consequences after the fact. This needs to be done logically, rationally, and unemotionally.

Students (and parents) need to recognise the slow, methodical consequence that will take place after the child has chosen. Teachers can take comfort in the outcome that is coming the way of the student. Do not allow the child to miss out on it. Do not minimise it, lessen the impact, or avoid uncomfortable conversations. It has been said that experience is the greatest teacher, in that it provides the test and then gives the lesson. After a child falls over while running on wet concrete, a lesson takes place. A lecture in advance means nothing to some students, and it wastes time for them and the teacher. The student made a choice, so let them know that they made it. After the choice has occurred, the consequence takes place, and the impact (sometimes an actual impact) will live long in their memory as a reminder.

The great aspect of choice and consequence is that it takes place every day and in every lesson. A lesson on cause and effect can lead to a behaviour lesson of a similar conversation. A sporting event where the consequence is that points are scored can be broken down into the choices the players made during the game that led to that result. The world is full of examples, but students are either not exposed to them often enough, or the consequences are glossed over or dealt with far out of proportion to the choice. The term "proportional response" is a key factor. Do not make the disciplinary action so small or large that the child misses the lesson.

The teacher should not be emotional about any of it. The parent and child will become emotional, and blame will be placed on many things. But the choice was made. It is the teacher's role to set the standard, explain the reasons, and establish the rules. Parents and students will continually seek justifications and explanations. If the teacher has provided a lack of information, this will mean that the teacher made a choice, and they, like the students, will experience the consequence, though theirs will be due to their inaction.

A teacher's well-being can often be caught up in feeling like the choices they provide are difficult and that they have provided unfair consequences. Feeling sorry for the student who made a poor choice and burdening yourself with responsibility for creating the choice in the first place is wasted time. Build relationships, seek the best in others, and always be optimistic. Build your own relationships first, seek the best in yourself, and offer what you can. Do not filter your life, dreams, and visions through students' poor choices and pre-warned consequences.

That was their move; create your own.

"Determining whether a decision is good or bad means examining the quality of the beliefs informing the decision, the available options, and how the future might turn out given any choice you make."
—Annie Duke

"Experience can be an effective teacher. But, clearly, only some students listen to their teachers."
—Annie Duke

"The benefit of failure is an objectivity that success simply can't offer."
—Maria Konnikova

Reflective Considerations

- Death is a part of life, as is failure
- Both death and failure can be emotional, but they can also produce learning, ideas and change.
- Peace is not a part of life, and will avoid you, unless you actively seek it, create it and hold onto it.
- A professional understands death, failure, peace and victory, and uses this knowledge to win or learn.
- A victory can never be achieved if it is not recognised, identified, respected and celebrated. Life is too short and too hard, so don't waste it on small, shallow wins or big, silent victories.
- But whatever happens, it will still be your move.

IX

Final Considerations

"The paradox of education is precisely this:
that as one begins to become conscious,
one begins to examine the society in which he is being educated."
—James Baldwin

"Everything's gonna go south ...
you can either accept that, or you can get to work.
That's all it is. You just begin. You do the math.
You solve one problem ... and you solve the next one...
and then the next.
And if you solve enough problems, you get to come home."
—The Martian

Consider Wisdom

(Recommended Reading: ***Wisdom Takes Work*** by Ryan Holiday)

"Knowledge is knowing that a tomato is a fruit.
Wisdom is knowing that a tomato does not belong in a fruit salad."
—Miles Kington

"Use your money wisely."
"Choose your time wisely."

These are comments often made by people who understand that they need to make good decisions. The emphasis is often placed on the importance of time or money, but not much is made of the importance of wisdom. It is impossible to use time or money wisely if you do not have the wisdom to decide or if you have no idea how to be wise in the context of time or money.

As this book draws to an end, it is important that the understanding and implications of wisdom are briefly explored. Teachers need to teach and develop wisdom in students, but they need to develop their insight first. As a teacher, our goal should not be to focus our students on improving their understanding of maths, language, science, and all the other subjects. Instead, we should be focused on beginning the creation of wisdom in students.

What is wisdom? It is the quality of having experience, knowledge, and good judgement. It is an ability to identify and act on truth with compassion and empathy, and to recognise the impact it can have on others.

- Intelligence is maths.
- Knowledge is using a calculator.
- But only wisdom will combine both to create a correct answer.

Wisdom is found through the intentional pursuit of learning and exploring. It is created through reading and writing. It can be developed through deliberately seeking out a variety of opinions, judgements, and positions to understand the reasons why. Wisdom begins within yourself, as the only person you can make wise is you. You cannot find it by trying to attain it. You must constantly search for it. Wisdom may find you; you will not find wisdom. It is developed by reflecting on your own thoughts and opinions and considering where they came from. Explore the philosophies of the ages and identify which relate to you and where your assumed thinking came from. Have conversations with others. Learn to be an observer who listens. Then listen again and again—to yourself, to others, to opinions, to perceived truth—and then experiment with the knowledge. Research its importance, relevance, and accuracy. This will take time, but wisdom is not found in a 30-second social media post. It is found with reflection and deliberate practice.

- A football player does not become a player in the middle of a game.
- A doctor does not become a surgeon in the middle of their first surgery.
- A lawyer does not become a lawyer by stepping untested into a court case.

We should not expect to become a wise human when thrust into the frantic flows of life.

Any profession takes time to develop the skills, and it is no less important—

in fact, it is more so—for human beings to take the time to understand themselves and their relationship with the world before dropping into the river of life.

As a teacher, there may be 15, 30, or 300 opinions and life experiences that are different from yours in the school that you can access and learn from. Listen to them and learn from them. Then reflect on how they impact and change the thinking in your life. It will be an excellent step towards gaining wisdom.

Read, reflect, review, re-engage, respect, restate, redirect, retain, and relearn.
Then read and listen some more.

It is vitally important that students begin the lifelong journey of being a learner with the possibility of becoming wise. They will not have the tools if you do not first embrace and encourage wisdom in yourself.

"The only true wisdom is knowing you know nothing."
—Socrates

Consider Being a Gardener

(Recommended Reading and Listening:
The Fourth Pillar by Harry Moffitt,
This is Strategy by Seth Godin, and
Sir Ken Robinson's **TED** talks)

"Planting a seed is a strategy,
but it is the culture that determines what happens next."
—Seth Godin

This book was written with the focus on the teacher as a warrior. It's true that a teacher should to be prepared, focused, disciplined, and strategic. The teacher also needs to employ a range of devices whilst simultaneously checking the environment to ensure that they make the best decisions. But the focus of the book could also be on a gardener who is also mindful of the environment and the culture. Yet, they do something that others do not: they grow something. So, to conclude the book, let's talk about gardening.

The interesting fact about gardeners and farmers is that there is nothing they can do about the seeds they plant. They cannot change the seed into a flower, plant, fruit, or grain. The gardener and farmer instead focus directly on the environment. They check the soil, water the ground, ensure there is enough sun and warmth, remove the weeds, and protect the plants from predators. Only under these conditions can seeds change and grow.

"The gardener does not make a plant grow.
The job of a gardener is to create optimal conditions for growth."
—Sir Ken Robinson

The farmer, like the warrior, must be tactical and strategic, patient and precise. The goal of their work is to create growth, improvement, and a product. The school must also follow the same protocols and processes as the farmer and the warrior. The leadership of the school should not focus on the strategies that they have, nor should they focus on the students. These are the seeds. Focusing on the seeds does not allow them to appreciate how they grow.

The school must emphasise the climate. What is the soil like? Is it fertilised and ready for learning, or is it hard, crusty, and indifferent to the seeds in the ground? Are the seeds watered every day with feedback, positivity, and relationships? Is there enough sun to allow for the scientific growth process? Is the area free of weeds that can suffocate learning, which take the precious resources of food, water, and sunlight away from the plants that are trying to grow? Does the farmer ensure that the weeds are constantly removed to allow room for growth? And is there a fence around the plants to protect them from outside influences that may be negative or suffocating?

"The real role of leadership in education ...
is not and should not be command and control.
The real role of leadership is climate control, creating a climate of possibility."
—Sir Ken Robinson

The focus in schools and among leadership teams should be on creating, maintaining, and improving the culture. School strategies may focus on reading, writing, or Maths, but they cannot grow by themselves. The school needs to have a culture and environment that enable students to persist and build momentum through all weather conditions.

What is the culture around the strategies that will enable these seeds to grow? Who are the farmers working on these seeds? This becomes the story the school tells the community. It is the story the school tells the teachers. It is the story the school tells the students. The seeds of reading or Maths grow in the environment, and the results come from the culture.

"Culture eats strategy for breakfast."
—Anonymous

The climate set by the leadership team must help teachers grow and reach their potential. Teachers also need differentiated support. They need to be watered, and their soil must be maintained. They also need the warmth of the sun and protection from weeds and predators. Recognising the different needs that teachers have goes a long way towards creating the culture that parents, students, and other schools notice. A creative, innovative, and learner-driven environment that enables students to grow comes from how the teachers are treated.

Supporting the teacher's well-being, and recognising their impact, helps the seeds (students) in their class to grow. The school leadership team has very little direct impact on students. There are too many children. Instead, the school should create more farmers, gardeners, and leaders. The seeds are plentiful, but the professionals are not. Those professionals water the seeds. Their feedback notes who needs more sun and who needs weeds removed around them. These teacher gardeners monitor, control, and adjust the climate.

"You cannot predict the outcome of human development.
All you can do is, like a farmer,
create the conditions under which it will begin to flourish."
—Ken Robinson

The teacher, in much the same way, needs to be their own gardener. Every teacher has their own seeds, ideas, or potential. But potential, like seeds, does not grow unless there is a climate and environment for it to grow in.

Teachers need to be just as conscious of the soil, climate, water, sun, weeds, and predators that can affect their mental and psychological seeds as farmers are with their physical seeds. Teachers need to plant their ideas and potential in productive soil—soil that is ready to accept the positive version of themselves, someone who can see the potential and wants to grow.

Teachers need to keep the idea watered through reading, experimenting, and sharing with others. They need feedback on their growth through mentoring with people who challenge them and want them to be successful. Teachers need the warmth of relationships, positive feedback, and recognition of the small positive gains taking place in their lives. Most importantly, teachers need to remove the weeds that can manifest as negativity through other people, social media, books, television shows, or movies. They must protect their idea of who they are and what they can achieve, leaving a gate that allows themselves and others to escape when it is appropriate.

"In the garden we don't make anything grow;
rather, we create the conditions for growth."
—Harry Moffitt, The Fourth Pillar

- We cannot make the school grow, and we cannot make our strategies grow.
- We cannot make our students grow educationally in the classroom.
- We cannot make ourselves grow psychologically or educationally.
- We cannot improve our mental health, well-being, or self-image.
- **But we can change the environment.**

We can change the climate and focus on the garden of our world, becoming farmers and gardeners of change.

When I focus on the deep surroundings of my seed or potential, I may be shocked even to consider growing anything. Or I may be surprised to discover how much more potential I have to change everything.

"We need the right conditions for growth in our schools, ...and in our individual lives. If the conditions are right, people grow in synergy with the people around them and the environments they create... Finding and nurturing them is the surest way to ensure our growth and fulfilment as individuals."

—Ken Robinson, The Element

Consider Myself in the Future

"It just astounds me that I learn the simplest things
and look back at the entirety of my life and I'm like,
No one told me about this?
Human beings have all of this knowledge,
all of this other knowledge, and no one told me about this?"
—Amanda Palmer

A soldier is trained in the latest tactics and equipment, or else they will experience loss and failure in their environment. Doctors no longer use leeches and bloodletting to solve medical problems. Engineers do not use mud bricks to build buildings anymore. Architects now use computer imaging to create buildings.

These, and many other professions, have been developed because they have embraced new ideas, research, experimentation, and the sharing of resources.

Teaching is also a profession. It should also embrace new ideas in thinking.

A teacher who wants to make a difference believes that they have all they need to teach. They believe that using all their personal knowledge and experience, from their training and time at school, is all they will need to create better learning. They are wrong.

A teacher who wants to learn embraces professional learning and development. They walk into a classroom and recognise a myriad of ways that students learn and will embrace learning themselves. They engage in neuroscience to understand how the brain processes, holds, and applies information. They learn about poverty mindsets, trauma-informed practices, and cultural differences. They try to understand family values and beliefs, generational impacts, and Indigenous influences.

Books, podcasts, and research will be imperative for a teacher who wishes to learn how to create better learning for students. Time spent engaging in these activities, on their own time, will create a thriving and prepared teacher who creates high-impact teaching for their students. A teacher who does not embrace personal professional development misses the most important parts of the process. The brain, relationships, family, culture, disabilities, ingenuity, trauma, and history of students are hidden inside research. Only teachers who are willing to learn, read, research, and engage in new thinking can identify them.

Being a teacher who does not engage in professional development is like being a soldier who believes they can confidently enter the field of battle with no weapon and their eyes closed. The lesson and the teacher will not only fail. The collateral damage will be considerable.

"You think your pain and your heartbreak are unprecedented
in the history of the world,
but then you read.
It was books that taught me that the things that tormented me most
were the very things that connected me with all the people who were alive,
who had ever been alive."
—James Baldwin

The Journey Begins...

You don't win on your potential.
You win by delivering a result.
You don't win by having an idea.
You win by creating something.
You don't even win by winning.
You win by achieving something that you have dreamt about.

Reflect on my values.
Reflect on my beliefs.
Reflect on my pedagogical advantages.
Reflect on my pedagogical weaknesses.
What are my pedagogical triggers?
How will I react to them?

Reflect on my relational strengths.
Reflect on my relational weaknesses.
Who are my triggers?
How will I react to them?

Reflect on my best environment for teaching.
Reflect on my most challenging environment for teaching.
How will I react in each environment?

Reflect on my personal history.

What other triggers do I need to identify?
How do I show myself publicly?
How do I see myself privately?
What battles need to be overcome?

How easily is my mental health affected by stimuli,
both positive and negative?
How do I react?
How quickly do I react?
How long does it take to rebalance after I react?

Teaching and mental health can be a battle.
I need to be aware and alert.
I need to be prepared as well as planned.
I need to recognise my strengths and weaknesses.
I need to identify the real enemy before I engage.
I need to be strategic and tactical.
I need to accept that I will lose and I will win.
I need to learn from failure and embrace success.
I need to define who I am.
I do not need to be defined by others, experiences,
or brief moments in time.
Nothing will prevent me from being a great person or a great teacher,
except myself.

There has never been a more important time to have professional educators. They are on the frontlines of a world that is seeking to understand and learn. The public, at large, is under attack from misinformation, disinformation, and those who seek to create their own facts. Teachers need to stand strong against thought bubbles, echo chambers, and groupthink. They must arm themselves with knowledge, information, and pedagogical approaches that deliver learning in such a way that it develops trust, opens minds, and widens perspectives.

A teacher who wants to make a difference will not effect meaningful change. The focus is on themselves as the only person who can deliver information.

The teacher who wants to be a learner will naturally engage in conversation, negotiation, compromise, seeking win-win scenarios, arguing socratically, and demonstrating patience. They will employ humour and discernment, identify facts from opinions, seek high-minded conversation, never resort to language that is abusive or negative, and most importantly, they will listen.

These are the teachers we need in the world right now, but they need to be prepared.

Teachers need to be strong in themselves and their well-being before they can be great at teaching. Their well-being will bring them the confidence to teach and try new things. It will give them the character to stand strong against harmful practices, but it will also allow them to learn from their mistakes. A teacher's well-being will create the shield that protects them from harm from students and parents, but it will also provide the weapons to ensure learning, relationships, and improvement continue to happen under all circumstances.

Teacher well-being needs to be strategically and tactically developed, planned, and implemented to ensure that success happens physically and psychologically.

Teachers need to be protected against psychological attacks. They need to create allies who will support them. They should never enter the field of learning without the tools, tactics, and equipment that will allow them to be successful. They need to be strategic in their work, recognise the environment, and adapt accordingly.

The world should be in awe of teachers, as I am every day. They put themselves on the front line for their students, for learning and for truth, and they create better children, families, and societies.

So put on your equipment: your weapons of learning and your gardening tools.

Teaching is a tough job, and only the best can do it.

Continue to train to be a warrior teacher.

Continue to shape your well-being.

We need you out here.

Acknowledgments

This book was written because of the inspiration of the authors who have been referenced throughout the book. It is on their shoulders that teachers teach, learners learn, and the science of reason and imagination is allowed to grow and progress. It is also important to name other influential people who have also played a role in the creation of this book about teachers:

Tim Ferriss, whose book Team of Titans I once picked up in a bookshop. He introduced me through his writings and his podcast to many interesting, professional, creative people who have enjoyed challenges and experienced heartbreak (far worse than mine). His story and his veritable plethora of influential conversations have, in no small way, provided the motivation for me to move forward in my well of being, teaching, and life.

Seth Godin has also provided his unique perspective to martketing, projects, and creativity, and his lessons have been the backbone to my writing. Steven Pressfield, whose book The War of Art created a wonderful counterpoint to the other book that interested me, The Art of War. Brene Brown through discovering vulnerability. Robert Greene with his work on Human Nature. And Carol Dweck, whose research started me on this journey.

I also welcomed the thoughts and feedback of Sue, Ben, and Michelle, as well as Michael, Jen, and Mike from the Reedsy team, who challenged me to restructure and rethink my writing.

References

Recommended Reading

Introduction

- Lee, S. (2020). **Be Water, My Friend**. Random House.
- Holiday, R. (2025). **Wisdom Takes Work**. Profile Books(GB).

Who Are you?

- Moffitt, H. (2025). **The Fourth Pillar**. Macmillan Publishers Aus.
- Sinek, S. (2009). **Start with why: how great leaders inspire everyone to take action**. Portfolio/Penguin.
- Ham, P. (2025). **The Soul**. PRHNZ Preview.
- Gerber, M. E. (2017). **The E-myth Revisited : Why most small businesses don't work and what to do about it**. Harper Collins E-Books.

Consider the Well-being of Teaching

- Jean-Pierre Weill, Osburn, M., & Emmanuel Yadin Klein. (2016). **The well of being: A children's book for adults**. Flatiron Books.
- Maté, G., & Maté, D. (2023). **The myth of normal: trauma, illness and healing in a toxic culture**. Vintage Canada.
- Medina, J. (2020). **Brain Rules (Updated and Expanded)**.

- van der Kolk, B. (2015). **The body keeps the score: brain, mind, and body in the healing of trauma.** Penguin Books.
- Sapolsky, R. (2004). **Why zebras don't get ulcers (3rd ed.).** Holt. (Original work published 1994)
- Looper. (2018). The Ending Of Sucker Punch Finally Explained. In YouTube. https://www.youtube.com/watch?v=hafjS7WSzes
- Anderson, L. (2024). **The Paramedic Mindset**. Macmillan Publishers Aus.
- Greene, R. (2018). **The laws of human nature**. Penguin USA.
- Burkeman, O. (2021). **Four Thousand Weeks: Time Management for Mortals**. Penguin Canada.
- Apple TV - **Shrinking**
- Greene, R. (2012). **Mastery**. Profile Books.
- Aurelius, M., & Waterfield, R. (2021). **Meditations**. Basic Books.
- Chu, C.-N. (2010). **Thick Face, Black Heart**. Hachette UK.
- Godin, S. (2024). **This Is Strategy**. Simon and Schuster.
- The Most Important Question of Your Life, https://markmanson.net/question, Mark Manson
- Duke, A. (2022). **Quit**. Ebury Press.
- Dixit, A. K., & Nalebuff, B. J. (2010). **The Art of Strategy: A Game Theorist's Guide to Success in Business and Life**. W. W. Norton & Company.
- Tzu, S. (2020). **Art Of War**. Flame Tree Publishing.
- Brown, B. (2025). **Strong Ground**. Random House.

The War of Teaching

- Haidt, J. (2012). **The righteous mind: why good people are divided by politics and religion**. Penguin Books.
- Goleman, D. (1996). **Emotional intelligence: Why it can matter more than IQ**. Bloomsbury.
- Manson, M. (2017). **The Subtle Art of Not Giving a F*ck**.

- Konnikova, M. (2013). **Mastermind: how to think like Sherlock Holmes**. Penguin Books.
- "Land mines are weapons of mass destruction in slow motion." —Human Rights Watch and Physicians for Human Rights, 1993 report, "Landmines: A Deadly Legacy"
- Kerr, J. (2013). **Legacy: What the All Blacks can Teach Us About the Business of Life**. Constable.
- Voss, C., & Raz, T. (2017). **Never split the difference: Negotiating as if your life depended on it**. Random House Business Books.

The Battle of Learning

- Lucius Annaeus Seneca, & Butler-Bowdon, T. (2024). **On the Shortness of Life**. John Wiley & Sons.
- Pink, D. (2018). **When.** Riverhead Books (a Penguin Random House imprint)
- Dobelli, R. (2017). **The Art of the Good Life**. Sceptre.
- L David Marquet. (2015). **Turn your ship around: a workbook for implementing intent-based leadership in your organization**. Portfolio / Penguin.
- Grant, A. M. (2016). **Originals: how non-conformists move the world**. Penguin Books, An Imprint Of Penguin Random House Llc.
- McChrystal, S. A. (2015). **Team of Teams: the Power of Small Groups in a Fragmented World**. Portfolio.
- Senge, P. M. (2014). **The fifth discipline: the art & practice of the learning organization**. Business Book Summaries.
- Lukianoff, G., & Haidt, J. (2018). **The Coddling of the American Mind: How Good Intentions and Bad Ideas Are Setting Up a Generation for Failure**. Penguin Books. (Original work published 2018)
- Harari, Y. N. (2015). **Sapiens: A Brief History of Humankind.** Harper Perennial. (Original work published 2011)
- Diamond, J. (2017). **Guns, Germs, and Steel**. W.W. Norton & Company.

- Kucharski, A. (2020). **The Rules of Contagion**. Basic Books.
- Sinek, S. (2020). **Infinite Game**. Portfolio Penguin.

The Barriers to Learning

- Pressfield, S. (2002). **The War of Art**. Black Irish Entertainment LLC.
- W. Timothy Gallwey. (2010). **The Inner Game of Tennis**. Random House.
- The Shawshank Redemption
- Taleb, N. N. (2016). **The Black Swan: the impact of the highly improbable**. Random House.
- Taleb, N. N. (2012). **Antifragile: things that gain from disorder**. Random House.
- Lamott, A. (1994). **Bird by bird: Some instructions on writing and life**. Anchor Books.
- Moneyball Movie
- Pinker, S. (2005). **The language instinct: how the mind creates language**. Penguin Books, [Post.
- Diamond, J. (2017). **Guns, Germs, and Steel**. W.W. Norton & Company.
- Crystal, D. (2012). **Spell it out: the story of English spelling**. Profile Books.
- Holiday, R. (2017). **Perennial Seller**. Penguin.
- Greene, R. (2006). **The 48 Laws of Power**. Profile Books.

How does it end?

- Clark, A. (2024). **The Experience Machine**. Random House.
- Duke, A. (2019). **Thinking in bets: making smarter decisions when you don't have all the facts**. Portfolio/Penguin.
- Klein, G. A. (2013). **Seeing what others don't: the remarkable ways we gain insights**. Public affairs.

- Duckworth, A. (2016). **Grit: The power of passion and perseverance**. Scribner.
- Schmidt, E., & Rosenberg, J. (2014). **How Google works**. Grand Central Publ.
- Covey, S. R. (2020). **7 Habits of Highly Effective People: Revised and Updated: Powerful Lessons in Personal Change**. Simon & Schuster, Incorporated.
- Holiday, R. (2025). **Wisdom Takes Work**. Profile Books(GB).
- Sir Ken Robinson's TED talks

Conclusion

"How are you feeling? Meh.
That feeling, that's the mundanity of a job well done.
Do you know how many wars there have been in the history of mankind?
No, of course not, cause most wars are forgotten.
All the men who fought in them, and all the medals they won,
Heroes and hardware fade to the back of the history books
because it is not about war.
This war never ends, there is no V day, there is no finish line.
The real battle in all of life is being someone that people can count on,
And that is not defined in a single moment.
You earn that with a lifetime of showing up.
These conflicts, they don't define you, you don't want them to.
Trust me."
—Devotion (2022)

"Tho' much is taken, much abides;
and though we are not now
that strength which in old days moved earth and heaven;
that which we are, we are; One equal temper of heroic hearts,
Made weak by time and fate, but strong in will
To strive, to seek, to find, and not to yield."
—Tennyson, Ulysses

www.ingramcontent.com/pod-product-compliance
Lightning Source LLC
LaVergne TN
LVHW052220200926
848481LV00001B/163